IMAGES
of America

CHARLES STREET JAIL

On the Cover: The Charles Street Jail, seen here in 1934, served as the jail for Suffolk County, Massachusetts, which includes the city of Boston, from 1851 until it closed in 1990. Today, it is a luxury hotel. (Photograph by the Metropolitan District Commission, courtesy of the Commonwealth of Massachusetts Department of Conservation and Recreation Archives.)

IMAGES
of America

CHARLES STREET JAIL

Joseph McMaster

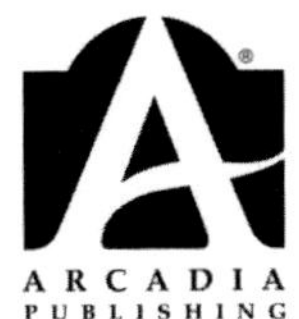

ISBN 978-1-4671-3413-2

Published by Arcadia Publishing
Charleston, South Carolina

Printed in the United States of America

Library of Congress Control Number: 2015935772

For all general information, please contact Arcadia Publishing:
Telephone 843-853-2070
Fax 843-853-0044
E-mail sales@arcadiapublishing.com
For customer service and orders:
Toll-Free 1-888-313-2665

Visit us on the Internet at www.arcadiapublishing.com

To all those who worked to improve conditions at the Charles Street Jail, all those who worked to preserve and restore the building, and Gretchen and Iain for giving me the time to take this journey

Contents

Acknowledgments

I would like to thank all those who so generously gave their time and/or provided images for use in this book, particularly Arthur Pollock, the *Boston Herald*; Jane Winton, Aaron Schmidt, Eve Griffin, Evelyn Lannon, and Tom Blake, Boston Public Library; Sean Fisher, Commonwealth of Massachusetts Department of Conservation and Recreation Archives; Elizabeth Roscio, the Bostonian Society; Marta Crilly, Boston City Archives; Margaret Sullivan, Boston Police Department; Richard Friedman, Carpenter & Co; Gary Johnson and Kwesi Budu-Arthur, Cambridge Seven Associates, Inc.; Suffolk Construction; the Liberty Hotel; and of course, Caitrin Cunningham at Arcadia Publishing for her patience and guidance. Photographs not attributed in the text are courtesy of the author.

INTRODUCTION

When it opened in 1851, the Charles Street Jail was hailed as one of the finest penal institutions in the country, if not the world. Boston was known for its support of social reforms, and the new jail serving Suffolk County, which includes the city of Boston, was the latest in a long list of local institutions and efforts aimed at improving society. Designed by the Boston architect Gridley James Fox Bryant and the leading prison reform crusader Rev. Louis Dwight, also of Boston, it was a grand, elegant structure built on equally grand principles. Newspapers reported that Bryant was so proud of it, he would often bring foreign visitors there "and point with proper pride to what he considered his masterpiece." One 1872 report called the jail an example of the "great advances which have been made in the treatment of criminals in the past few years," and praised the jail for "the perfect cleanliness of the rooms and inmates, the well-prepared food, and the treatment of the prisoners as human beings."

The jail's high reputation would not last, though. By 1906, the press was reporting that overcrowding was becoming a problem as two prisoners were being assigned to cells designed to hold only one. By the mid-1960s, so many problems had erupted that the jail had been investigated numerous times and was being called "a malignancy on the face of Boston" and "a haven of political patronage and a mockery of modern penology." Finding the jail's conditions so bad they violated inmates' constitutional rights by amounting to cruel and unusual punishment, the courts eventually ordered the jail to close. Once an embodiment of some of society's highest aspirations, it became a stark and depressing reminder of its deepest failures.

In an ironic twist, after finally closing in the early 1990s and then lying empty and deteriorating for about a decade, the building was gutted, rehabilitated, and turned into a luxury hotel where guests now choose to pay handsomely for the privilege of staying the night. More than 150 years after it was erected, the dilapidated building at last achieved a kind of reform and redemption similar to what the jail's high-minded builders hoped it would bring about in its inmates. Today, it has come full circle and is again a place that many Bostonians point to with pride—just as Gridley Bryant once did.

Richer even than the story of the rise, fall, and rise of the building are the stories of the thousands upon thousands of people unfortunate enough to spend time at the jail in its nearly century and a half of continuous use. Being a county jail and not a prison meant that most inmates at the Charles Street Jail were not convicts. Instead, they were people being held—innocent until proven guilty—while awaiting hearings and trials. Only a few inmates at any one time were serving longer sentences. As a result, the turnover in population was constant, and the rough granite walls were home to an unimaginably wide variety of inmates: from the most hardened murderers and thieves, to debtors, celebrities and everyday people charged with minor offenses.

If there are eight million stories in "the naked city," as the movie of that name famously concludes, there must have been countless stories at the Charles Street Jail. This book presents a collection of some of the more curious, well-known, and important ones: a convicted slave trader, future mayor of Boston, notorious killers, bank robbers, social activists, wealthy eccentrics, stage stars, a famous prizefighter, gangsters, mafia members, prisoners of war, traitors, hit men, the figure thought to have inspired the famous adventure novel *Around the World in 80 Days*, and the infamous imposter whose book and story was turned into the hit movie *Catch Me If You Can*, starring Leonardo DiCaprio, to mention just a few.

Of course, alongside these colorful or memorable characters were many more whose stories have been lost to time. There were multitudes that endured harsh and unspeakable conditions, spoke up for their rights, or worked tirelessly to do their best by inmates under conditions that became increasingly difficult.

Above all, though, the Charles Street Jail building is a survivor. It was unscathed in the Great Fire of Boston of 1872, left standing when much of its neighborhood—Boston's West End—was bulldozed during urban renewal, endured decades of decline, ardent calls for its demolition, and years of disuse. And just as the building, now designated a National Historic Landmark, was painstakingly preserved, perhaps this book can help preserve some of the remarkable stories and images that surround it.

One

The Birth of the Charles Street Jail

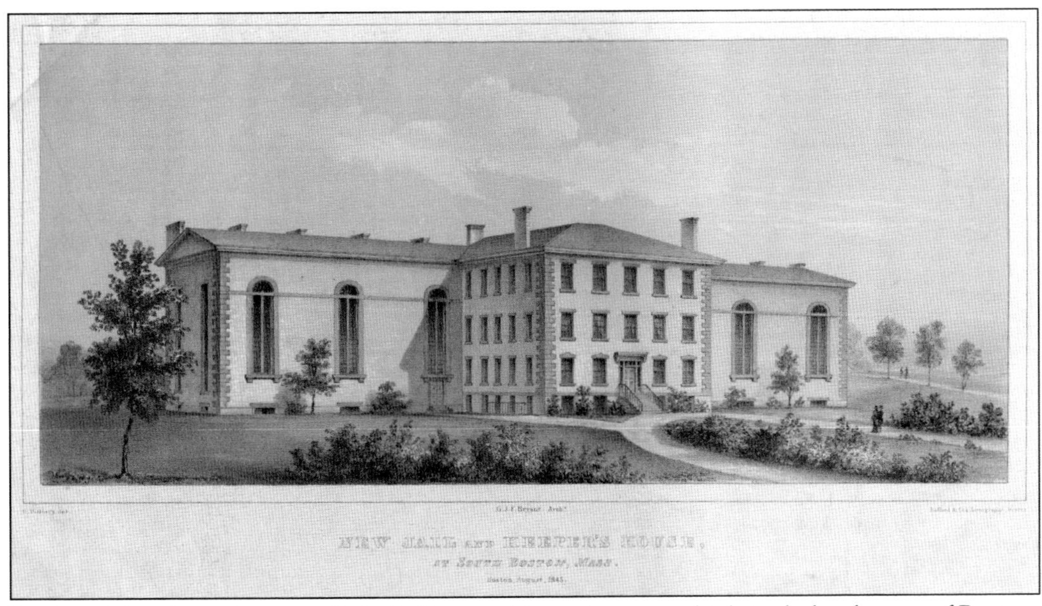

By the 1840s, the jail serving Suffolk County, Massachusetts, which includes the city of Boston, had become inadequate and out of date. When the city announced it was considering construction of a new jail, a local architect named Gridley James Fox Bryant submitted a proposal that included this rendering. Residents of South Boston opposed building the jail in their community, though, and plans for the site were dropped. (Courtesy of the Library of Congress.)

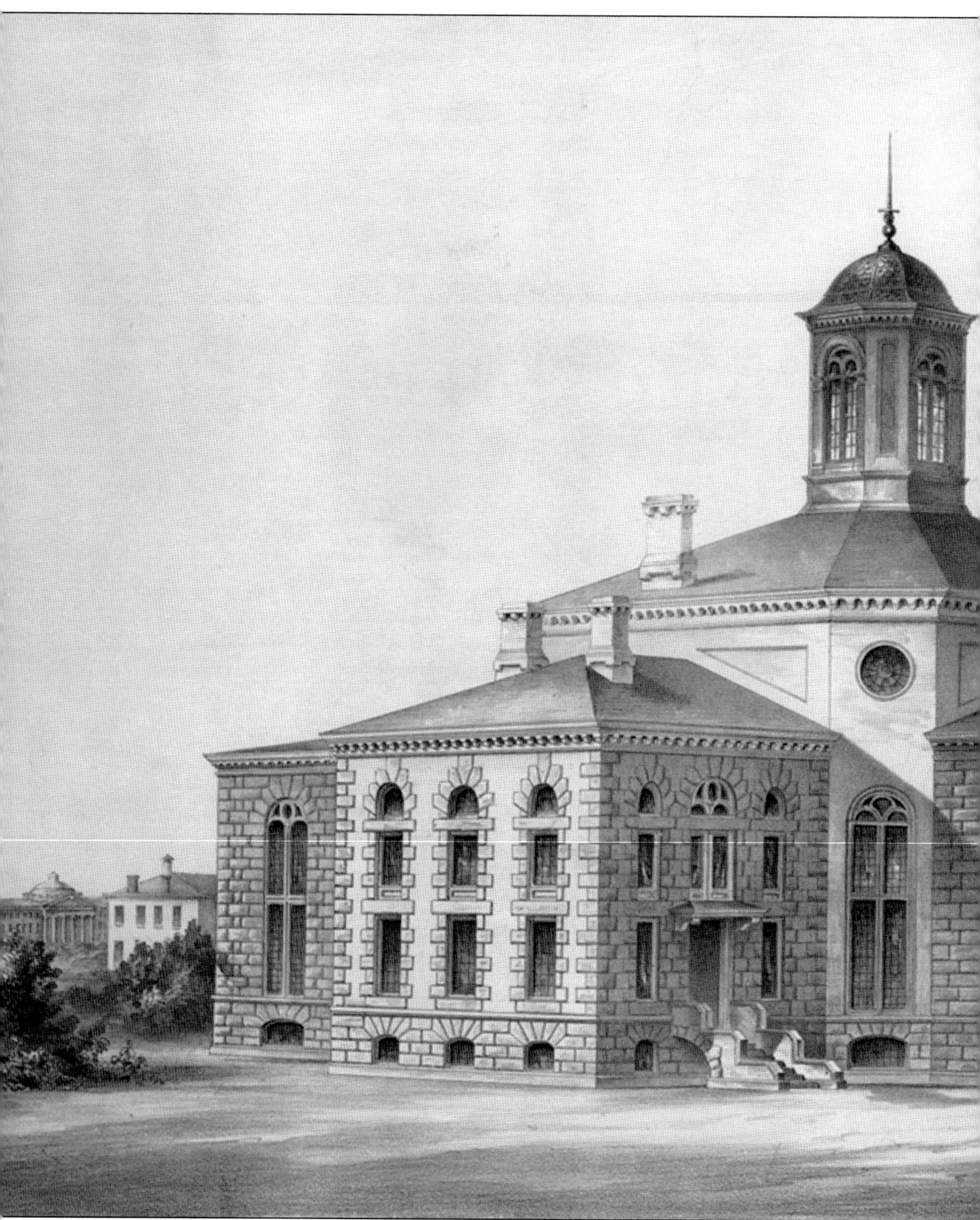

Working with a well-known prison-reform advocate and the founder of the Boston Prison Discipline Society, Rev. Louis Dwight, Bryant revised his plans and submitted this rendering for a new Suffolk

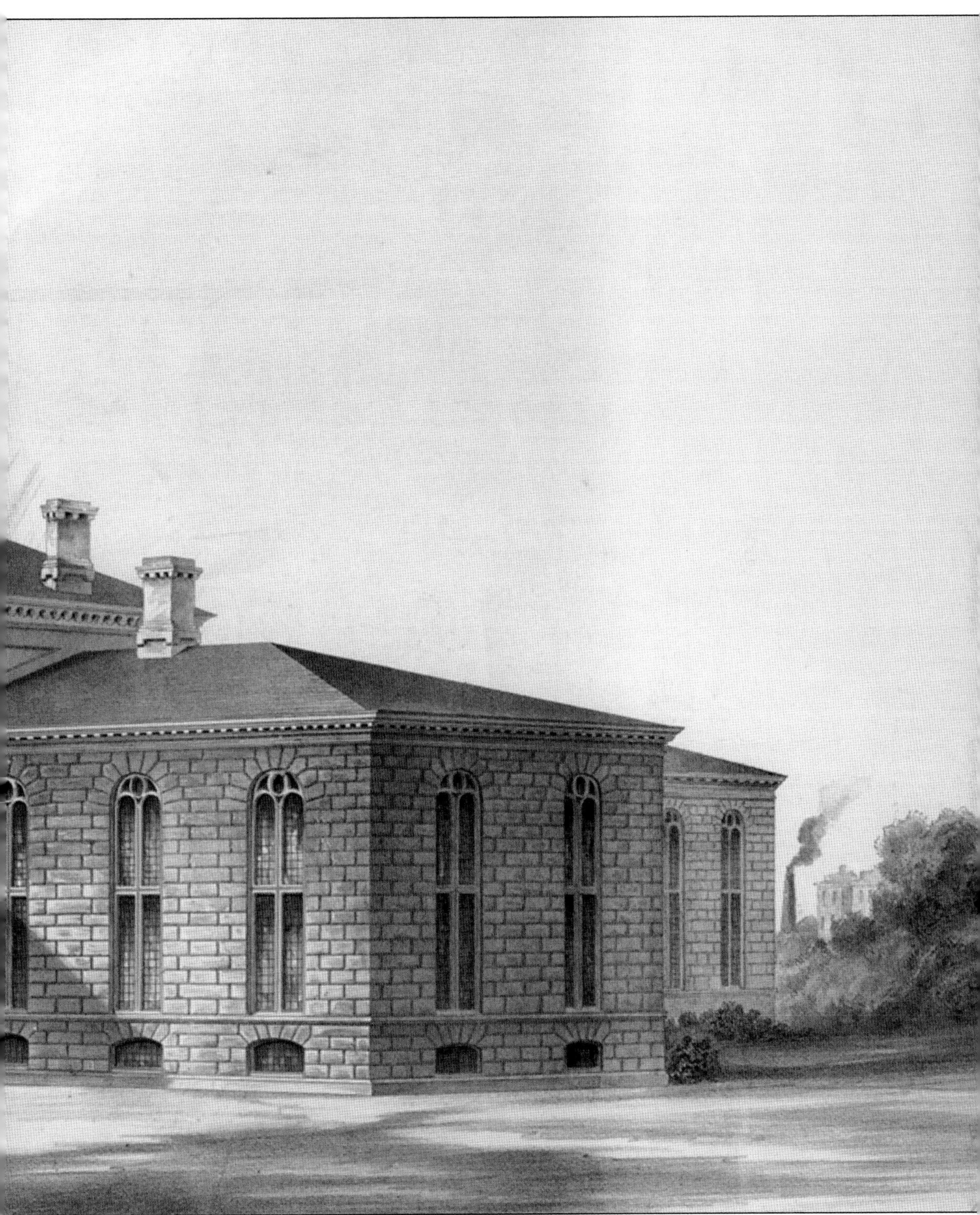

County Jail in 1848. Construction began in 1849. (Courtesy of the Boston Public Library.)

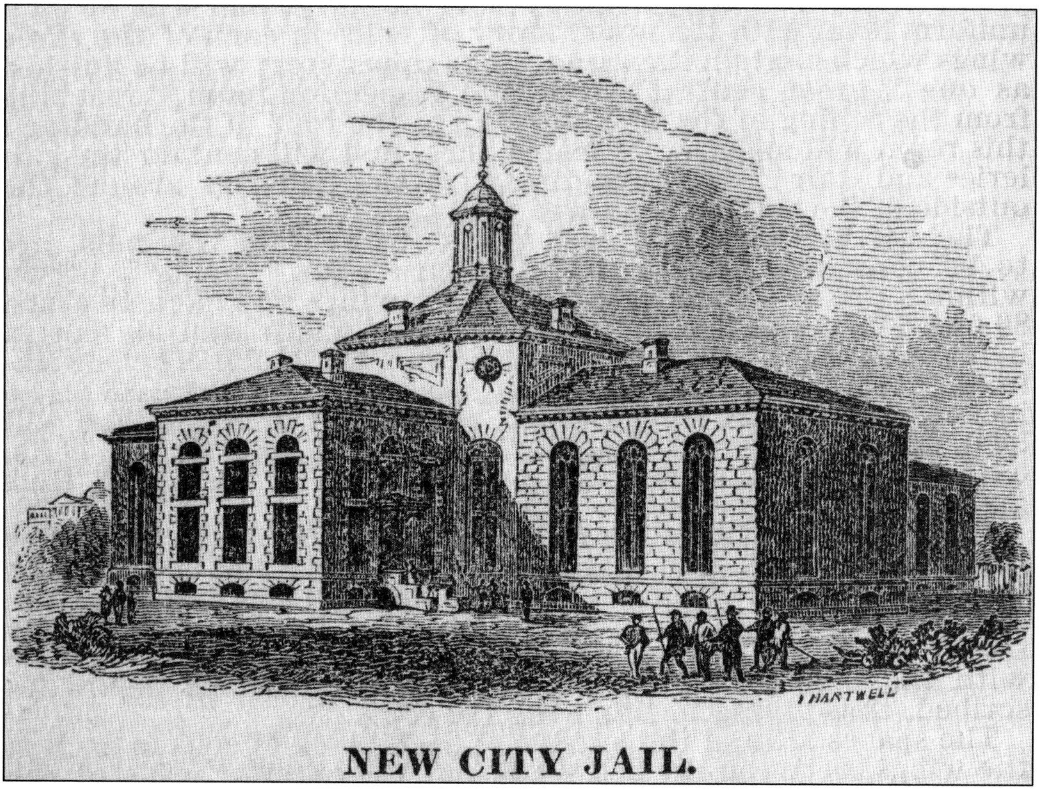

NEW CITY JAIL.

Periodicals from Boston to as far away as London carried news of the new jail—many of them publishing this image and a lengthy description of the building's dimensions, layout, and facilities.

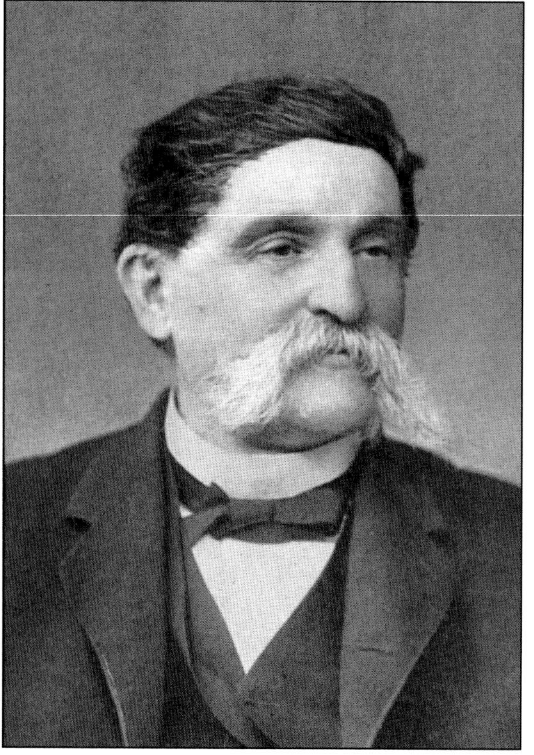

Gridley James Fox Bryant had worked as an architect in Boston for many years, though the jail would be his first large public project. Born in 1816, he was the eldest of 10 children and the son of a mason, contractor, and engineer also named Gridley Bryant.

The elder Bryant had worked on the construction of many notable Boston buildings, including the Bunker Hill Monument. When funds were being raised for the monument in the 1820s, he bought a granite quarry in Quincy, Massachusetts, to supply the stone. (Courtesy of the Boston Public Library.)

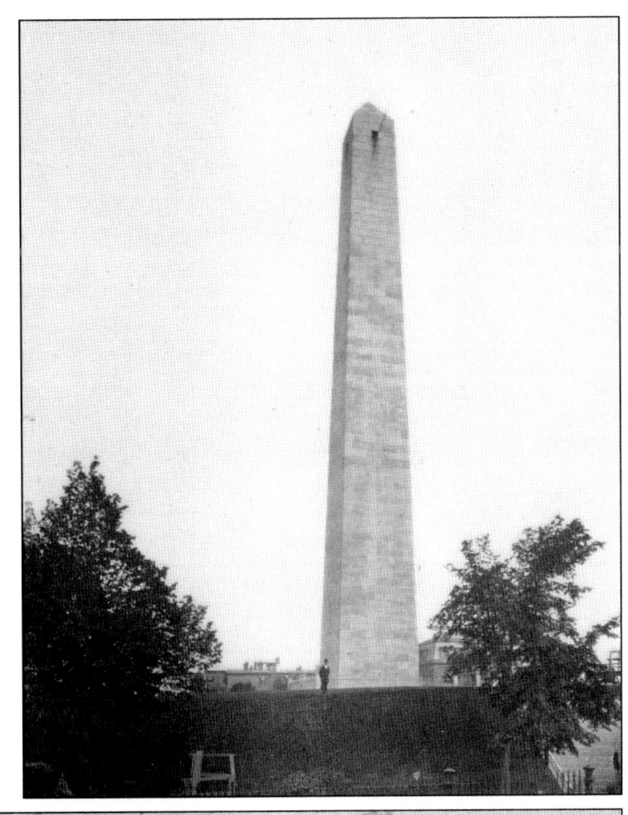

To move the stones from the quarry to a nearby river where they would be taken to Boston by boat, he constructed what many consider the country's first commercial railroad, called the Granite Railway. He also invented a special railroad car to transport such heavy loads. (Courtesy of the Quincy Historical Society.)

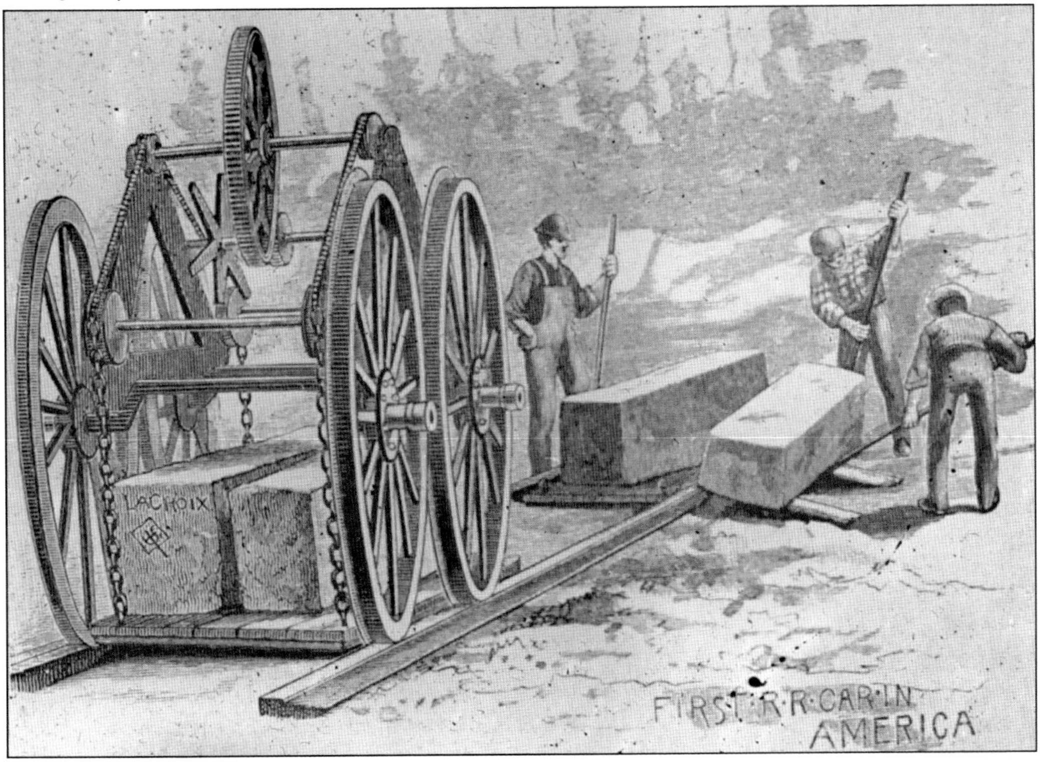

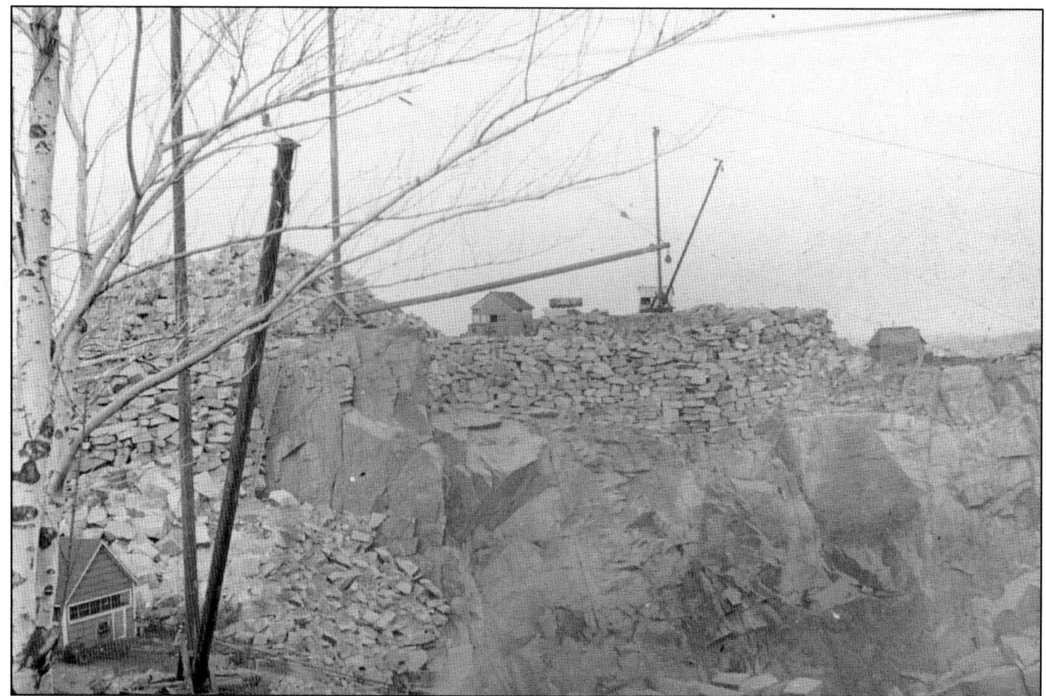

The younger Gridley Bryant was well acquainted with granite construction, and his design for the new Suffolk County Jail called for an exterior made entirely of Quincy granite. Here, workers at the Granite Railway quarry extract stone using techniques that would have been familiar to Bryant's father. (Courtesy of the Quincy Historical Society.)

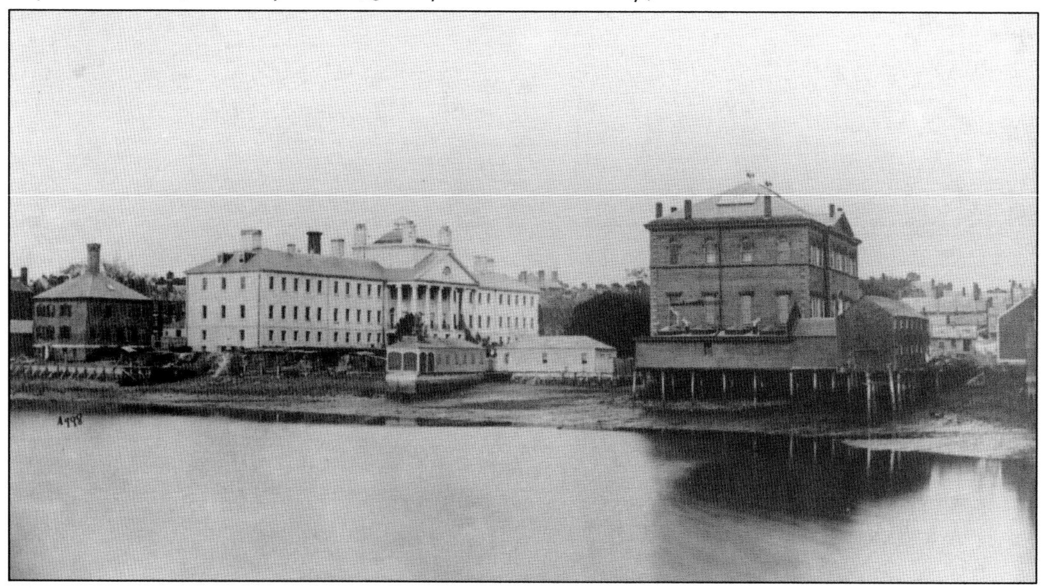

The new jail was to be built on a site on the Charles River in Boston near the Massachusetts General Hospital (left) and the Harvard Medical School (right), which Bryant had designed. As this photograph shows, these two buildings were constructed on pilings that were exposed at low tide. The jail would be just to the right of the medical school, on a site that was to be created from landfill. (Courtesy of the Boston Public Library.)

This 1846 map of Boston, made before the landfill project began, shows the site where the new jail would be located. The plot, on the corner of Cambridge Street and North Grove Street, is identified as "Jackson's Wharf." Boston has a long history of filling in mudflats and marshland along the river to create more buildable ground. The city's Back Bay section would be made this way, and creating land in front of the jail and the hospital would continue over the coming decades. (Courtesy of the Norman B. Leventhal Map Center at the Boston Public Library.)

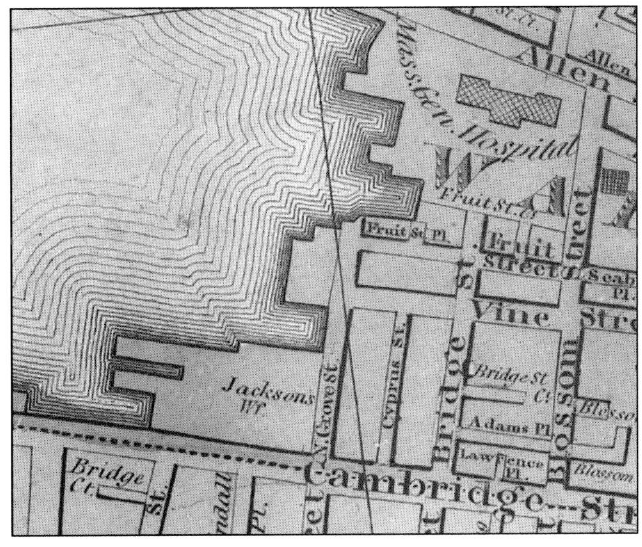

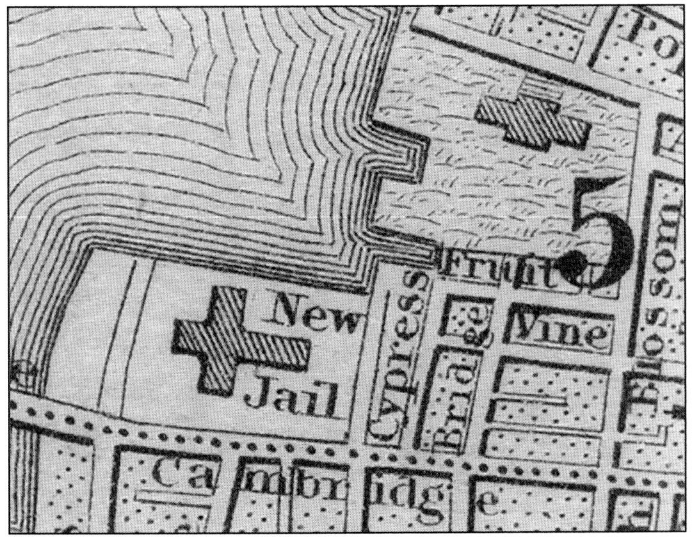

To create land for the jail, a granite seawall was built and then the area behind it was filled. This map from 1851 shows the location of the jail after the land was created. Charles Street was extended in front of the jail, which soon became known as the Charles Street Jail, though its official name was always the Suffolk County Jail. (Courtesy of the Norman B. Leventhal Map Center at the Boston Public Library.)

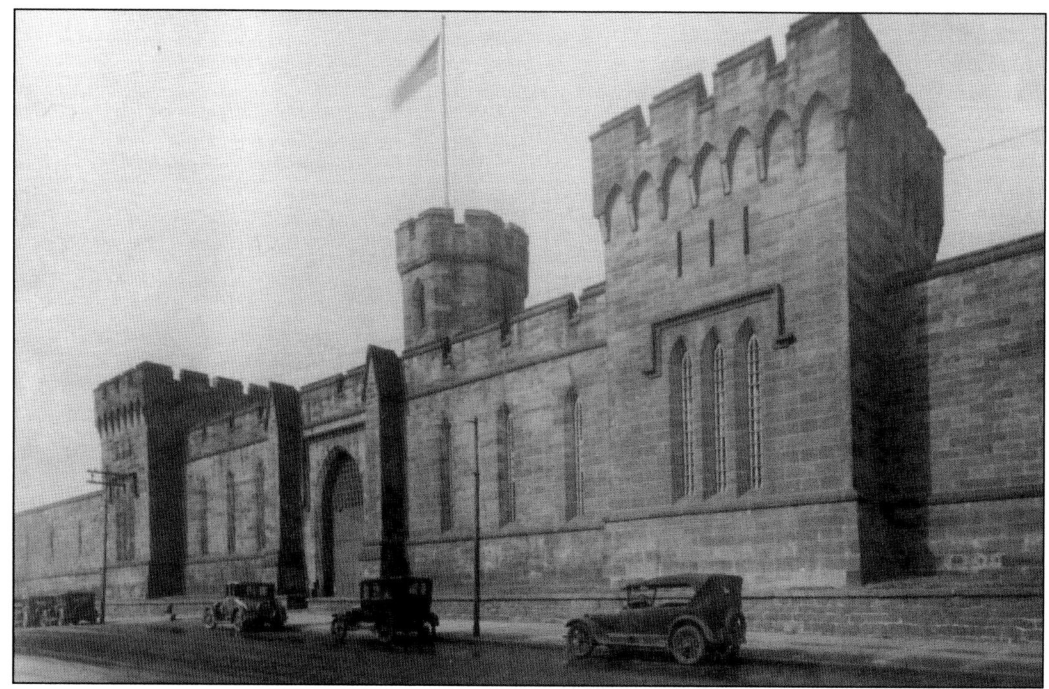

At the time that Bryant and Dwight designed the Charles Street Jail, there were two competing schools of thought about prison design. One—called the Pennsylvania Plan, after this building, the Eastern State Penitentiary in Philadelphia, Pennsylvania—held that prisons should be forbidding and severe. Prisoners were to spend their days and nights in solitary confinement, where they were supposed to reflect on their misdeeds. (Courtesy of the Eastern State Penitentiary Historic Site.)

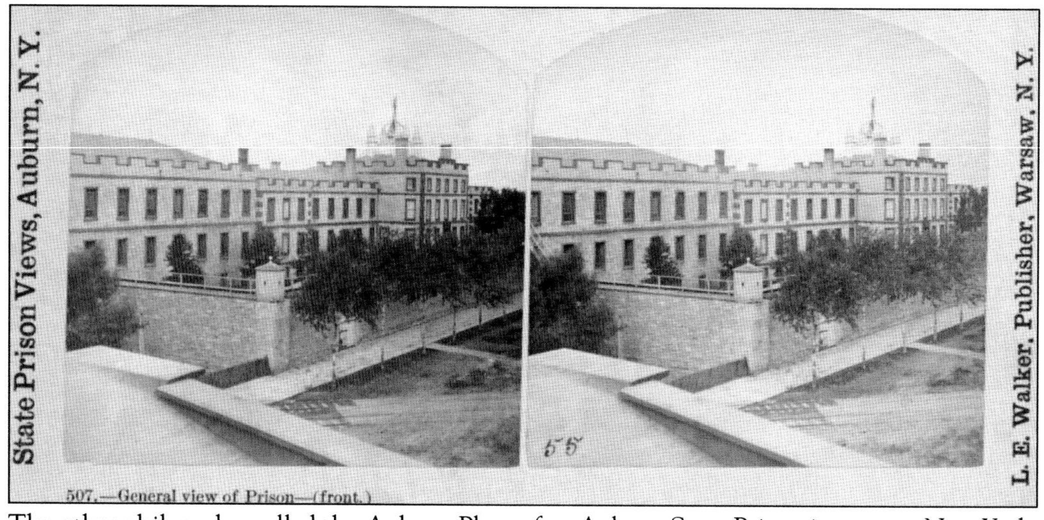

The other philosophy, called the Auburn Plan, after Auburn State Prison in upstate New York, grew out of the era's progressive social reform movements. Rev. Louis Dwight was a leading proponent of the Auburn Plan, which called for more humane treatment of prisoners. Auburn Plan prisons were to be less severe in appearance, more focused on rehabilitation of prisoners, and constructed so prisoners spent nights alone in their cells, but engaged in useful work with others during the day.

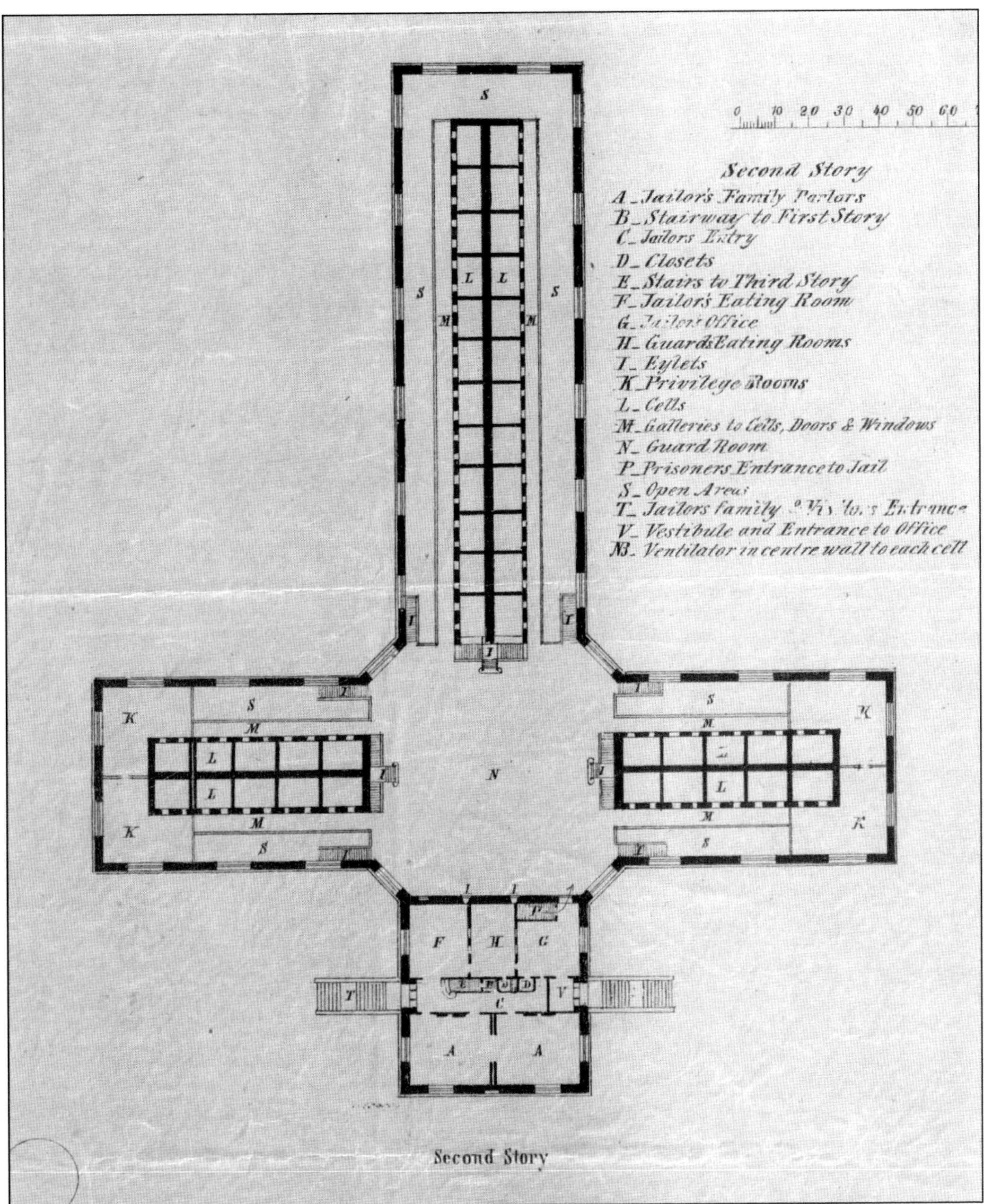

The Auburn Plan heavily influenced the design of the Charles Street Jail. The floor plans called for a building in the shape of a cross with a central, octagonal rotunda. Jail cells occupied three of the wings while the jailer's living quarters, offices and other facilities such as a chapel occupied the fourth. (Courtesy of the Boston Public Library.)

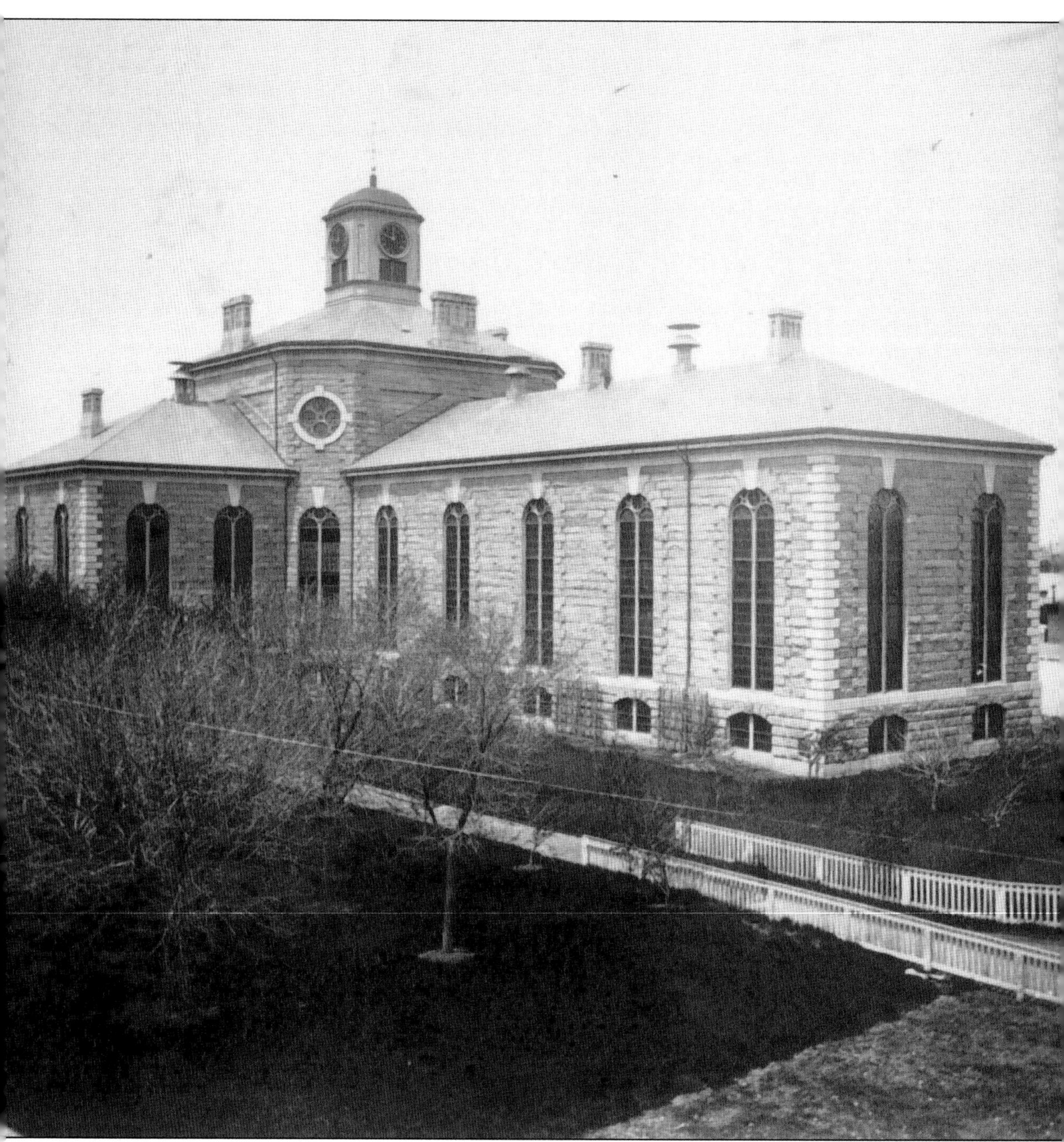

The Charles Street Jail opened November 25, 1851, and was hailed as the most advanced institution of its kind. Made of solid stone, it was considered virtually fireproof. Thirty windows, each 10 feet wide and 33 feet high, yielded "an amount of light to the interior of the cells probably four times as great as any prison yet constructed upon the Auburn system," proclaims one report. "There are no dark and dismal places in it," says another. Windows opened to allow fresh air and breezes from the river. The cupola appearing in Bryant's original design, which would have admitted even more light, was never built. Instead, a smaller clock tower was erected in its place to cut costs. (Courtesy of the Boston Public Library.)

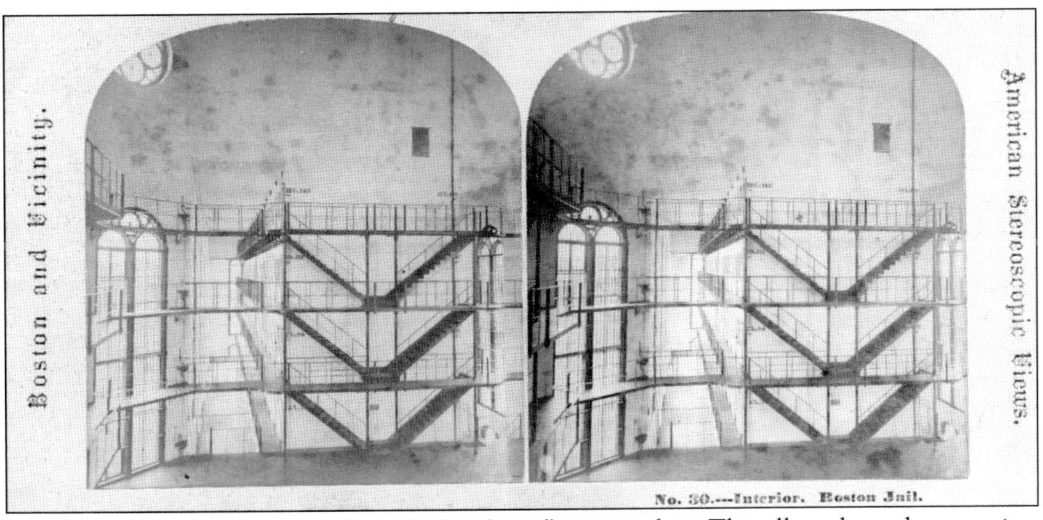

The open, central octagon was about 85 feet from floor to ceiling. This allowed guards to monitor each wing and gave prisoners a place to gather for work during the day. Iron galleries encircled the outer walls, connecting to similar galleries outside of the cells in each wing. Circular ocular windows above the multistory windows admitted more light. (Courtesy of the Bostonian Society.)

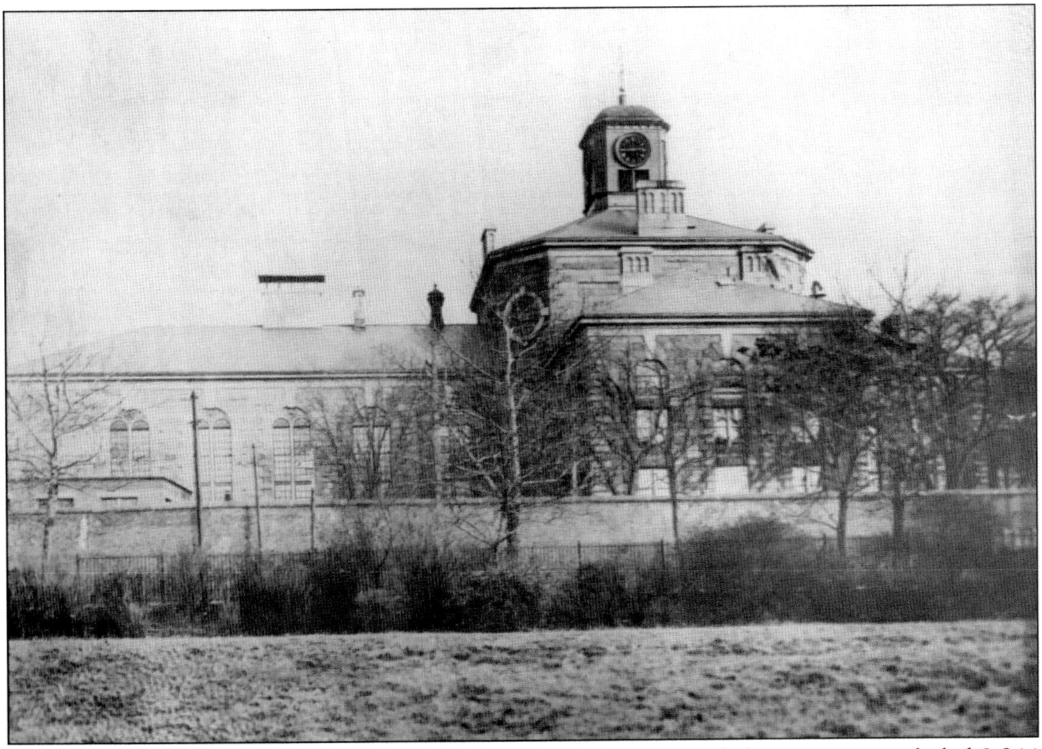

During the first six months of the jail's operation, papers reported that inmates included 2,344 criminals, 162 witnesses, and 320 debtors. Drunkenness topped the list of offenses with 242 people charged or convicted, though everything from assault and battery (155), to keeping brothels (32), interring a dead body in the city without a license (1), and throwing snowballs in the street (5) landed residents of the area in the jail during that time. (Courtesy of the *Boston Herald*.)

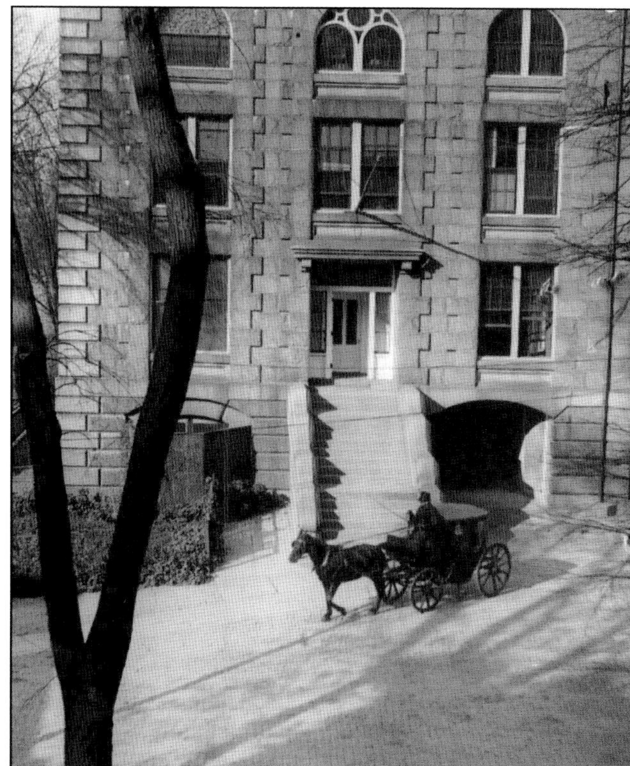

The sheriff of Suffolk County, who was in charge of the jail, was expected to live on the premises. The new building provided private quarters for the sheriff and his family, including a kitchen, washrooms, closets, parlors, a dining room, and bedrooms. (Courtesy of the *Boston Herald*.)

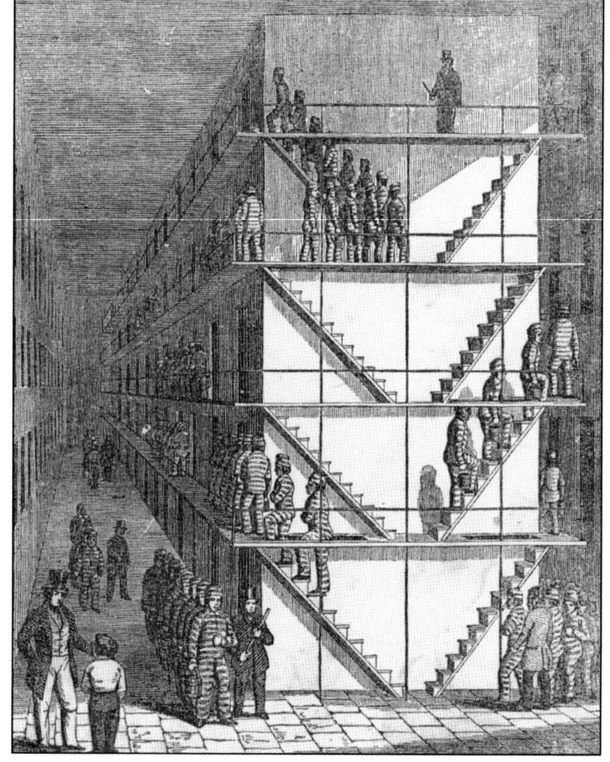

This lithograph of prisoners circulating through a prison with iron galleries very much like those at the Charles Street Jail gives a sense of how the place would have looked when first in use. According to an 1878 report, inmates were instructed "not to talk to any prisoner or communicate in any way without permission." Those charged with "perpetration of an infamous crime" were segregated from the rest of the population. Women were housed in a different area, and minors were "kept separate from notorious offenders, and from those convicted of a felony."

Though this image of a cell at the Charles Street Jail is relatively recent, little had changed since the time the building opened. Most cells were 8 feet by 11 feet, designed for single occupancy, and had a window and door facing the outer walls. Though there was no running water in the cells until decades after the jail was built, it had steam heat, and prisoners were allowed a bath once a week, according to an 1878 article. (Courtesy of the Library of Congress.)

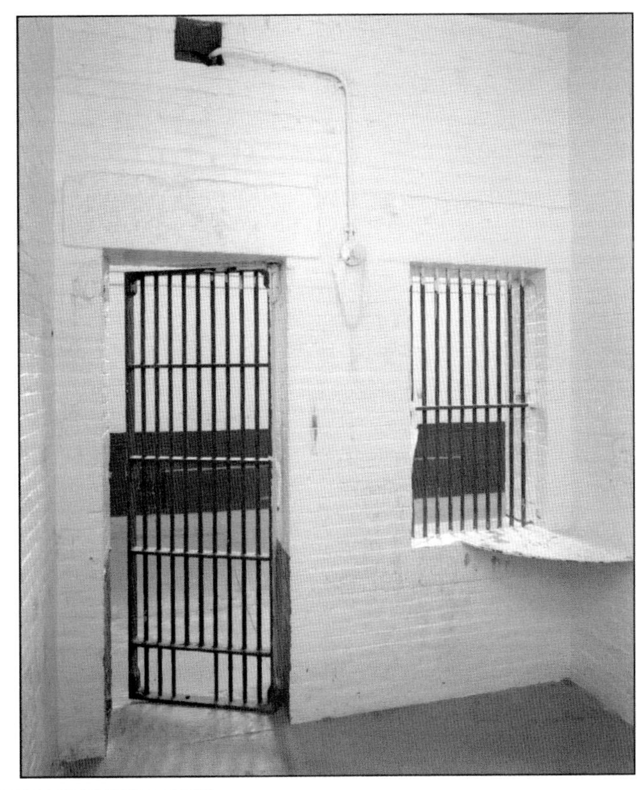

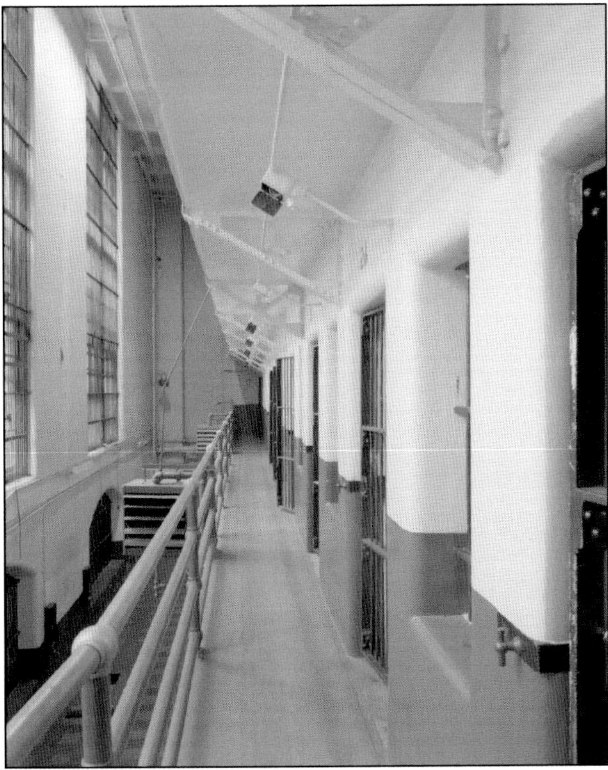

As part of the Auburn Plan, cells were arranged in rows down the middle of each wing. The area between them and the exterior walls was open from the bottom floor to the top, creating an airy feeling and what the Prison Discipline Society called "a prison within a prison." (Courtesy of the Library of Congress.)

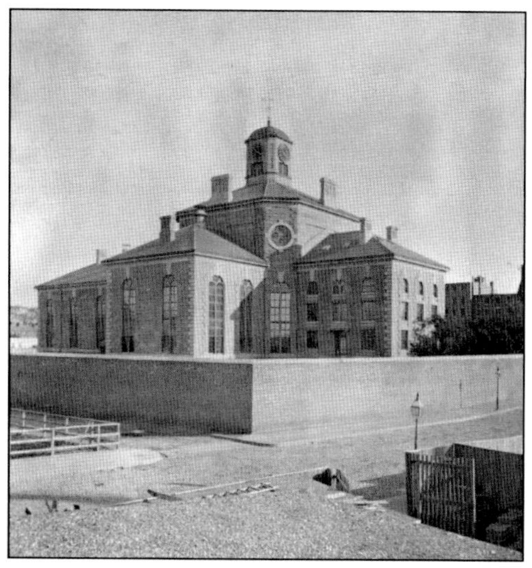

The cost of the finished building, including land filling, was reported to be $409,545, though the real figure may have been about $493,000. Officials from around the country and abroad visited the Charles Street Jail, proclaiming it "the model prison of the age." "The crime is punished, but the man himself is respected," one marveled. (Courtesy of the Bostonian Society.)

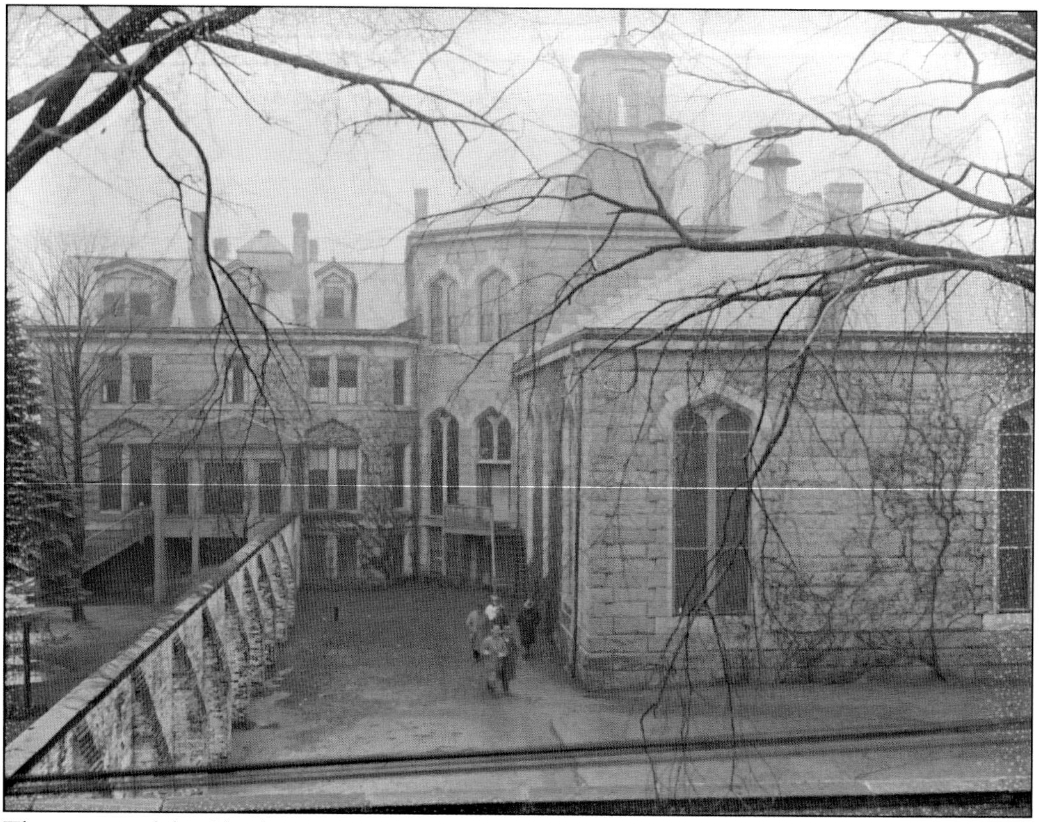

The success of the Charles Street Jail led to Bryant and Dwight receiving commissions for many other buildings, including jails and similar structures, in Massachusetts and beyond. In the 1850s, they substantially remodeled the Norfolk County Jail in Dedham, Massachusetts, commonly called the Dedham Jail, which bears a striking resemblance to the Charles Street Jail. The building became famous as the jail that held anarchists Nicola Sacco and Bartolomeo Vanzetti while waiting for trial. Closed in the early 1990s, the jail was converted into luxury condominiums. (Courtesy of the Boston Public Library.)

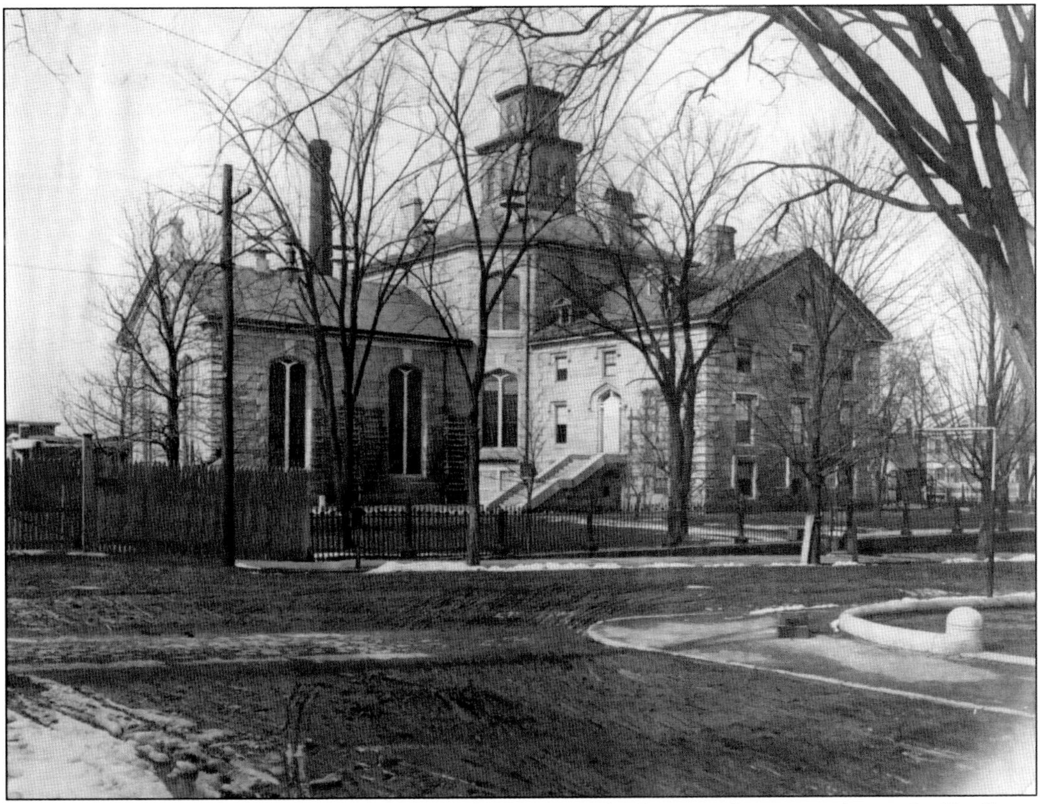

The Essex County Jail in Lawrence, Massachusetts, was built on a scheme similar to the Dedham and the Charles Street Jails. Constructed in 1853, it was torn down in the 1980s. (Courtesy of the Lawrence History Center.)

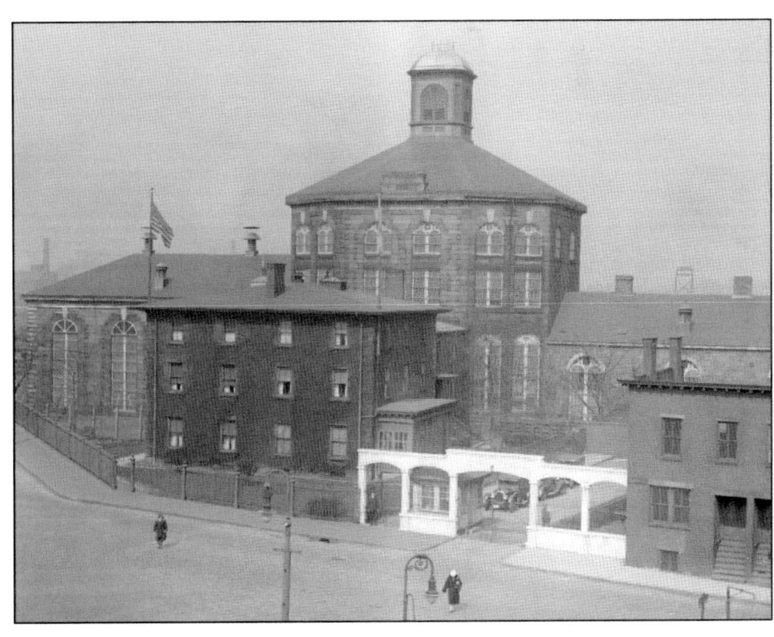

Before the Charles Street Jail was finished, Bryant and Dwight redesigned the Massachusetts State Prison in Charlestown. Among their contributions was the addition of a central octagon, like at Charles Street. (Courtesy of the Boston Public Library.)

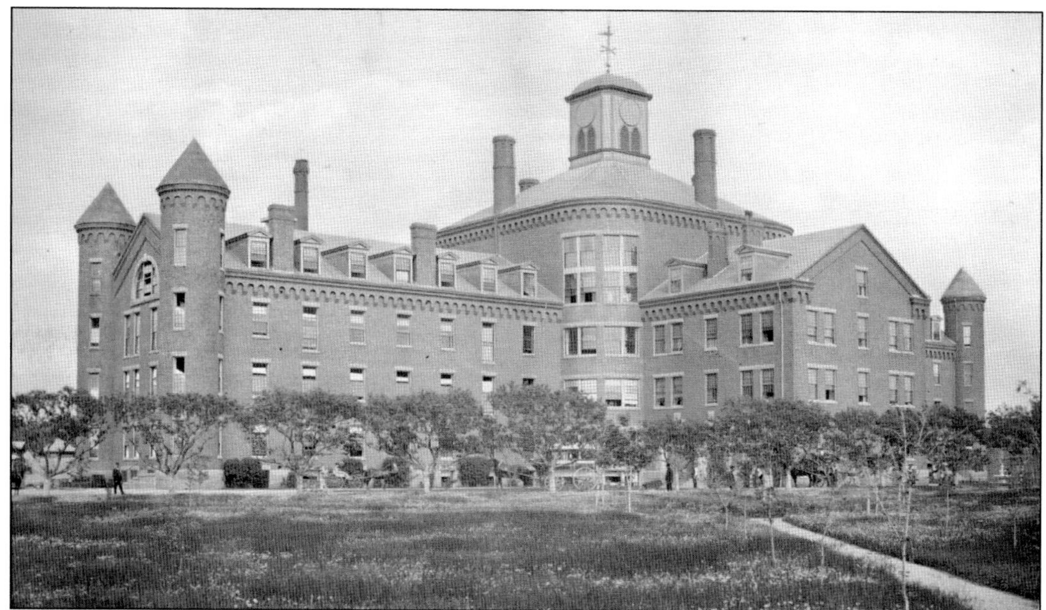

Another project begun while construction of the Charles Street Jail was still underway was the Deer Island Almshouse. Located on an island in Boston harbor and built to house paupers, it was later converted to a prison. Like the Charles Street Jail, it consisted of four wings and a central octagon. Bryant and Dwight designed a similar almshouse in Cambridge, Massachusetts, which is used as a school building today. (Courtesy of the Boston Public Library.)

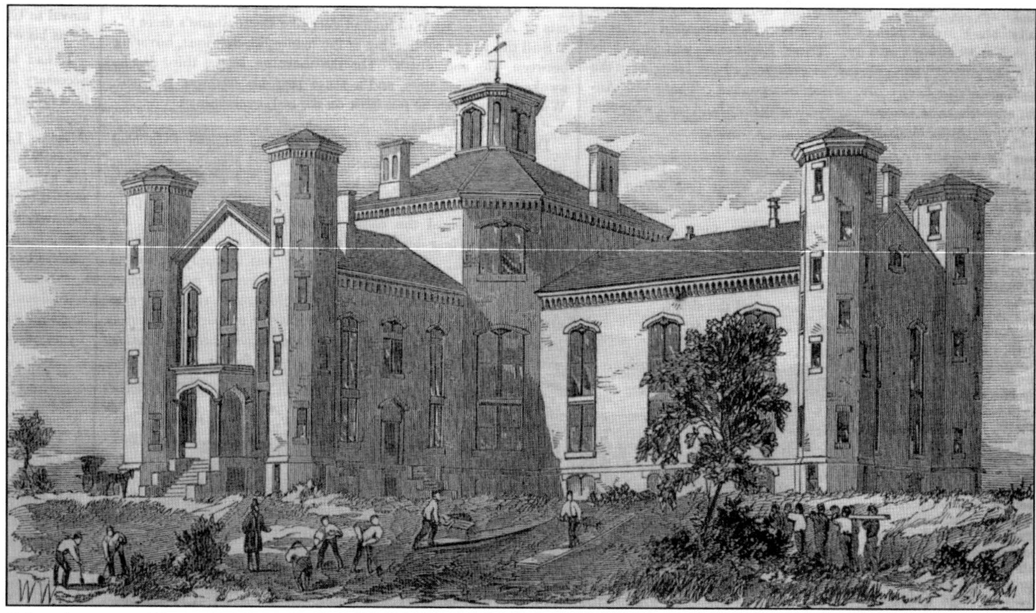

Clearly resembling the Deer Island Almshouse, the Maine State Reform School (known by various names, including the State School for Boys) was another Bryant building commissioned in the wake of the Charles Street Jail. The four wings and a central octagon housed boys ages 7 to 19 who were charged with everything from "Sabbath breaking" and "malicious mischief" to serious offenses, according to the school's annual reports. Located in South Portland, it was constructed in 1853 and repurposed as a medical office building in 2008.

Throughout his career, Bryant teamed up with other architects for important commissions. For the iconic Arlington Street Church in Boston, completed in 1861, he worked with well-known architect Arthur Gilman. The church is located in Boston's Back Bay section, an area that was created from landfill in the same way as the land for the Charles Street Jail. This photograph was taken soon after the landfill project was finished and before the surrounding area was developed. (Courtesy of the Boston Public Library.)

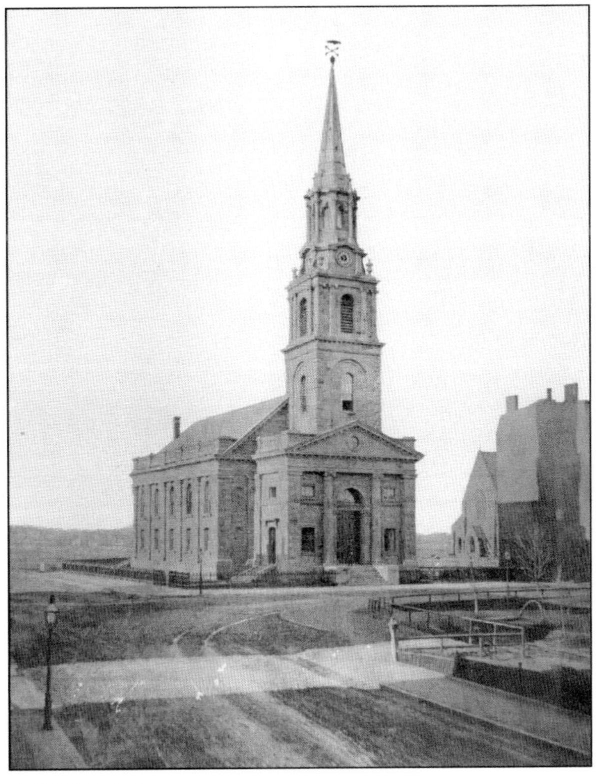

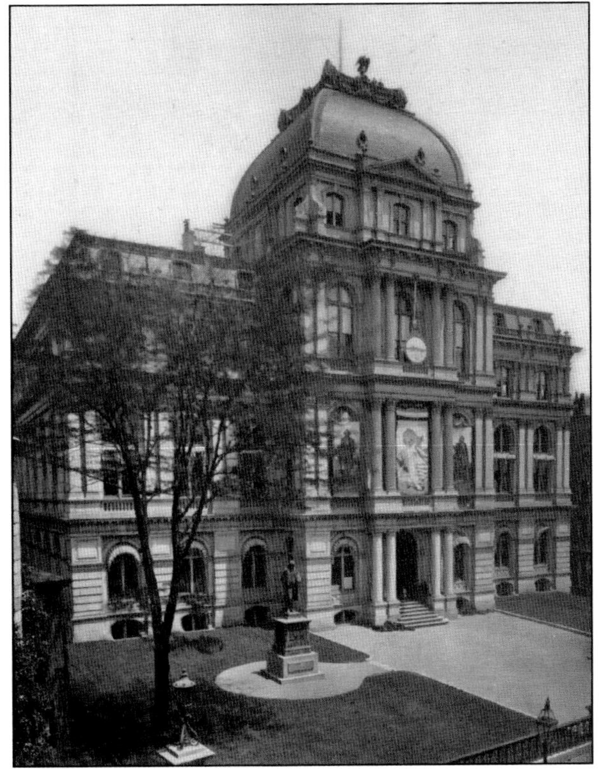

Designed by Gilman and Bryant, Boston's old city hall was completed in 1865. As the home of the city council and mayor's office, the ornate, granite structure was the seat of city government for more than 100 years. One of the first major examples of French Second Empire architecture in the United States, it became nationally known and inspired the designs of many other public buildings. After Boston's city government moved to new quarters in 1969, the building was renovated and converted into a restaurant and offices. (Courtesy of the Boston Public Library.)

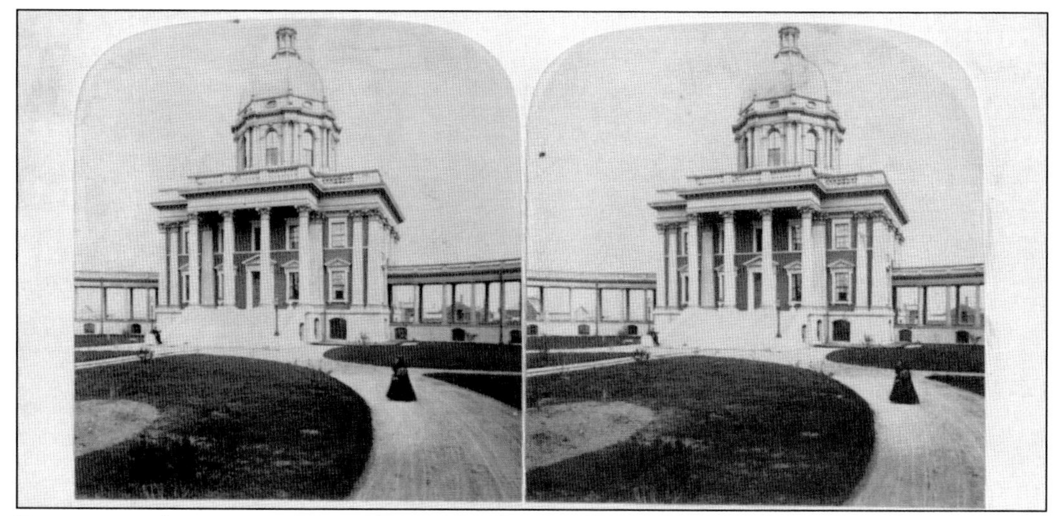

Bryant won the commission to design the Boston City Hospital, which opened in 1864 and included this grand, domed administration building. A free hospital for what benefactors called the "worthy poor," it was the first municipal hospital in the United States and an outgrowth of the same progressive reform movement that gave rise to the Charles Street Jail. The administration building no longer exists, but the hospital's original mission lives on in its successor, the Boston Medical Center, which states that it serves "all in need of care, regardless of status or ability to pay." (Courtesy of the Boston Public Library.)

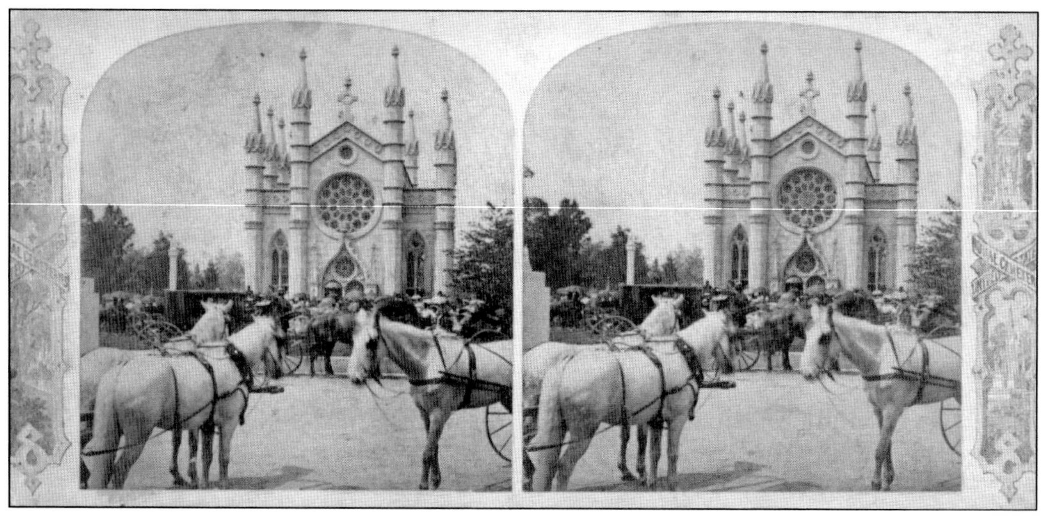

With 14 stone pinnacles, this picturesque Gothic Revival chapel at Mount Auburn Cemetery in Cambridge, Massachusetts, reflects a different side of Gridley Bryant's talents. Bryant designed the chapel with Dr. Jacob Bigelow, a physician and botanist who founded the idyllic rural cemetery. Known as Bigelow Chapel, it was built from Quincy granite in 1845 and rebuilt in 1858 due to structural problems. In addition to the chapel, Bryant designed a number of monuments and tombs at Mount Auburn. Coincidentally, the cemetery is also the burial place of Bryant's collaborator on the Charles Street Jail, Rev. Louis Dwight, who died in 1854. (Courtesy of the Boston Public Library.)

By the end of the 19th century, Bryant had designed and constructed countless buildings around Boston. Since many of them were made of granite, he is considered one of the greatest practitioners of what came to be known as the "Boston Granite Style," as exemplified by the Charles Street Jail. Unfortunately, 152 of his buildings were destroyed by the Great Boston Fire of 1872, which decimated about 65 acres of the city. (Courtesy of the Boston Public Library.)

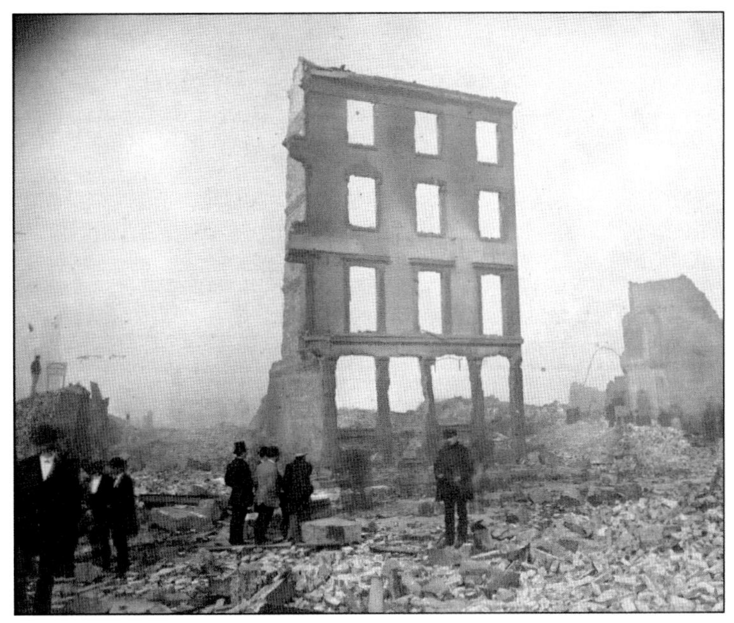

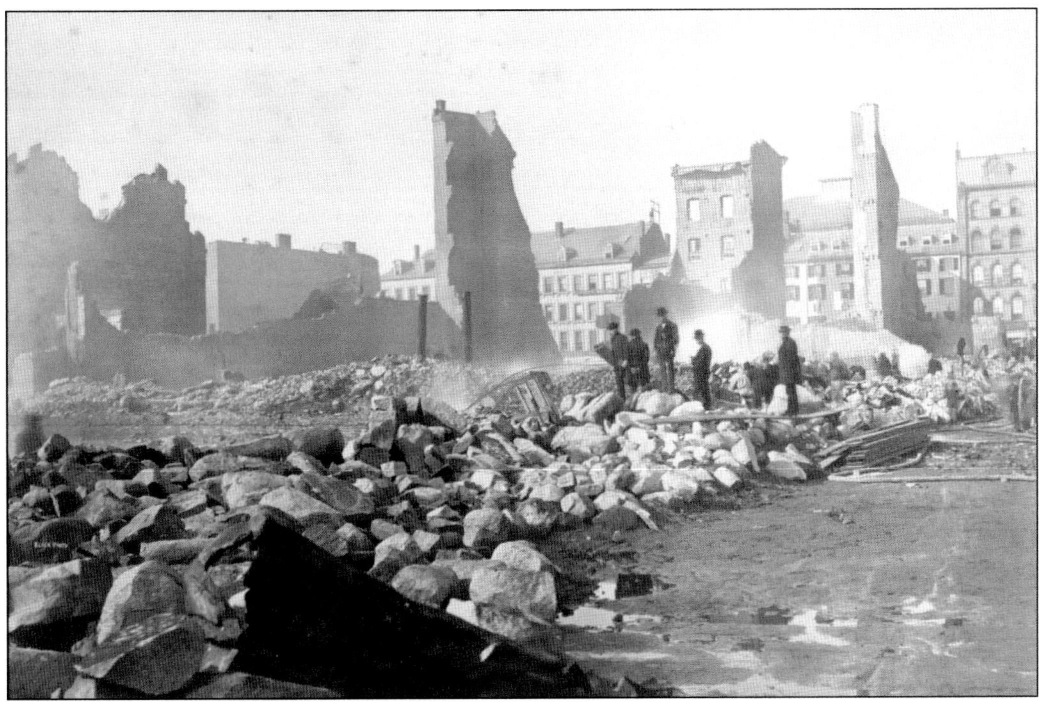

Newspapers reported that "after the big fire that visited Boston swept away his labor of years," Bryant was immediately commissioned to rebuild 110 of the buildings he had designed. (Courtesy of the Boston Public Library.)

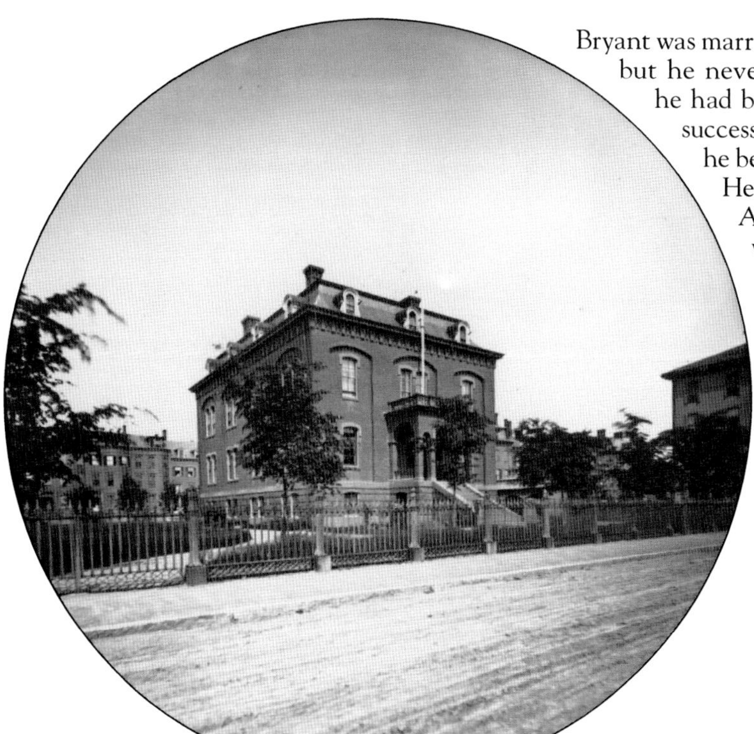

Bryant was married for more than 40 years, but he never had children. Though he had been one of Boston's most successful and prolific architects, he became destitute late in life. He moved into the Home for Aged Men, a facility for what its founders called "respectable aged and indigent men." Ironically, the home was located in a building Bryant had designed in 1860 as a hospital for women. (Courtesy of the Boston Public Library.)

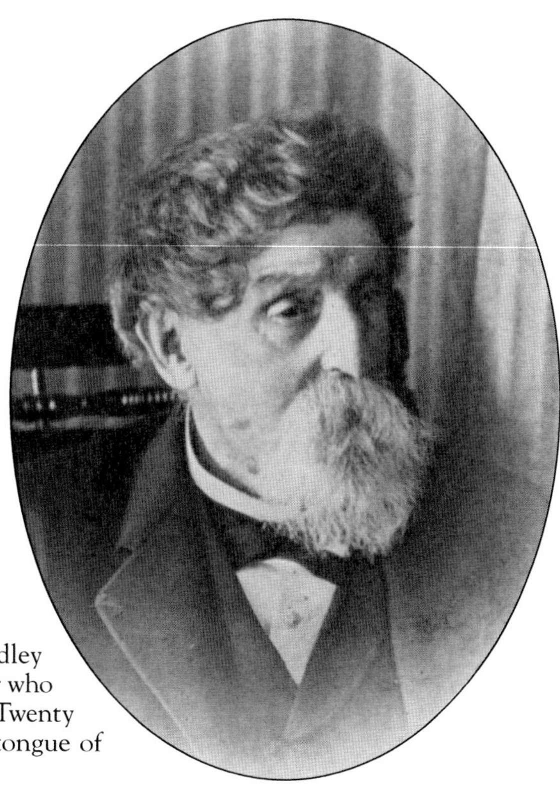

This is said to be the last portrait of Gridley Bryant prior to his death in 1899. A reporter who visited him shortly before he died wrote, "Twenty years ago Mr. Bryant's name was on the tongue of almost everybody; today he is forgotten."

Two

THE JAIL IN THE CITY

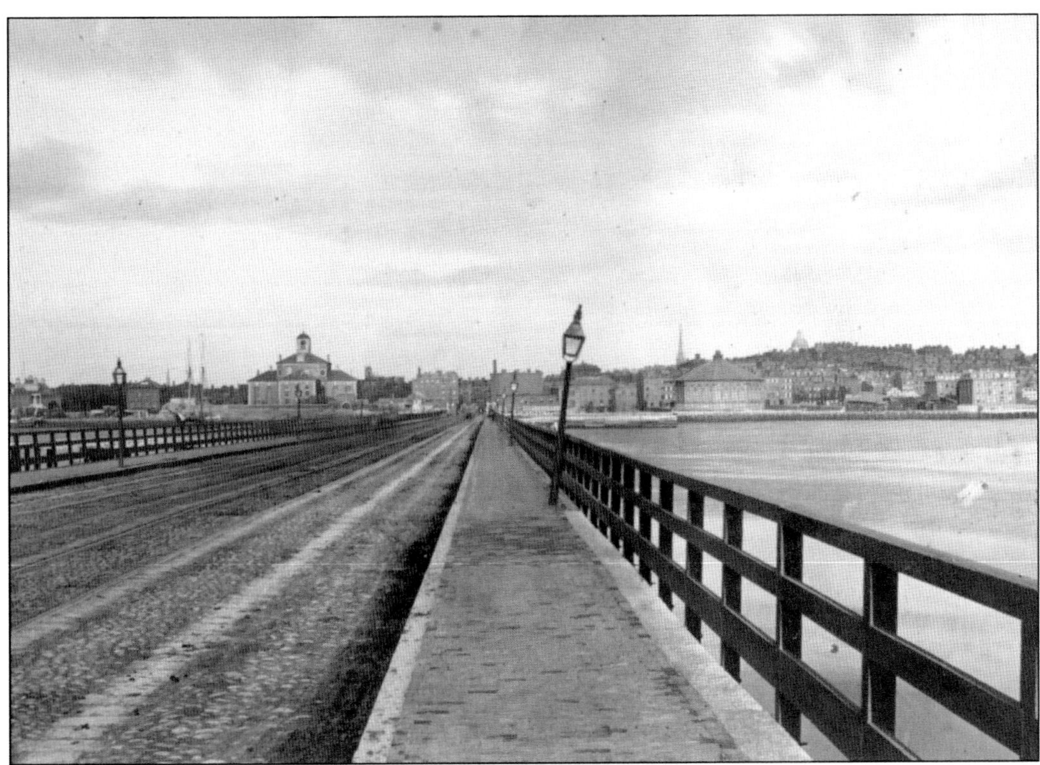

As soon as the Charles Street Jail was completed in 1851, it became an important component of the Boston skyline. From this vantage point across the Charles River in Cambridge, the jail appears even more prominent than the statehouse dome atop Beacon Hill to the right. (Courtesy of the Boston Public Library.)

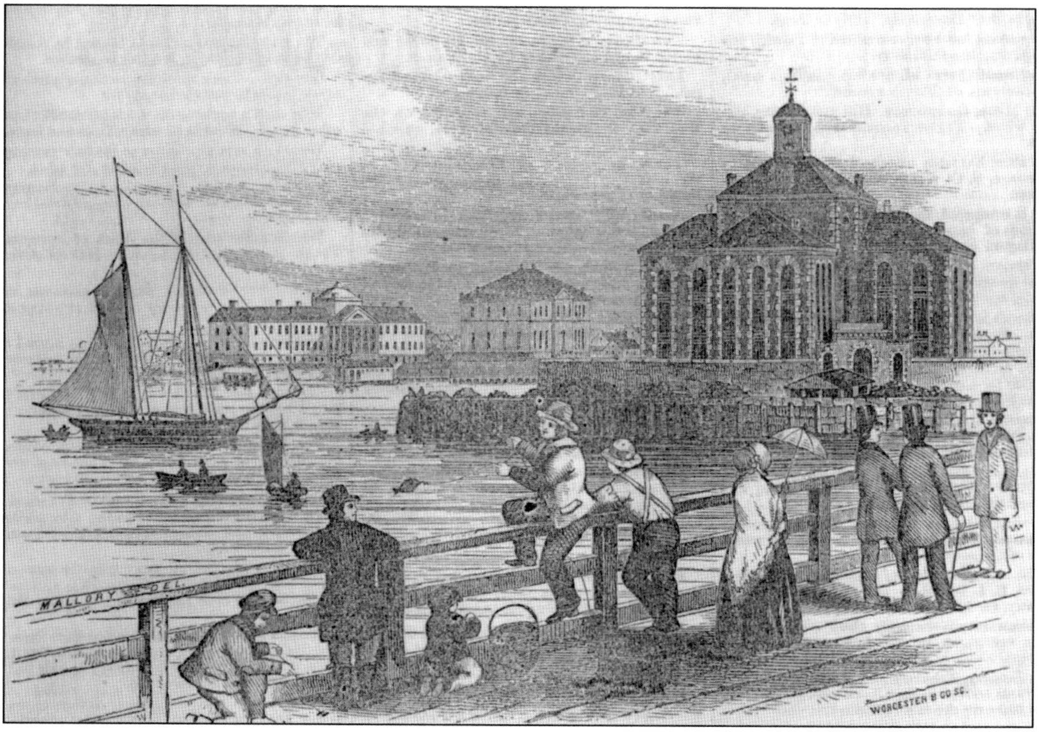

Published the same year the jail was finished, this scene shows the landfill on which the jail was built and suggests the building quickly became an integral part of Boston. The image also depicts the jail as a point of pride for Bostonians and a pleasant backdrop for fishing, conversation, and other activities – a remarkable contrast with how the jail would come to be seen in the decades ahead.

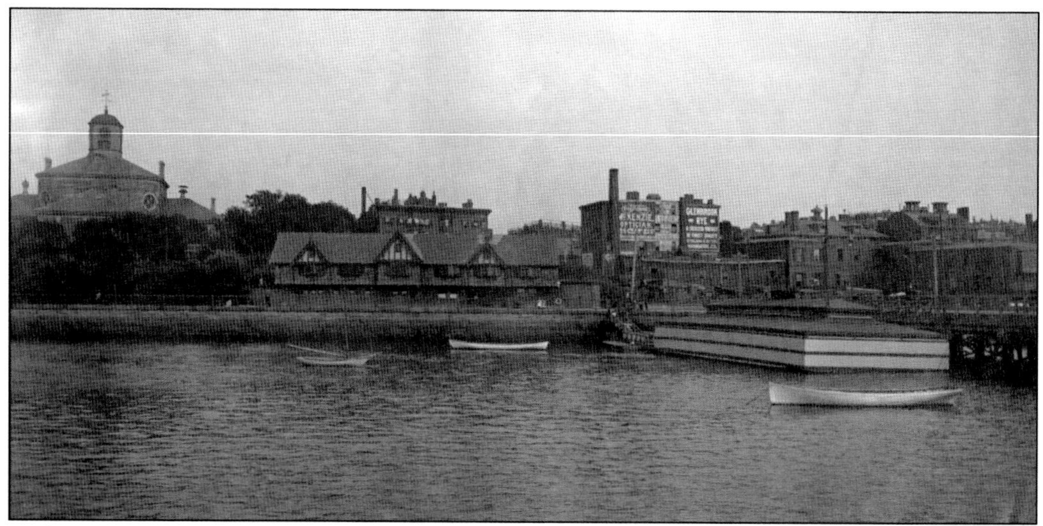

In the 1880s, more land was created directly in front of the Charles Street Jail. Called Charlesbank, it was turned into a park designed by Frederick Law Olmsted. Charlesbank was built primarily so residents of the nearby West End, a crowded, urban neighborhood of immigrants and tenements, would have outdoor space for fresh air and recreation. (Courtesy of the National Park Service, Frederick Law Olmsted National Historic Site.)

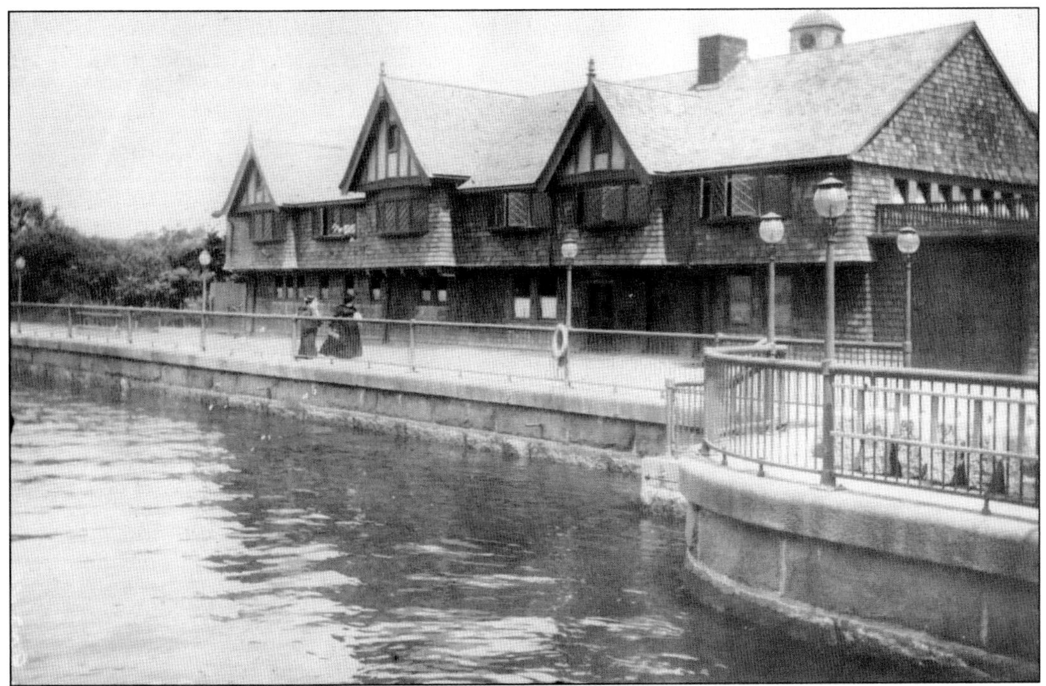

Charlesbank included separate recreational areas for men and women and the first free, open-air gymnasiums in the country. This building, located on the river in front of the Charles Street Jail, was the "administration lodge" for the women's gymnasium. Here, women and children could take advantage of exercise classes (accompanied by piano), games, lockers, and baths. (Courtesy of the National Park Service, Frederick Law Olmsted National Historic Site.)

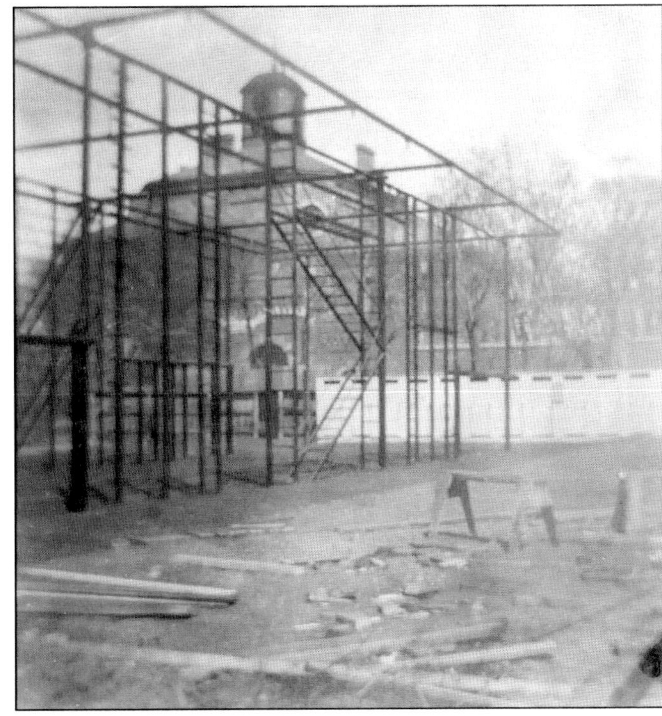

Behind the administration lodge was the gymnasium for women and children. In this image, the gym appears to be under construction, with the Charles Street Jail directly behind it. (Courtesy of the National Park Service, Frederick Law Olmsted National Historic Site.)

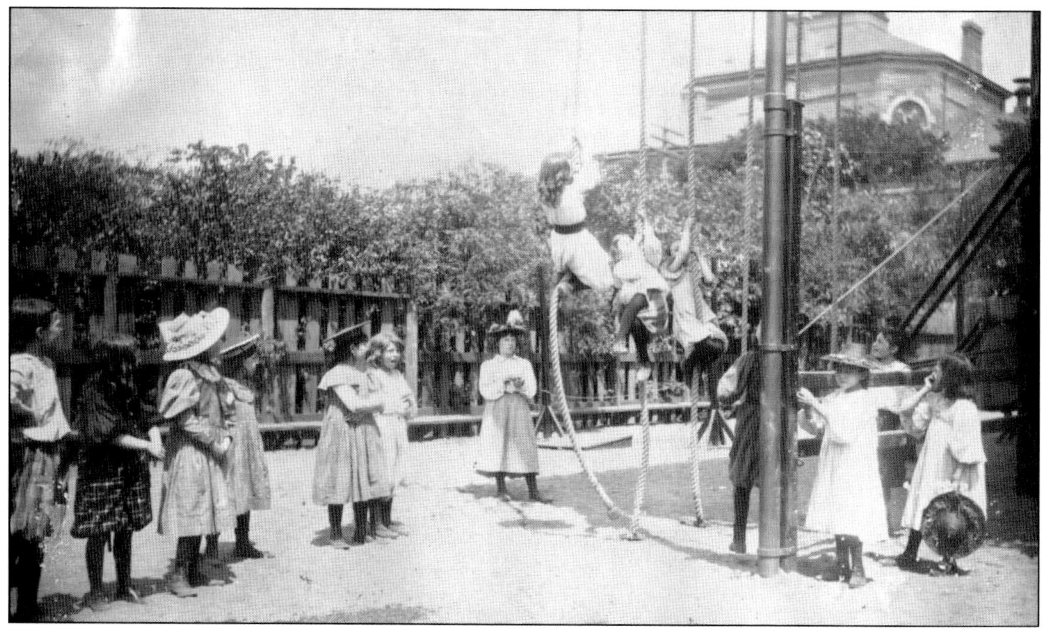

The caption for this photograph in the Olmsted Archives photograph album reads, "A race upon the ropes—the beginning." In addition to rope climbing, the women's and children's gym also offered sandboxes, swings, poles, ladders, and seesaws, all in the shadow of the jail. (Courtesy of the National Park Service, Frederick Law Olmsted National Historic Site.)

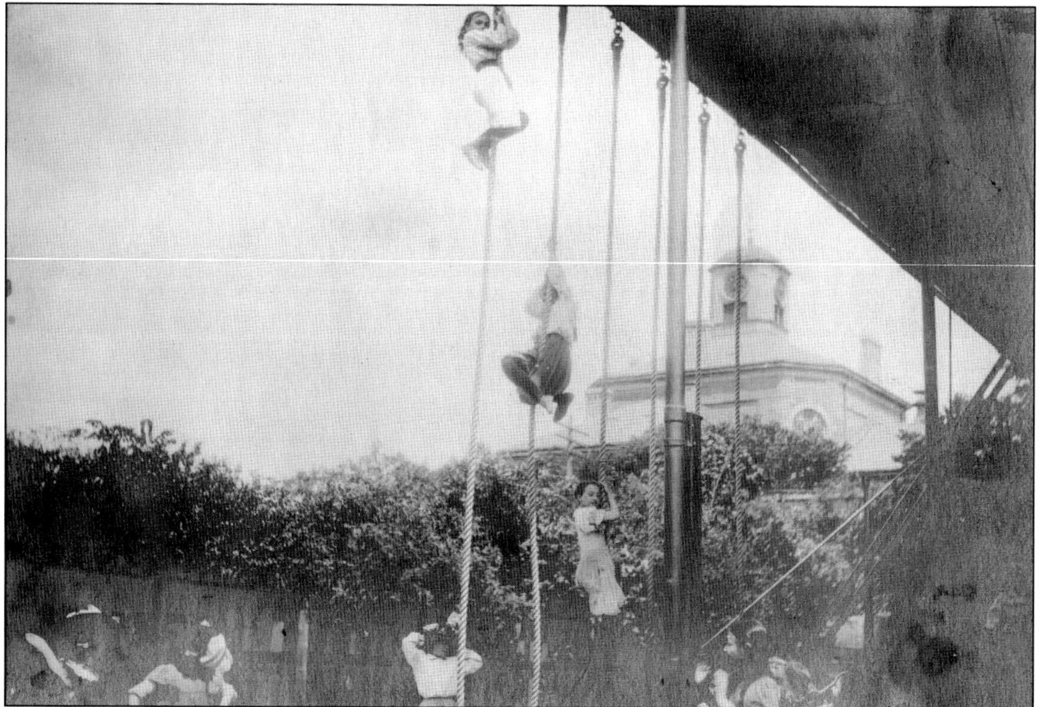

With the Charles Street Jail as witness, another rope race seems to have concluded. In 1894, the women's and children's gymnasium received an average of 900 visitors a day. (Courtesy of the National Park Service, Frederick Law Olmsted National Historic Site.)

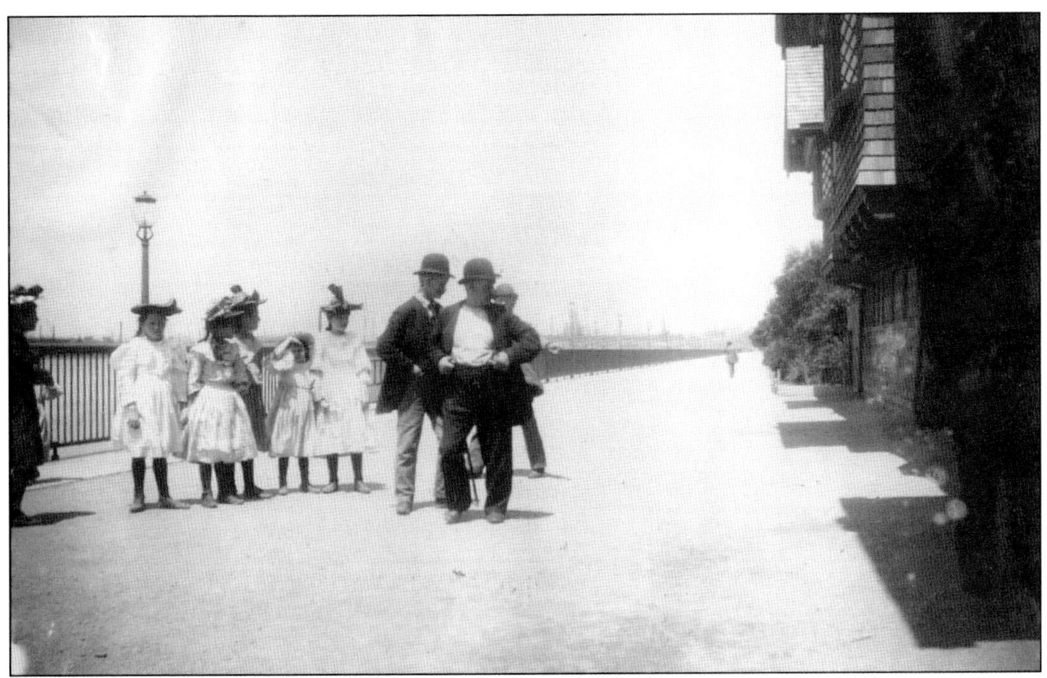

In front of the administration lodge and running throughout the park was a wide promenade, popular with residents of the West End. (Courtesy of the National Park Service, Frederick Law Olmsted National Historic Site.)

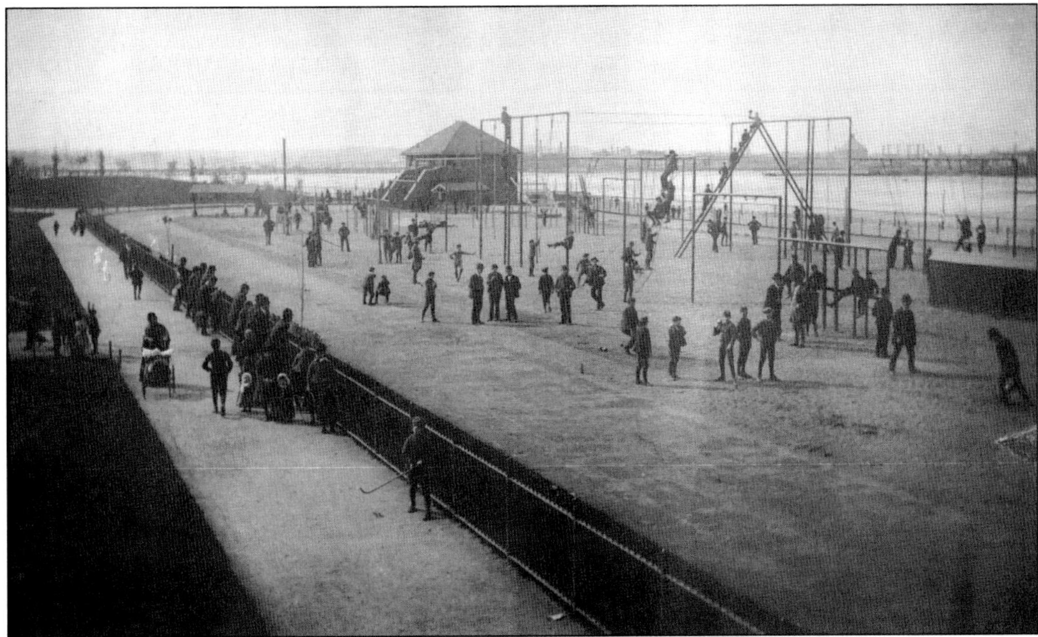

Olmsted worked with a Harvard physical fitness expert to design the park in front of the jail for active recreation. At the men's gymnasium, seen here, amenities included a track for running and bicycle riding, tall swing sets, an assortment of climbing and exercise structures, pole vaulting, and the shot put. (Courtesy of the National Park Service, Frederick Law Olmsted National Historic Site.)

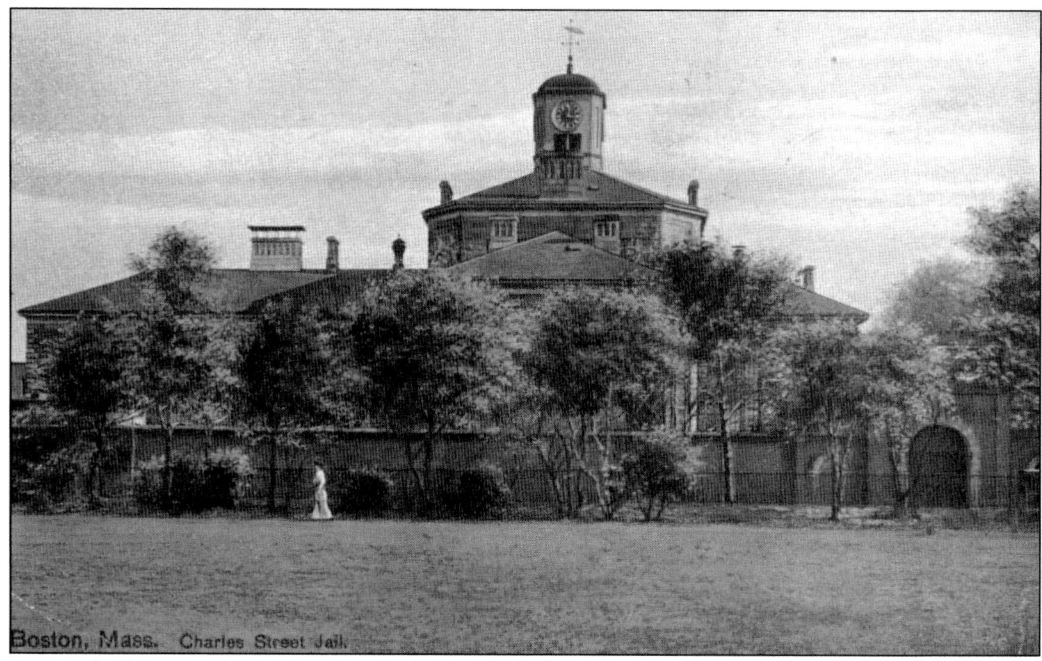

Postcards depicting the jail were not unusual. This one, probably from about 1910, shows the area around the jail as an idyllic and safe place for a woman to stroll.

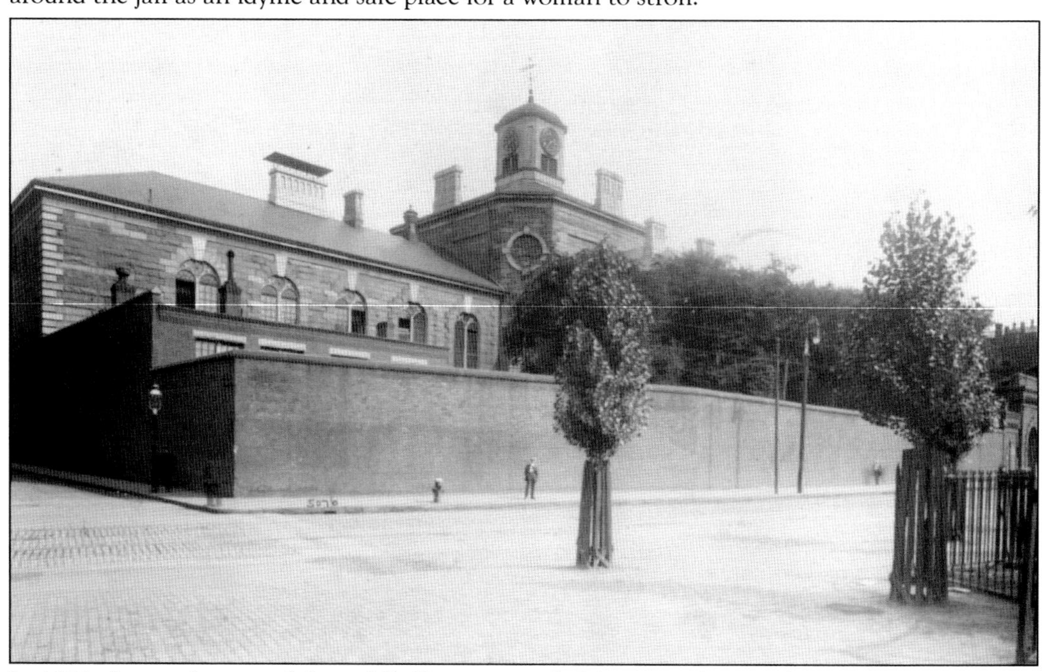

In 1902, the north wing of the jail (left) was extended from two bays to five to create a separate, adjoining facility exclusively for women. "The watchers were to be all women, and no male attendants will be here unless called for," one newspaper reported. Before this, women were segregated from men at the jail but housed within the same building. The first floors of the enlarged wing contained 72 cells, and the fifth floor was a new hospital for inmates. (Courtesy of the Boston Public Library.)

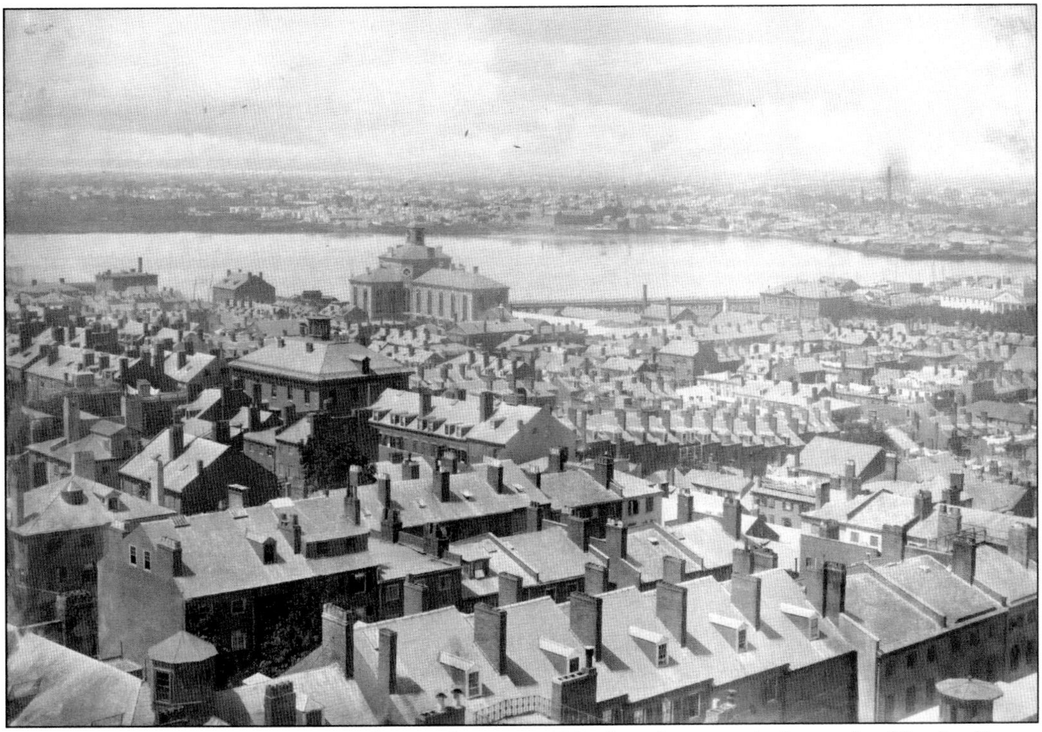

Taken from the cupola of the statehouse dome in 1858, this photograph shows the Charles Street Jail with the densely packed housing of Beacon Hill and the West End in the foreground. Land in front of the jail was not yet completely filled, and Charles Street appears in this photograph to be a raised road. (Courtesy of the Bostonian Society.)

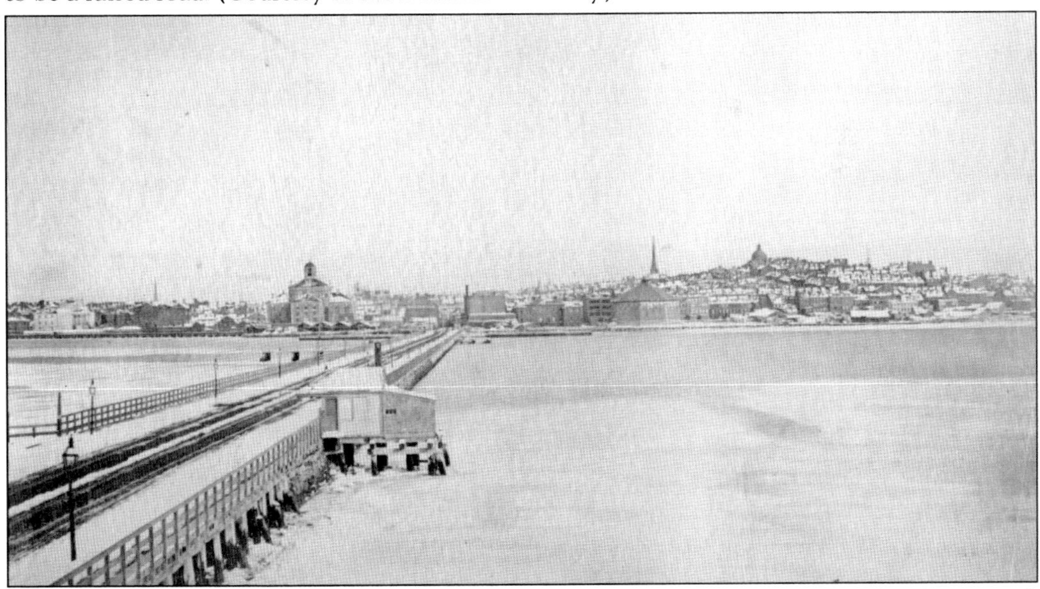

This 1864 image shows the Charles Street Jail with the West Boston Bridge in the foreground. Henry Wadsworth Longfellow wrote his poem "The Bridge" about the West Boston Bridge. It begins, "I stood on the bridge at midnight, / As the clocks were striking the hour, / And the moon rose o'er the city, / Behind the dark church-tower." (Courtesy of the Bostonian Society.)

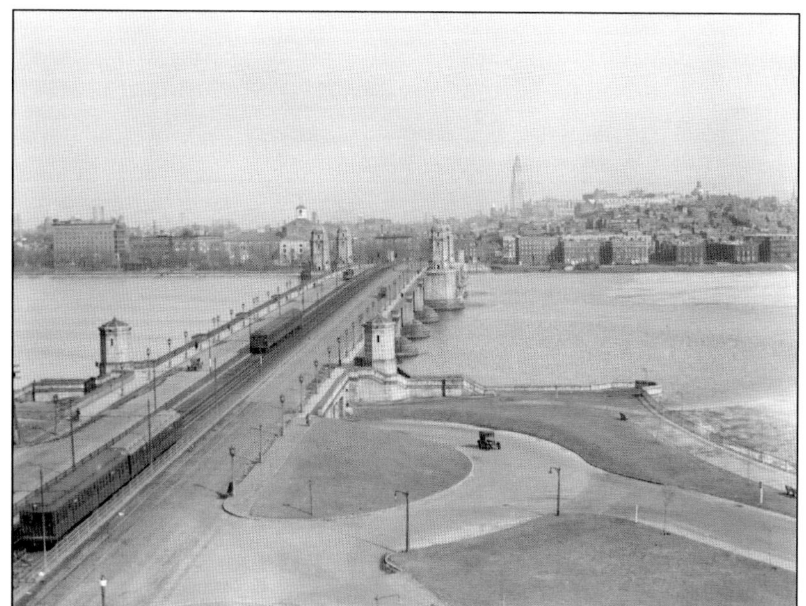

The West Boston Bridge was replaced by the Longfellow Bridge, which was completed in 1907. Seen here in the 1920s, the elevated railway and streetcars ran down the middle, connecting Cambridge and Boston. (Courtesy of the Boston Public Library.)

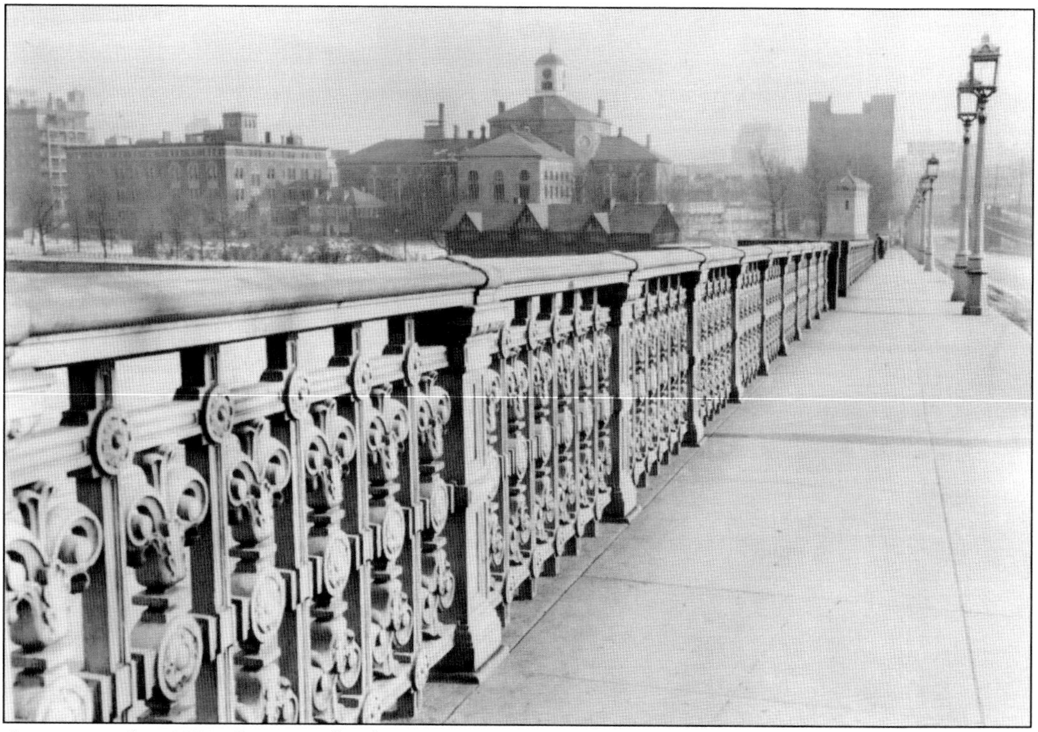

As seen in this 1931 photograph, the Longfellow Bridge and the Charles Street Jail became two of the defining features of Boston. In 2008, some of the Longfellow's handsome ironwork that had been removed in preparation for the bridge's restoration was stolen. Before it could be recovered, the metal was sold as scrap and melted or cut up. The thieves reportedly received about $12,000 for the metal. The cost to re-create these elements was estimated at about $500,000. (Photograph attributed to Arthur A. Shurcliff for the Metropolitan District Commission, courtesy of the Commonwealth of Massachusetts Department of Conservation and Recreation Archives.)

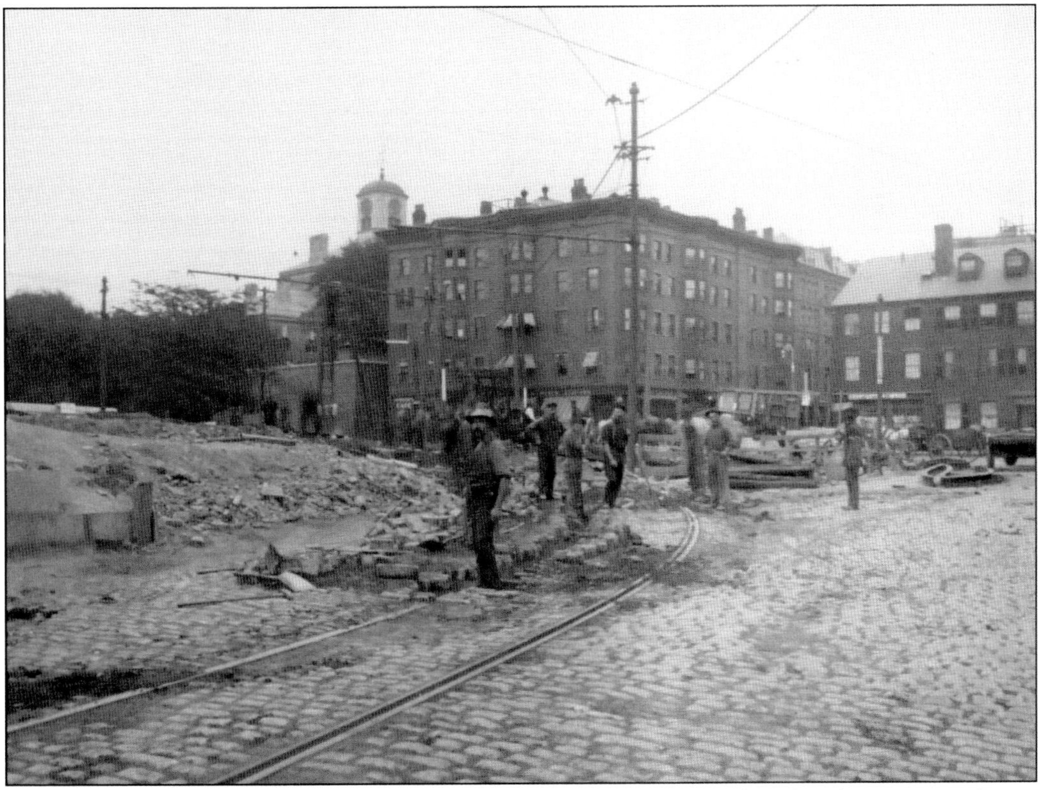

On the other side of the river, streets around the jail have been widened and repositioned over time. Houses and businesses were torn down to accommodate increased traffic and public transportation. Shortly after this photograph was taken, the apartment block next to the jail was removed. (Courtesy of Boston City Archives.)

After crossing the Longfellow Bridge, the train ran right past the jail. In 1918, funding was approved to expand the west wing (left) from three bays to six. Formerly the home of the sheriff, this part of the jail was turned into an administration building. The newer granite used in the addition is visible in this 1930 photograph. (Courtesy of the Boston Public Library.)

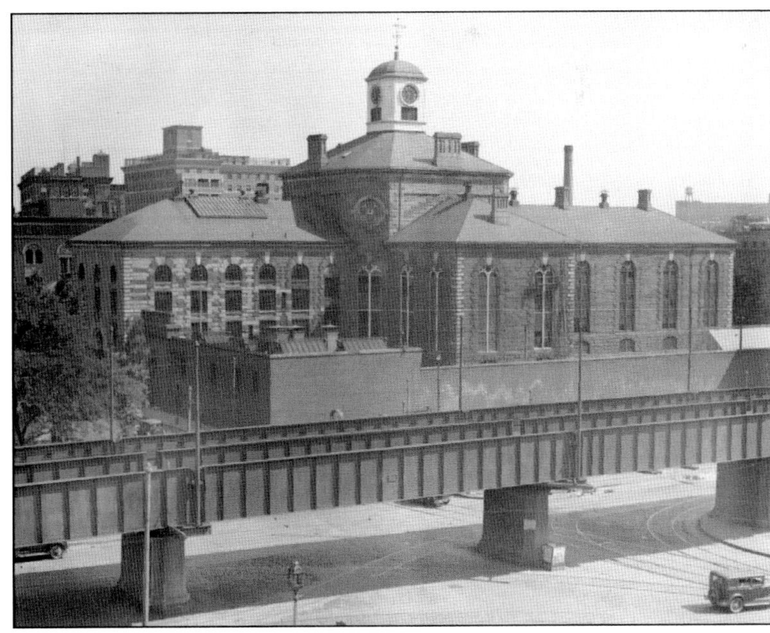

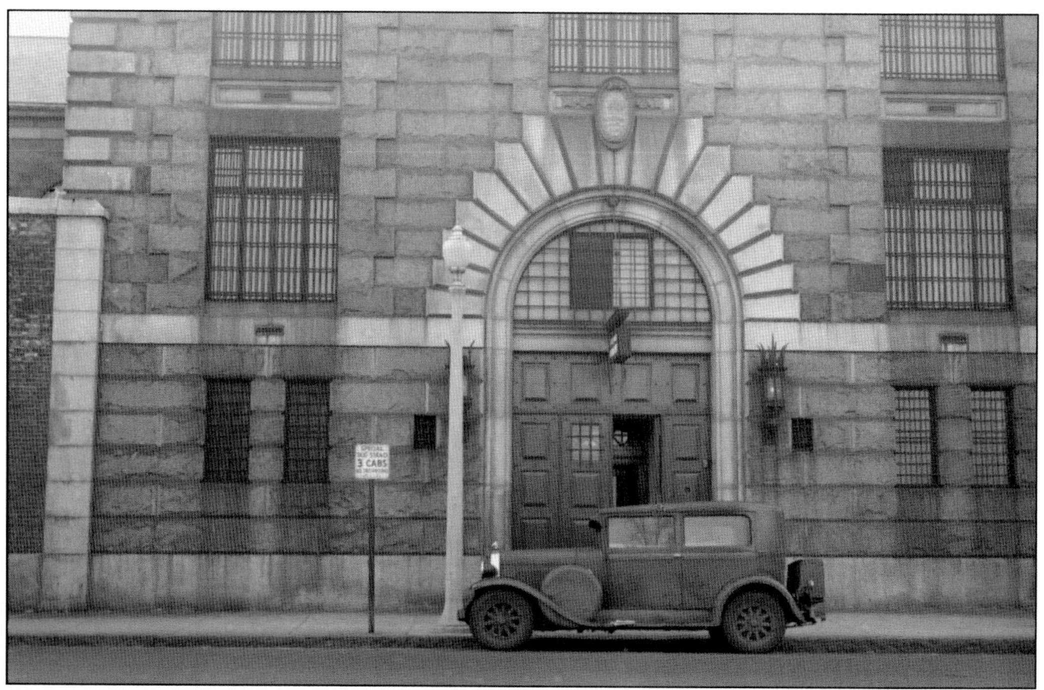

The front of the administration building, with its formal entrance for visitors, faced directly on Charles Street. This 1932 image clearly shows the addition's rough-hewn granite, which was cut to match the original. (Courtesy of the Boston Public Library.)

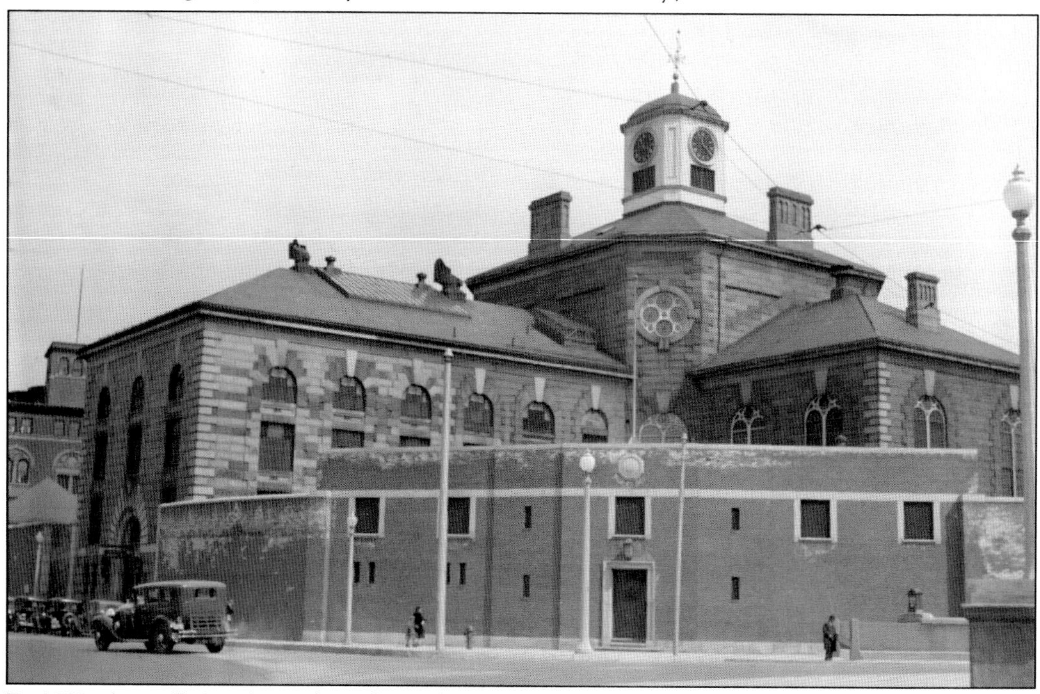

By 1932, the wall that formerly took a right angle turn in front of the jail had been replaced with a curving wall that followed the contour of the street. Appearing fortress-like, this new wall seems to hide the jail more fully from the public. (Courtesy of the Boston Public Library.)

Taken from Boston's Custom House Tower around 1930, this image shows the jail's diminished prominence on the skyline as the city grew up around it. (Courtesy of the Boston Public Library.)

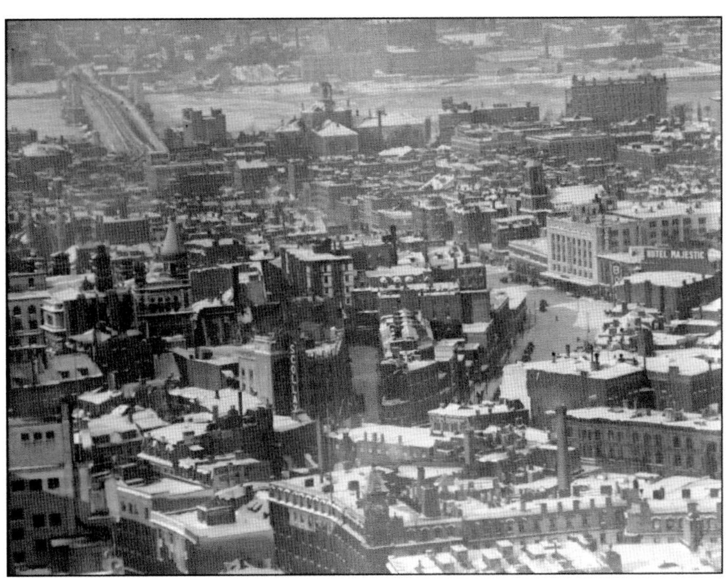

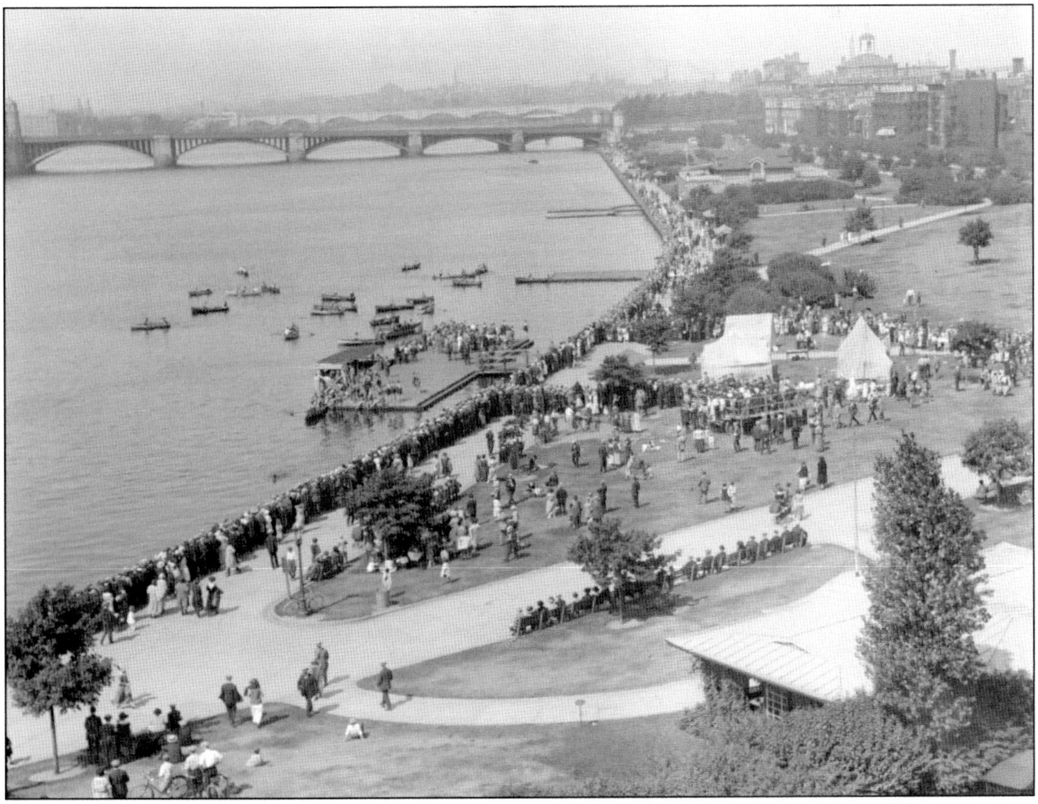

Throughout its history, the Charles Street Jail has been a silent witness to many of the activities of Boston. This 1923 image shows the jail in the background of a "swimming carnival" on the Charles River. (Courtesy of the Boston Public Library, Leslie Jones Collection.)

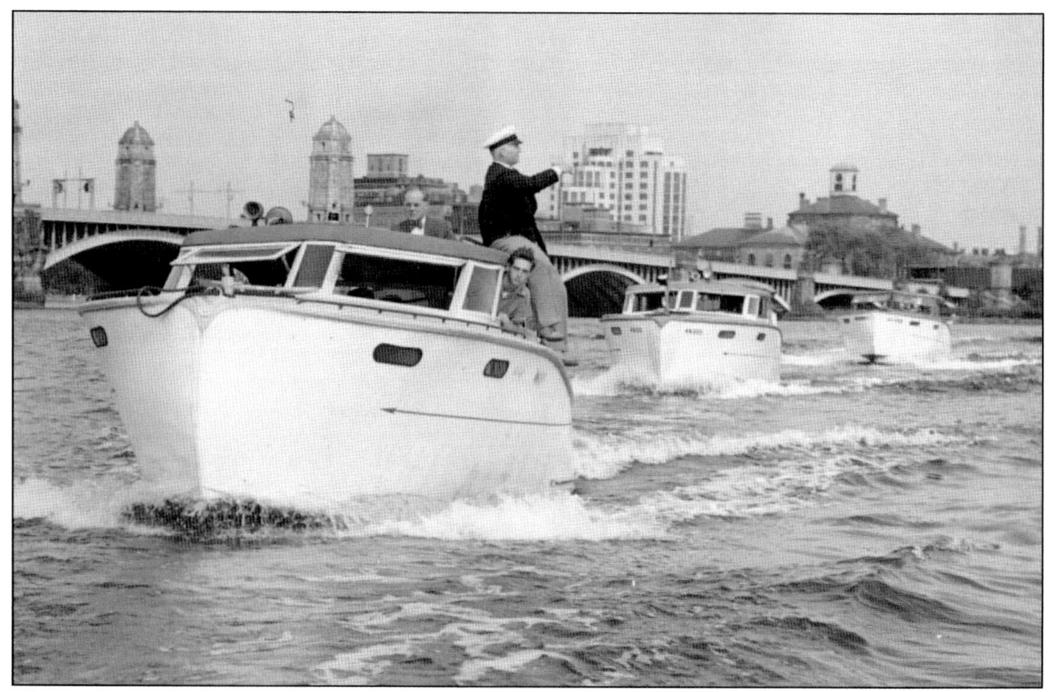

The Charles River has always been a place of recreation. Here, boaters enjoy a day on the water (probably between 1935 and 1950) with the jail in the background. (Courtesy of the Bostonian Society.)

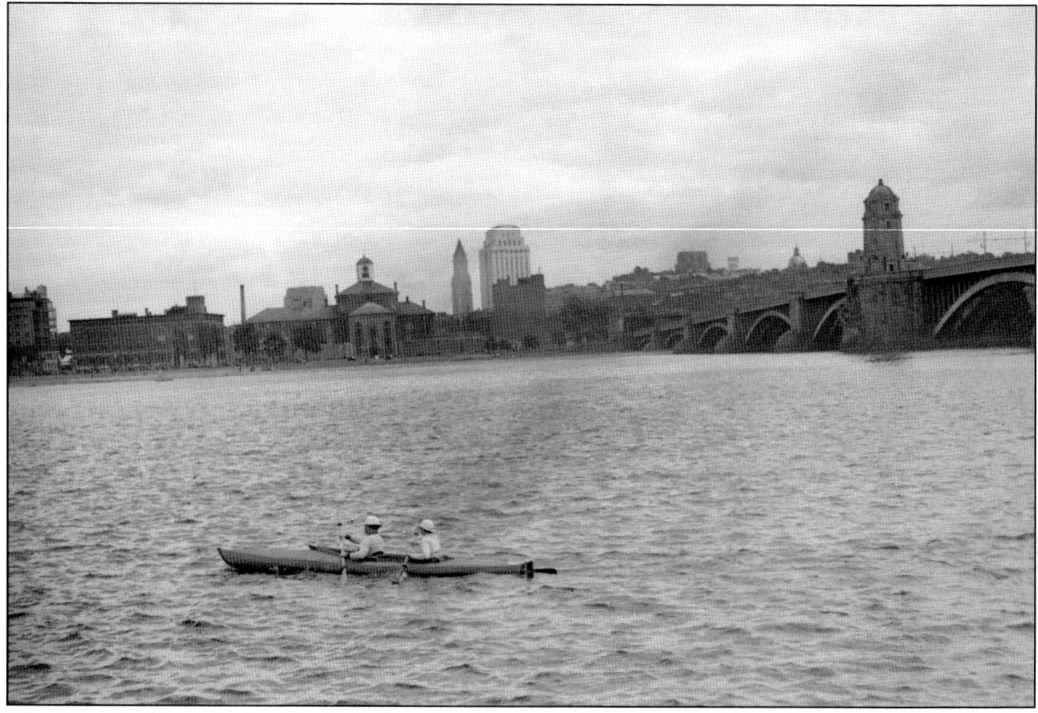

The Charles Street Jail is the backdrop for this pair of kayakers on the Charles River. (Courtesy of the Boston Public Library, Leslie Jones Collection.)

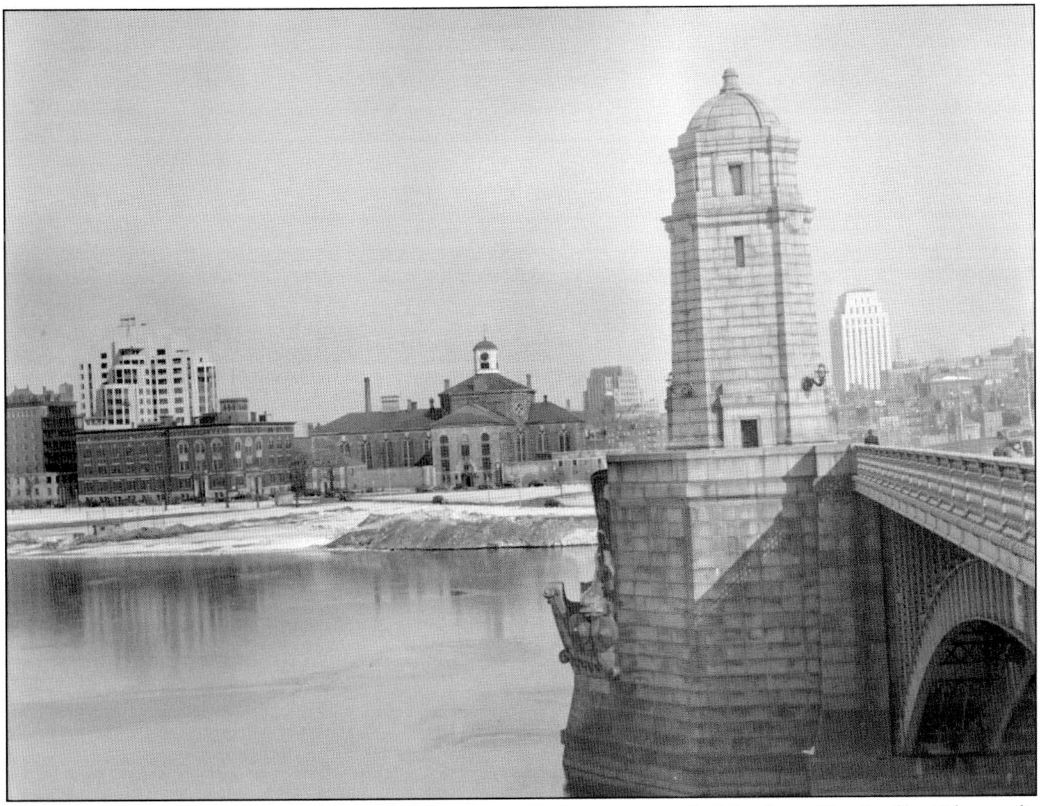

In the 1930s, land in front of the Charles Street Jail was extended farther. Gradually, Olmsted's vision for Charlesbank Park gave way to roads and traffic circles. The area was about to change even more radically. (Courtesy of the Boston Public Library, Leslie Jones Collection.)

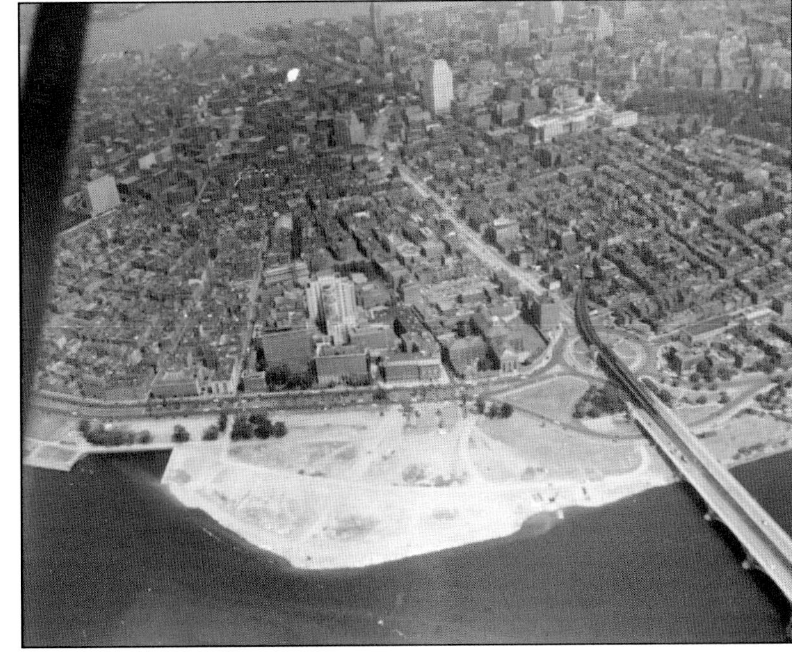

Taken around 1950, this aerial photograph shows even more land had been created in front of the jail and the extent to which Olmsted's plan had been abandoned. (Courtesy of the Boston Public Library.)

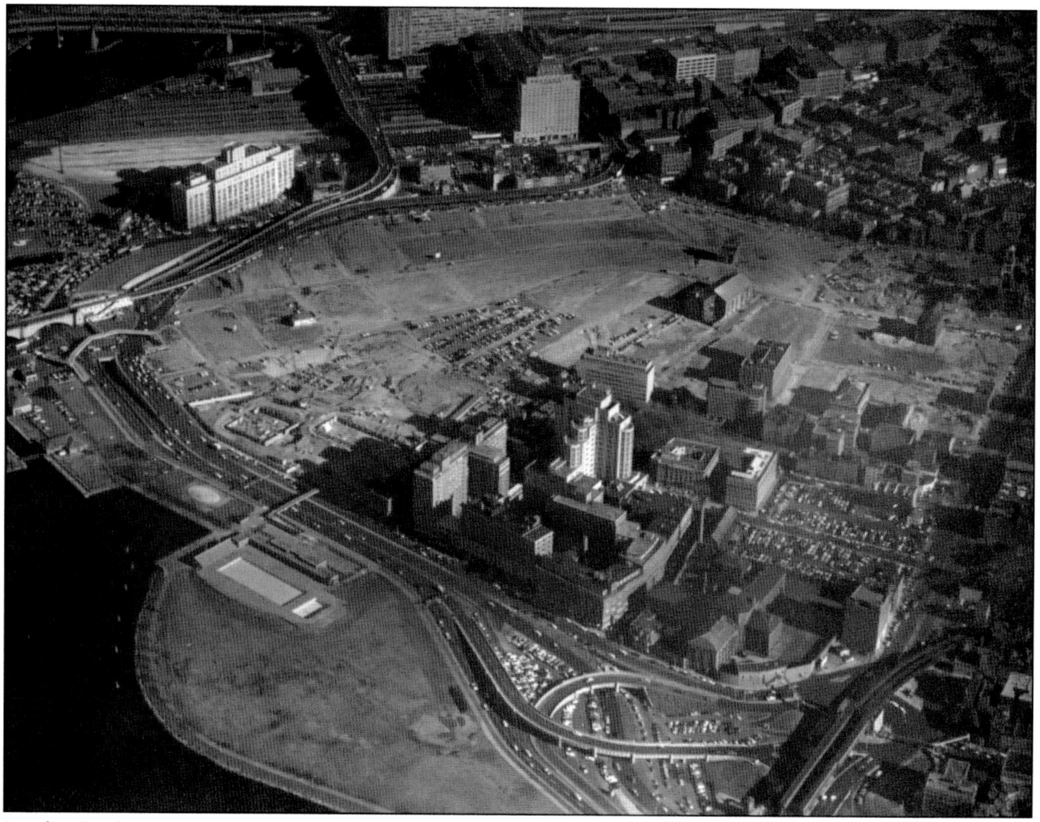

In the Early 1950s, Storrow Drive was constructed along the river, and more land was created near the jail to compensate for land lost to the highway. This image also shows one of the most drastic changes in Boston's history: the urban renewal that leveled most of the West End, the neighborhood that includes the jail. About 50 acres of urban landscape were cleared, and thousands of people were displaced. The jail is one of the few older West End buildings to survive. (Courtesy of the City of Boston Archives.)

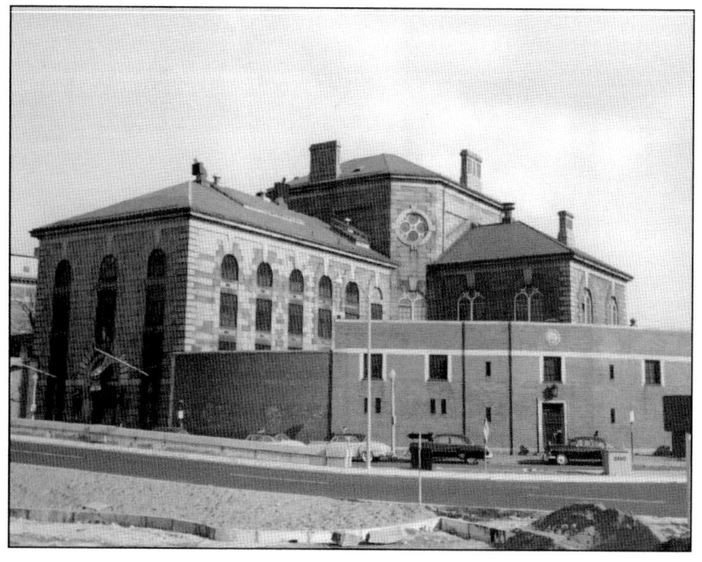

Around 1950, the clock tower was removed from the Charles Street Jail. By the time this photograph was taken in 1952, many of the nearby buildings had fallen to urban renewal, leaving the area around the jail sparsely populated. (Courtesy of Boston City Archives.)

By 1970, the area had lost much of its original character. The subway tracks and Storrow Drive left the jail cut off from the river and its surroundings. (Courtesy of the Bostonian Society.)

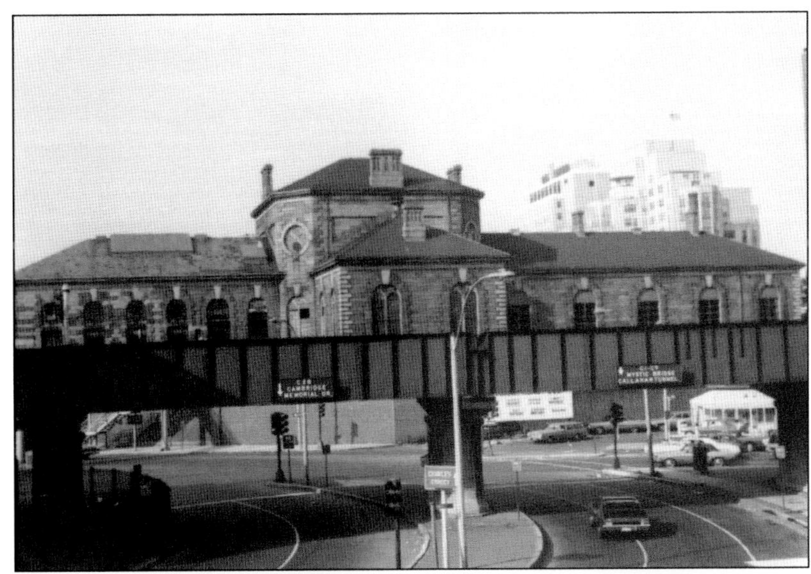

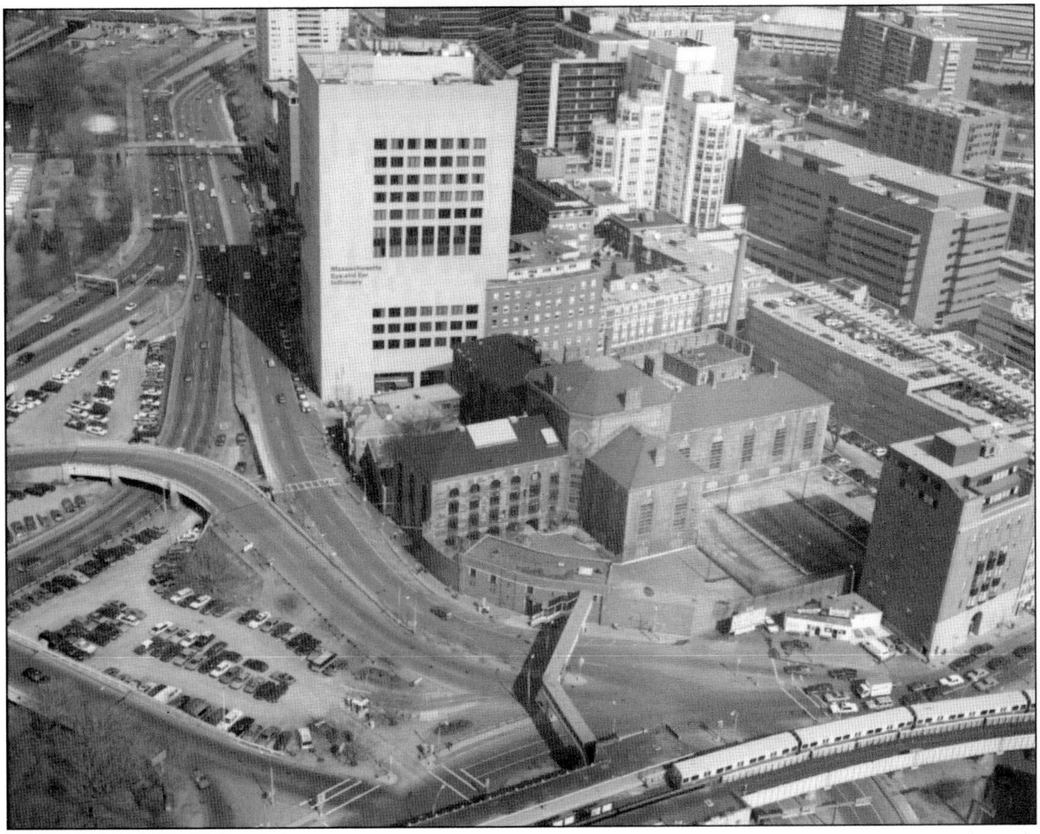

This aerial photograph shows how barren the area had become by the late 20th century. Though thousands drove by the jail every day and a pedestrian bridge brought subway passengers within feet of the jail's high brick wall, few had reason to linger in the area. The exceptions were patrons of the late night take-out restaurant called Buzzy's Fabulous Roast Beef, the small white building seen here nestled against the wall just outside the jail yard. (Courtesy of the Library of Congress.)

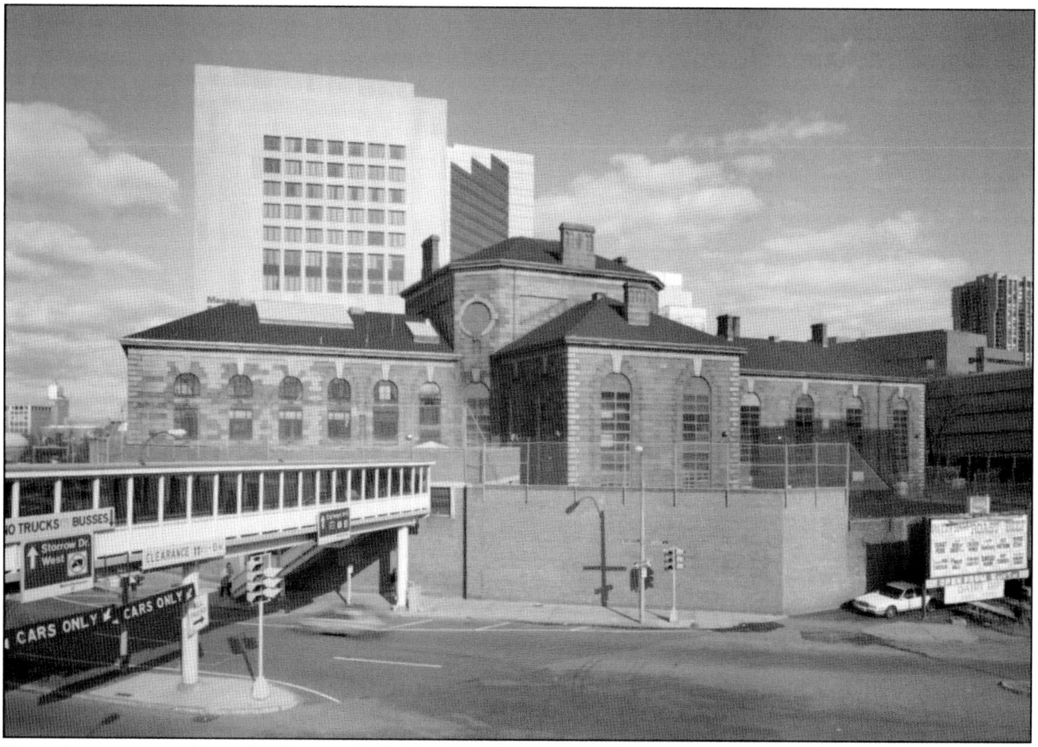

Buzzy's was open from 8:00 a.m. to 5:00 a.m., and much of its menu was posted on the billboard seen in this photograph. It had a varied following from students to revelers closing down the bars. Jay Leno talks of hitting Buzzy's for a late-night meal in his days in Boston. "You'd buy three Buzzy Roast Beef sandwiches; you'd eat two and then you'd throw one over the wall to the prisoners," he told a reporter. (Courtesy of the Library of Congress.)

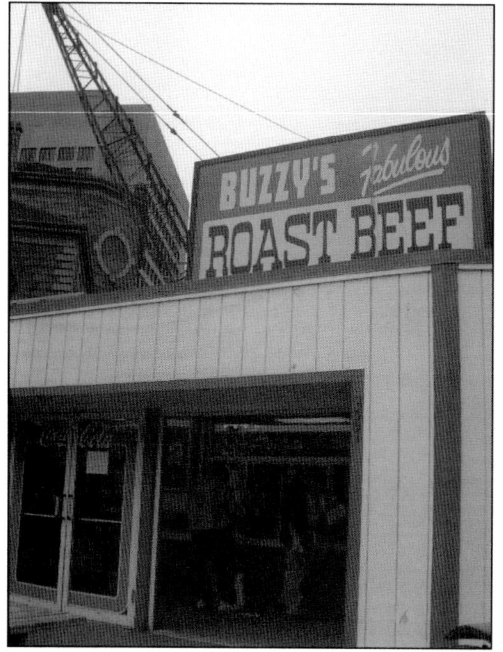

This picture of Buzzy's shows the restaurant in its last days while the Charles Street Jail building was being converted to a hotel. Buzzy's closed not long after this, and Massachusetts General Hospital bought the valuable parcel of land. (Courtesy of RobertandChristina.com.)

Three

Daily Life at the Charles Street Jail

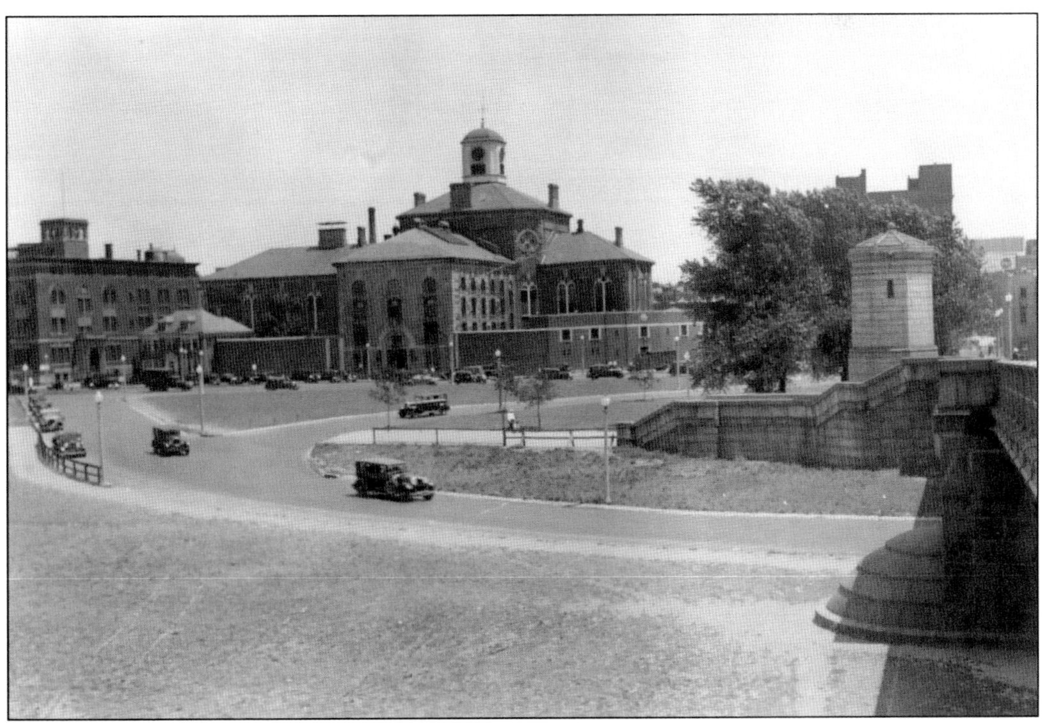

The sheriff of Suffolk County was in charge of the Charles Street Jail, and it was his job to make sure the place ran in an orderly way. With the conversion of the west wing from the sheriff's residence to an administration building in the 1920s, a new house, seen to the left of the jail in this photograph, was built for the sheriff and his family. (Photograph by the Metropolitan District Commission, courtesy of the Commonwealth of Massachusetts Department of Conservation and Recreation Archives.)

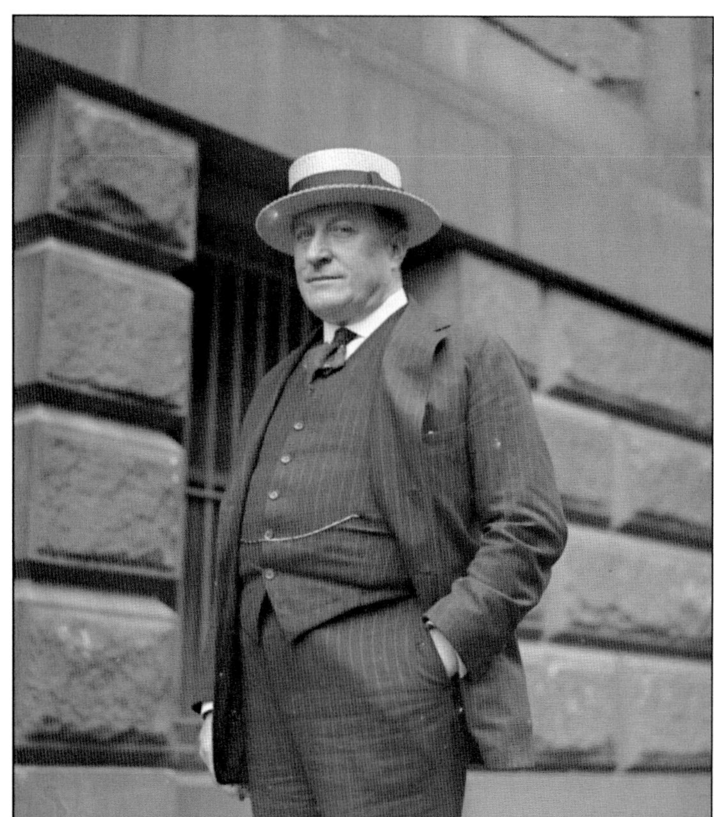

Sheriffs of Suffolk County were elected, and one of the most popular with voters and inmates was Sheriff John Keliher, seen here in 1921 outside the jail. "We in Boston pride ourselves on being liberal in the matter of reform, but the conditions some years ago were something to make a Bostonian bow his head in shame," he told a reporter. Keliher instituted many changes at Charles Street, and after he had been in office just a few years, a Boston newspaper proclaimed he had made the jail "as humane within as it is cruel-looking without." (Courtesy of the Boston Public Library, Leslie Jones Collection.)

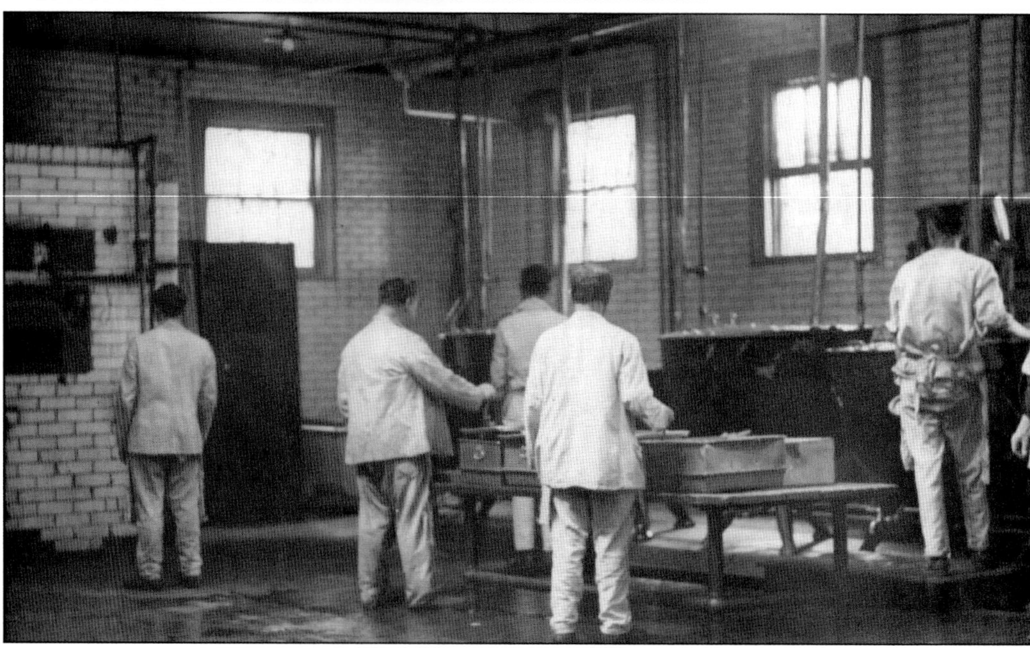

Under Sheriff Keliher, a new kitchen was installed. Improvements to the menu included fresh bread baked daily for prisoners. "I would not mind eating here myself," Keliher told a reporter. (Courtesy of the *Boston Herald*.)

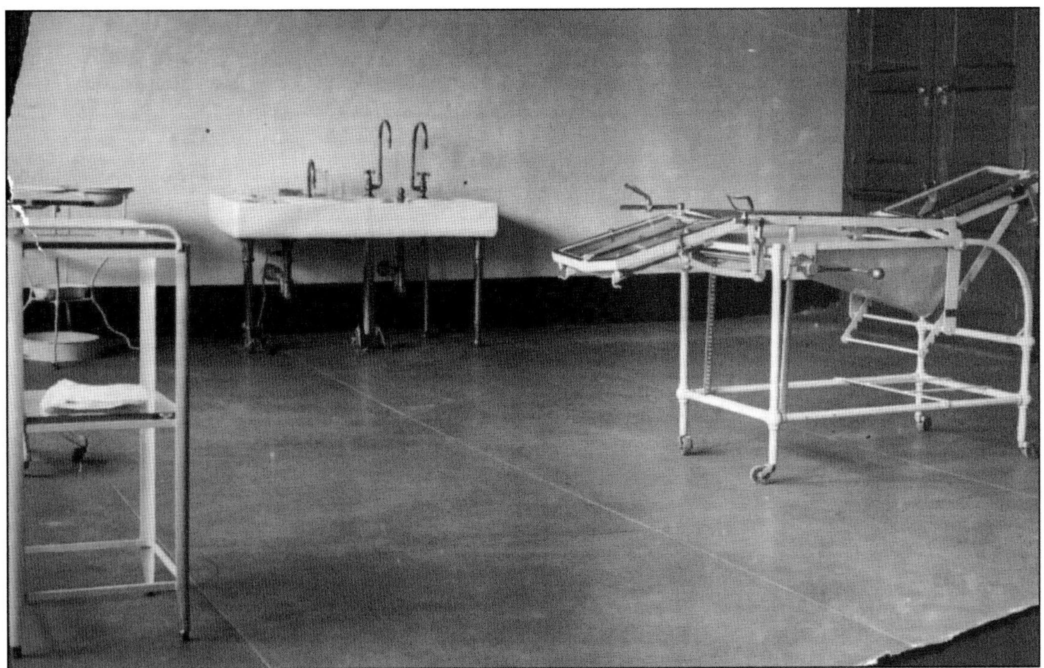

The expansion of the west wing also allowed the outfitting of a new hospital with dental equipment. No longer would sick inmates be sent to area hospitals where doctors "were not exactly enamored with such cases," as Keliher described it. (Courtesy of the *Boston Herald*.)

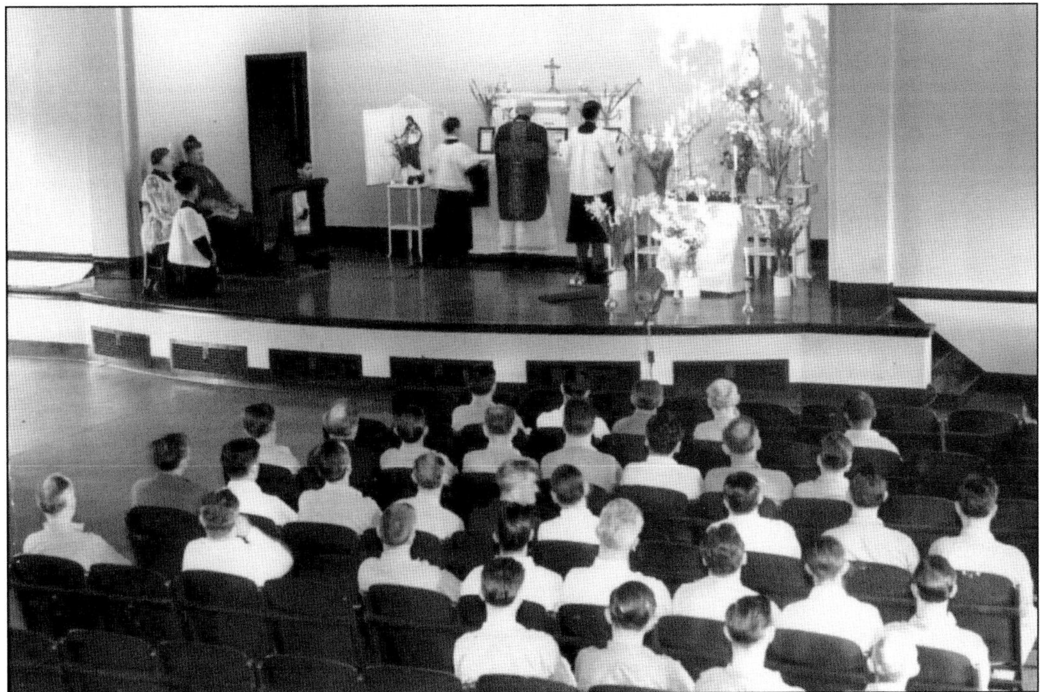

On the top floor of the new wing was an auditorium. Here, Keliher showed inmates movies once every three weeks and religious services, like this one in 1946, were held. (Courtesy of the *Boston Herald*.)

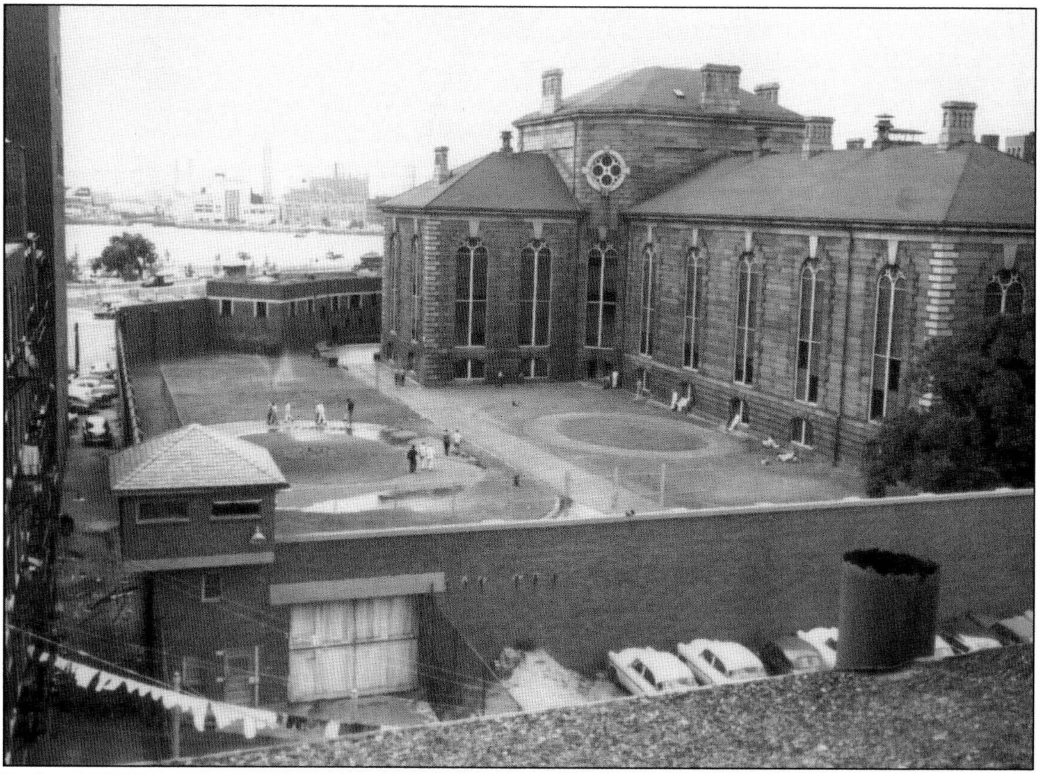

Before Keliher, no outdoor exercise had been allowed for quite some time. Now inmates awaiting trial were allowed out for an hour and a half each morning while those serving sentences could spend time outdoors in the afternoon. Activities including baseball, handball, and quoits (tossing a ring over a small upright post) were available, though by the time this photograph was taken in 1956, those recreations seem to have disappeared. (Courtesy of the *Boston Herald*.)

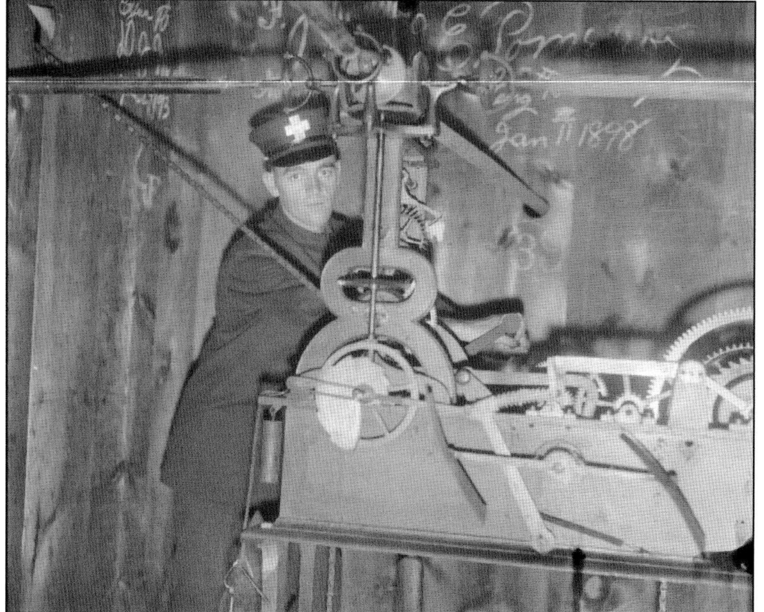

The Boston Fire Department was responsible for winding the clock atop the Charles Street Jail, as seen here in the 1930s. Providing the time of day was considered a public utility and a government function, so many public clocks, including the jail's, were owned and maintained by the city. (Courtesy of the Boston Public Library, Leslie Jones Collection.)

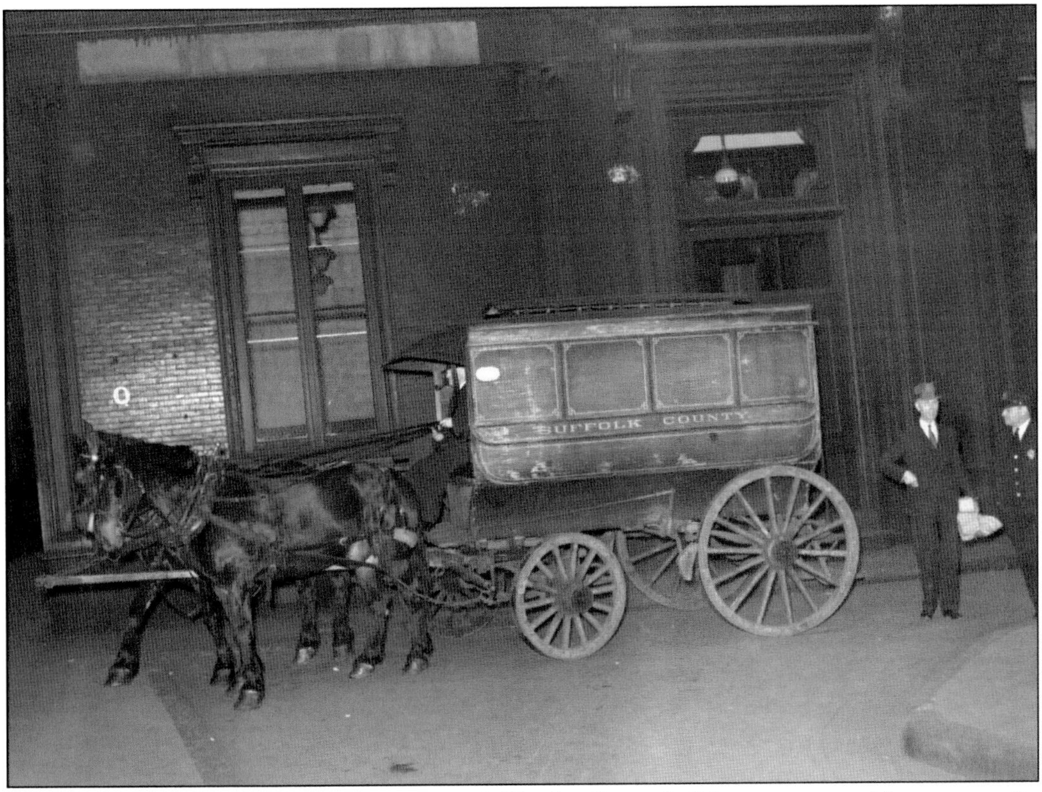

For years, this horse-drawn van transported Charles Street Jail inmates to and from court. In 1930, Sheriff Keliher replaced the wagon, pulled by a team of horses known as Bill and Pete, with automobiles, which he felt would be safer in the heavy street traffic. (Courtesy of the Boston Public Library, Leslie Jones Collection.)

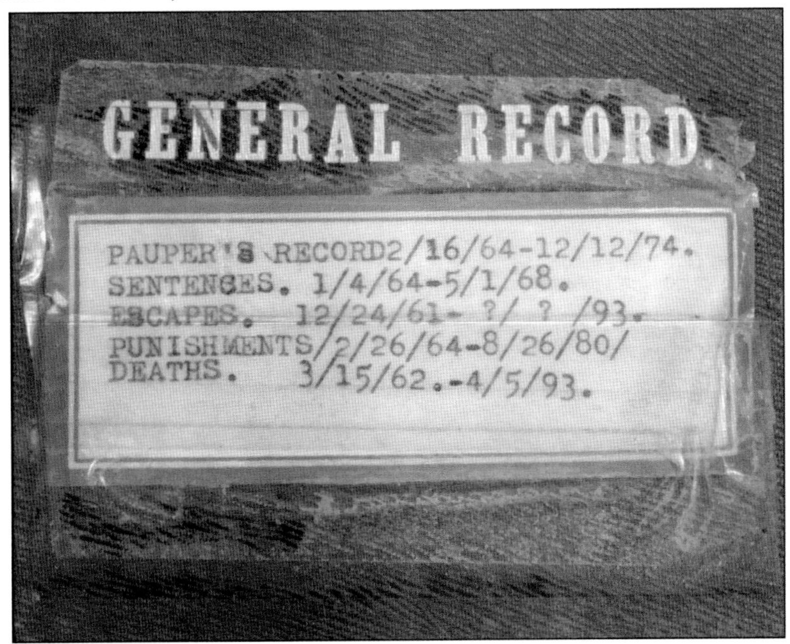

Daily operations at the Charles Street Jail included keeping meticulous records, many of which have survived. This is the label on the cover of one record book, which includes entries from 1861 through 1893. (Photograph by the author, record books courtesy of Boston City Archives.)

The record book begins with a list of paupers, and the heading of the page states: "To the Keeper of the Commonwealth Jail in the County of Suffolk. Sir, I claim support of my Creditors as a Pauper, not being able to support myself in Jail." (Photograph by the author, record books courtesy of Boston City Archives.)

This page from 1864 lists names of male and female inmates, the lengths of their sentences, and the offenses they were charged with, including "Common Drunkard," "Larceny," "Assault & Battery," "Breaking & Entering," "Night Walker," "Receiving Stolen Goods," "Noisy House," and "Manslaughter," among others. (Photograph by the author, record books courtesy of Boston City Archives.)

Of course, no jail is immune to escape attempts, and these were well documented at the Charles Street Jail. The record books include the names of escapees and the methods of escape, which include "escaped from jail van at So. Boston Ct. House," "cutting a hole through roof," "escaped by cutting bars of cell," and "escaped over the brick wall of the jail." (Photograph by the author, record books courtesy of Boston City Archives.)

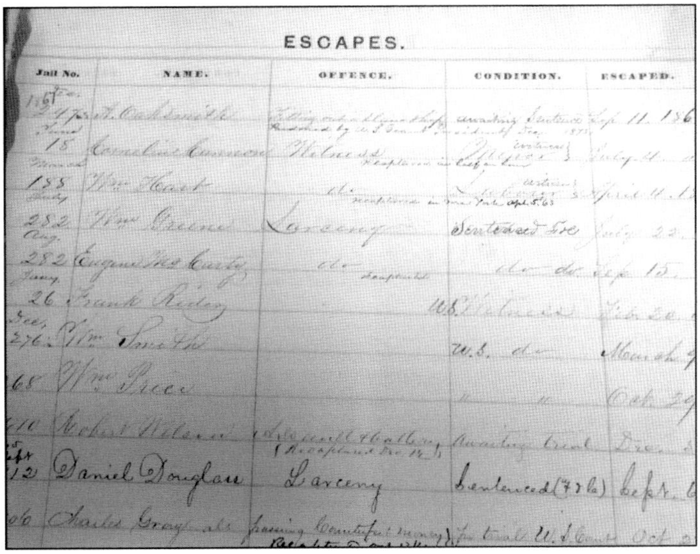

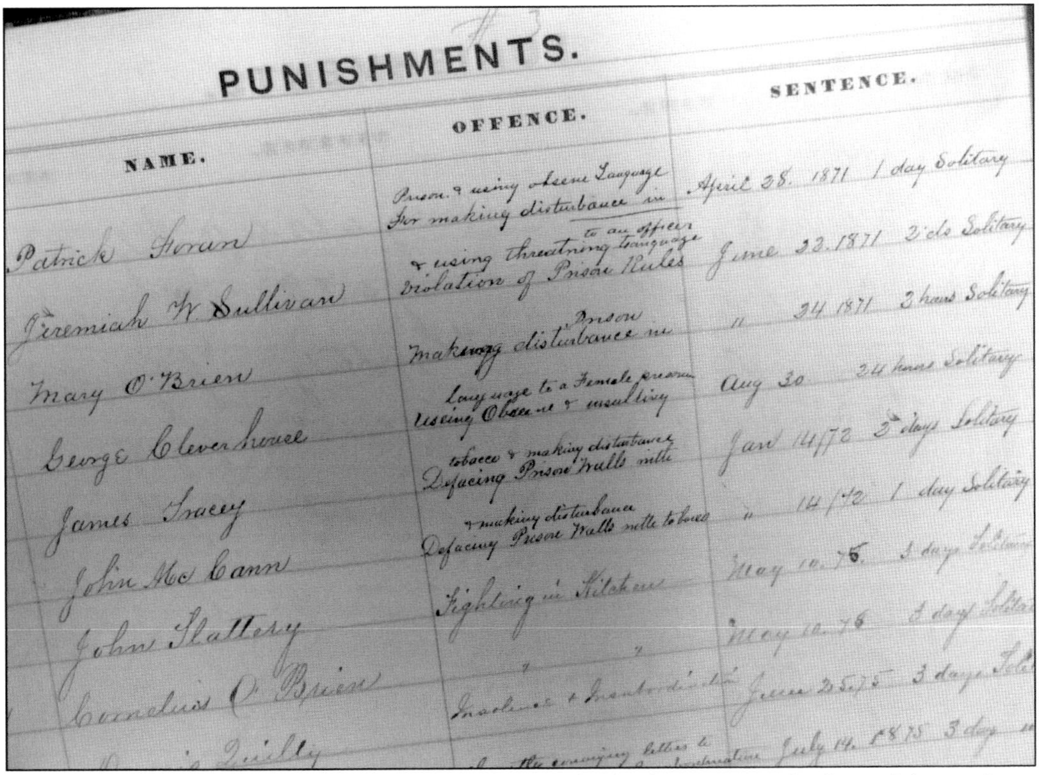

This page from 1864 lists names of men and women who broke various jail rules and the resulting punishment. Offenses include "Insubordination and vile language and profanity," "destroying bedding," "writing letters to female prisoners," "smoking in cell and threatening officer," "shouting in court," "fighting," and an attempt "to make tools to dig the bricks from his cell walls." Punishments listed were all varying amounts of time in solitary confinement. (Photograph by the author, record books courtesy of Boston City Archives.)

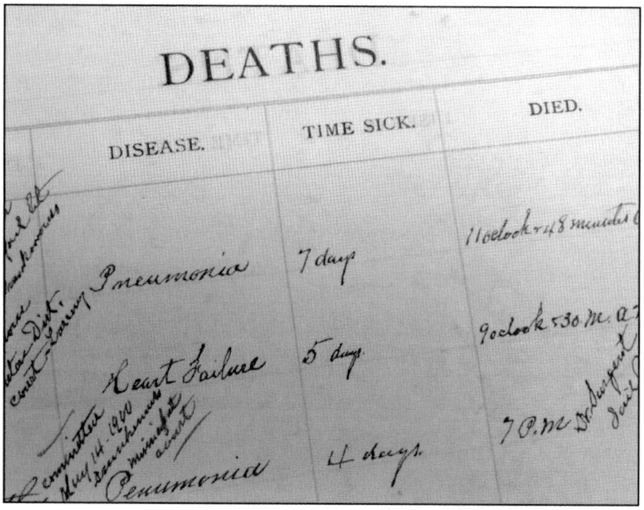

Names of those who died in jail, cause of death, how long they had been sick, and when they died were also recorded. "Diseases" ranged from "Delirium tremens," "suicide by hanging," "typhoid fever," "intemperance," "small pox," "consumption," "apoplexy," and "pneumonia," to "judicial execution." Occasionally, more information is given. For a man who died of typhoid fever in 1882, the jailer noted, "father was with him when he died." (Photograph by the author, record books courtesy of Boston City Archives.)

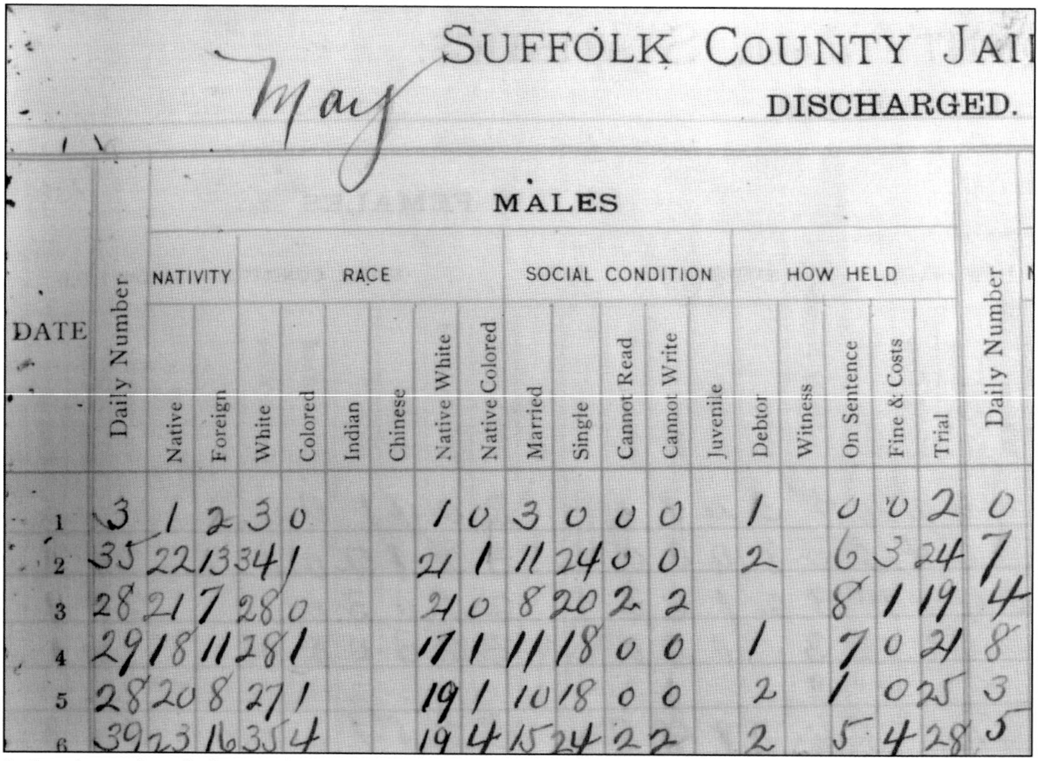

Jailers kept detailed records of prisoners' comings and goings to court, as well as the names of those who were released after serving their sentences or being bailed out. Daily statistics on the prison population were also kept, including "Nativity" (native and foreign), "Race" (white, colored, Indian, Chinese, native white, and native colored), "Social Condition" (married, single, cannot read, cannot write, and juvenile), and "How Held" (debtor, witness, on sentence, fines and costs, and trial). (Photograph by the author, record books courtesy of Boston City Archives.)

April 1903 SUFFOLK COUNTY JAIL.

Date.	1st Jail Watch.	2d Jail Watch.	Outer Office Watch.	Day Duty on Sundays. Steward.	Jail.	Outer Office.
1	Reardon	Shurtleff	Hatch			
2	Kelley	Callahan	Hatch	Day Finley		
3	Burke	Shurtleff	Single	Day Lowell night Morrison		
4	White	Callahan	Single	Day Morrison night Finley		
S. 5	Fallon	Shurtleff	Hatch	Day Lowell night Finley	Fallon	McCann Morrison
6	McCann	Callahan	Single	Day Morrison night Lowell		
7	Reardon	Shurtleff	Hatch	Day Finley night Morrison		
8	Kelley	Callahan	Single	Day Lowell night Finley		
9	Burke	Shurtleff	Hatch	Day Morrison night Lowell		
10	White	Callahan	Single	Day Finley night Morrison		
11	Hunter	Shurtleff	Hatch	Day Lowell night Finley		
S. 12	McCann	Callahan	Single	Day Morrison night Lowell	McCann	Reardon Finley

Records include which jailers were on duty for each watch, as well as miscellaneous notes such as "rained all day" and "commenced using hard coal," on this page from 1903. (Photograph by the author, record books courtesy of Boston City Archives.)

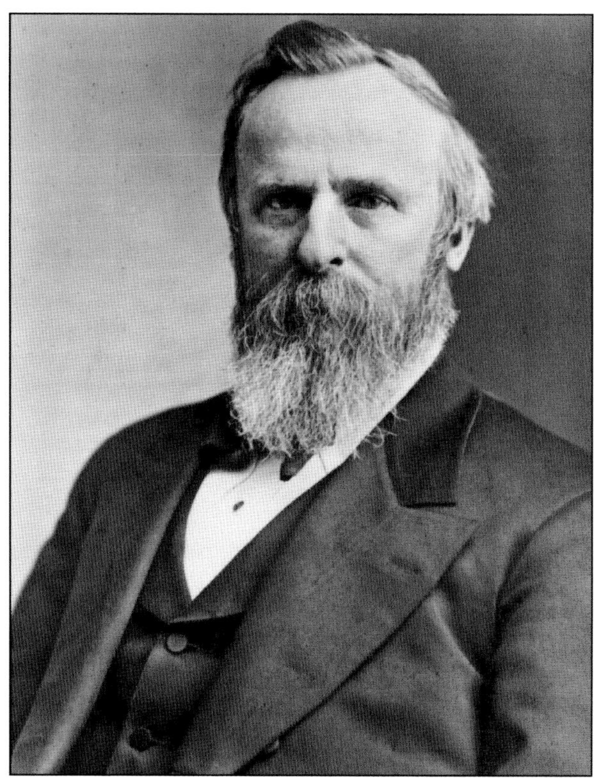

The Charles Street Jail was considered so well run that in 1888, the National Prison Association, headed by former president Rutherford B. Hayes, declared "Suffolk County Jail is a wonderful institution. It is the best in the United States." (Courtesy the Library of Congress.)

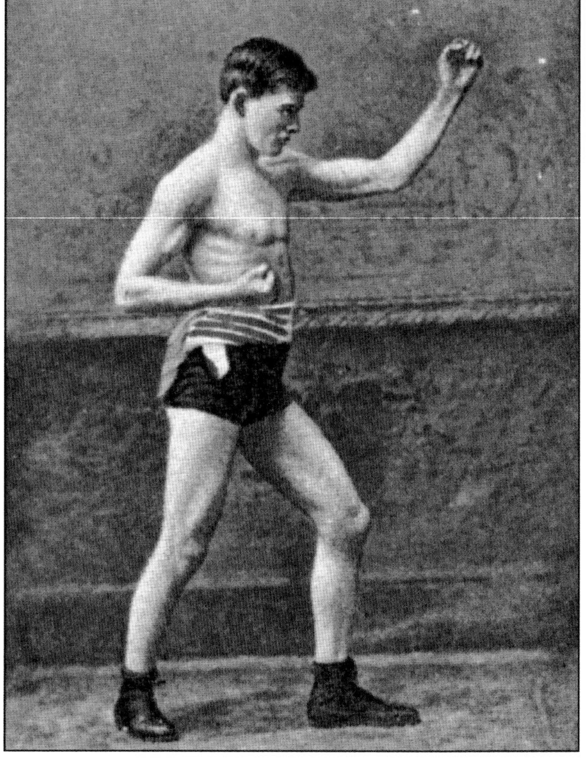

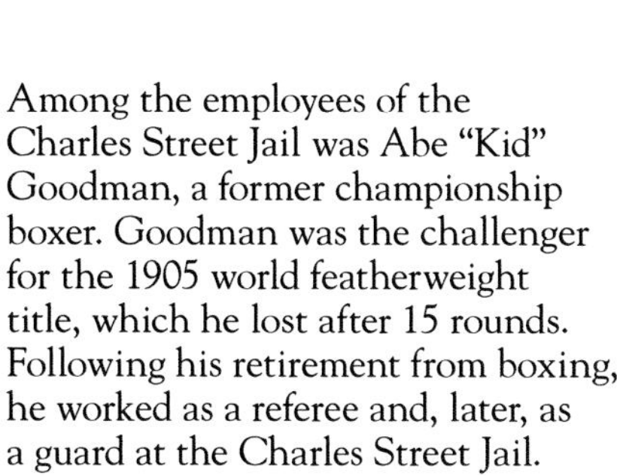

Among the employees of the Charles Street Jail was Abe "Kid" Goodman, a former championship boxer. Goodman was the challenger for the 1905 world featherweight title, which he lost after 15 rounds. Following his retirement from boxing, he worked as a referee and, later, as a guard at the Charles Street Jail.

Life at the Charles Street Jail occasionally included visits from celebrities. In 1926, Babe Ruth toured the jail. According to the press, he saw a cell, the jail yard, the hospital, and preparation of bread, coffee, baked beans, and fish. "It isn't like a jail—it is like a hotel," he told reporters. (Courtesy of the Boston Public Library, Leslie Jones Collection.)

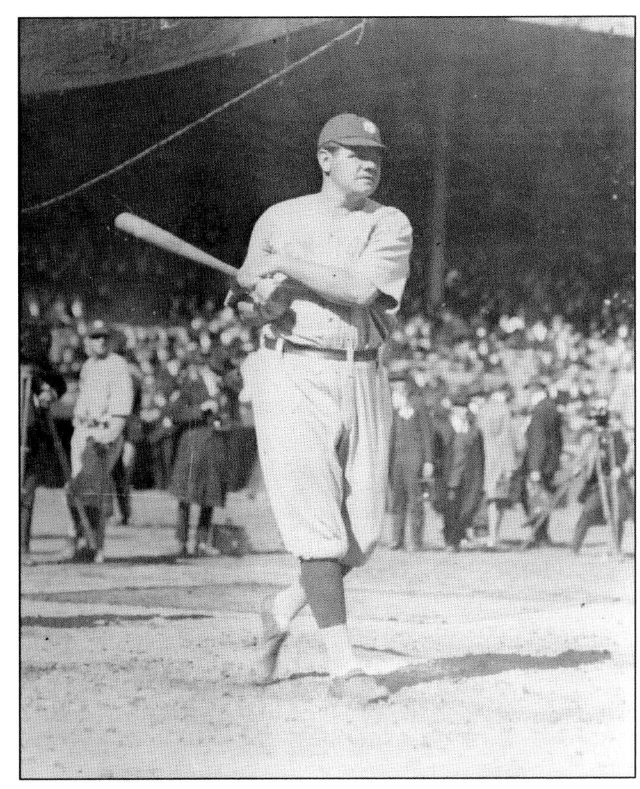

For the most part, the jail changed little over the decades. Cells received a new coat of whitewash from time to time. Running water and flush toilets were installed in all cells by the early 1920s. Otherwise, few improvements were made to the original plan. (Courtesy of the Library of Congress.)

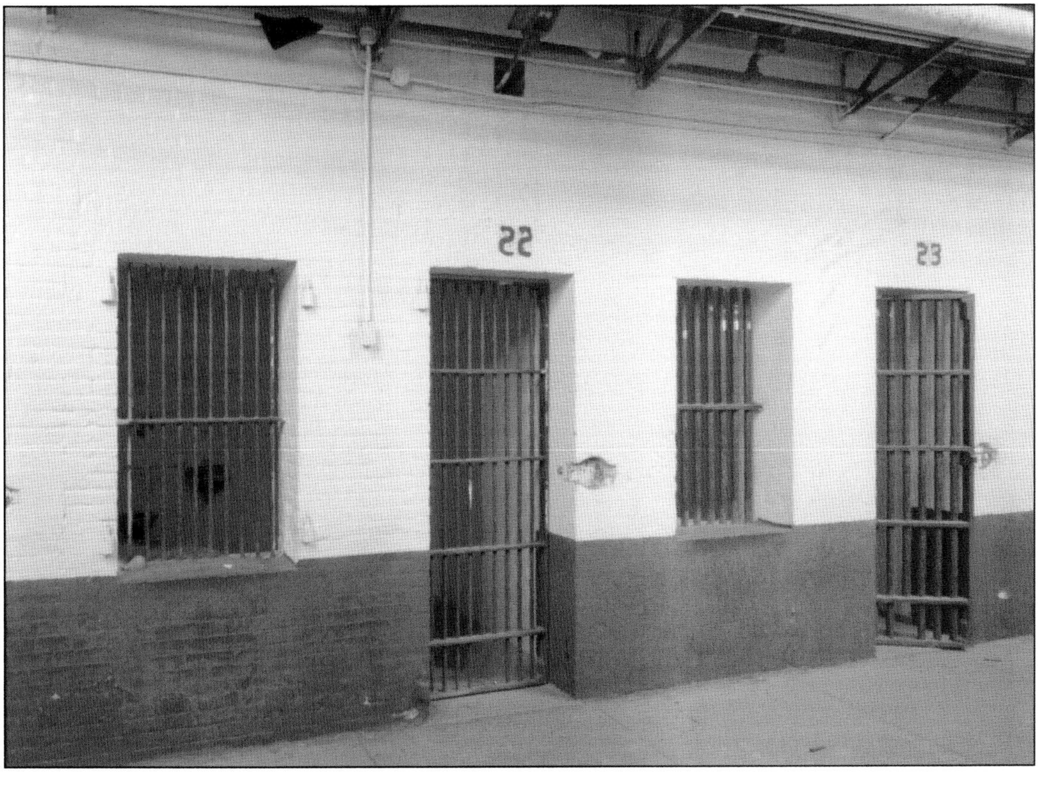

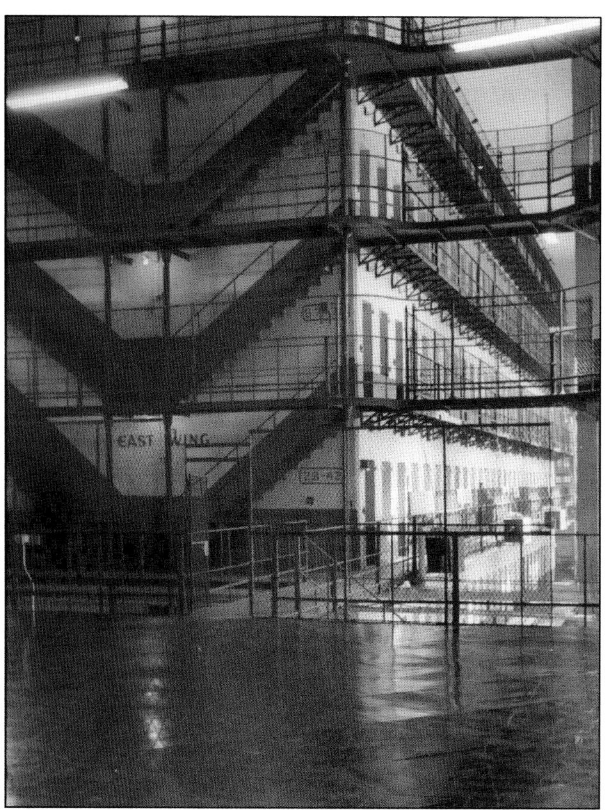

This image of one wing of cells, as seen from the rotunda, was taken in the 1970s. (Courtesy of the *Boston Herald*.)

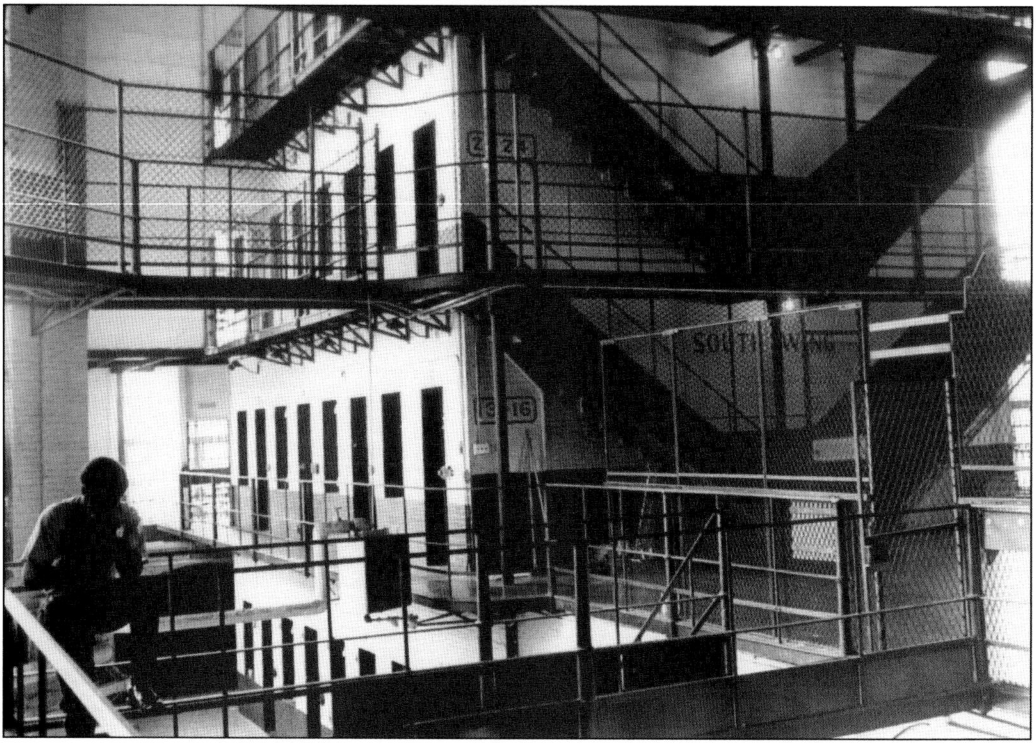

One noticeable change to the inside of the jail was the installation of chain-link fencing on the catwalks to prevent prisoners from jumping over the rails. (Courtesy of the *Boston Herald*.)

Four

Home of the Famous and Infamous

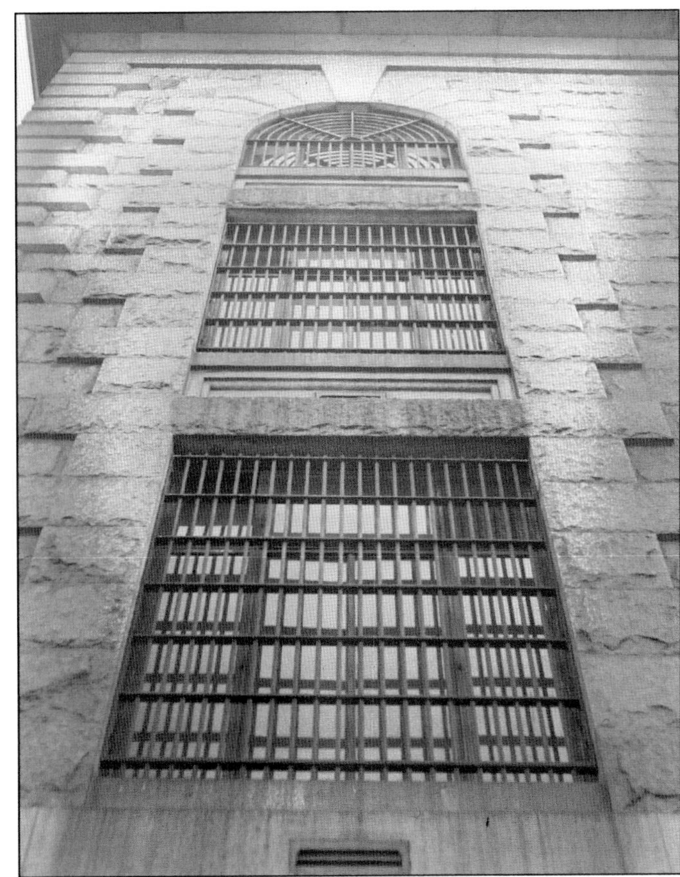

The Charles Street Jail operated from 1851 until 1990. During that time, it was home to all sorts—from petty thieves and paupers to some of the most hardened criminals. Because the building was a jail, not a prison, it served principally as a temporary holding place for those who were arrested and awaiting a hearing or trial, those en route to other houses of correction, and those serving relatively short sentences. As a result, the population turnover was enormous. Almost anyone who got into trouble in Suffolk County had a reasonable chance of spending at least some time here. (Courtesy of the Boston Public Library, Leslie Jones Collection.)

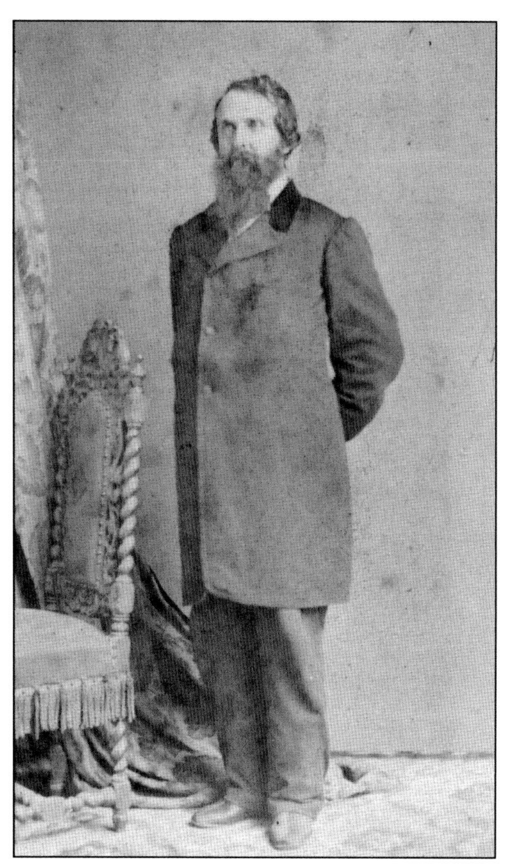

Appleton Oaksmith was jailed in 1861 for outfitting a slave ship in Boston. Convicted in 1862, he escaped from the Charles Street Jail, reportedly disguised as a workman. Among other ventures, he had supplied arms to revolutionaries in Cuba, helped in the brief takeover of Nicaragua by American general William Walker, served as captain of a blockade runner in the Civil War, and owned several slave ships. His mother, a prominent writer and abolitionist, appealed to Abraham Lincoln to pardon him for his crimes in Boston. Lincoln refused, but Pres. Ulysses S. Grant granted him a pardon in 1872. (Courtesy of the David M. Rubenstein Rare Book & Manuscript Library, Duke University.)

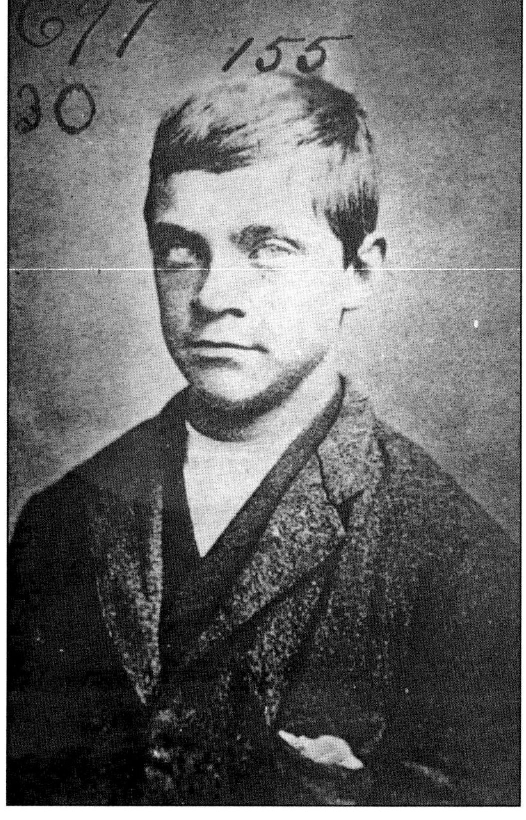

In 1874, Jesse Pomeroy, 14 years old at the time, was charged with the murder of a four-year-old boy and sent to the Charles Street Jail to await trail. This photograph was taken on the day he was arrested. Pomeroy confessed to an additional murder and was sentenced to hang. He was the youngest person in Massachusetts convicted of first-degree murder, and his case was national news. Given his age, his sentence was commuted to life in prison in solitary confinement. He spent more than four decades in solitary at Charlestown State Prison and died in 1932. (Courtesy of the Historical & Special Collections, Harvard Law School Library.)

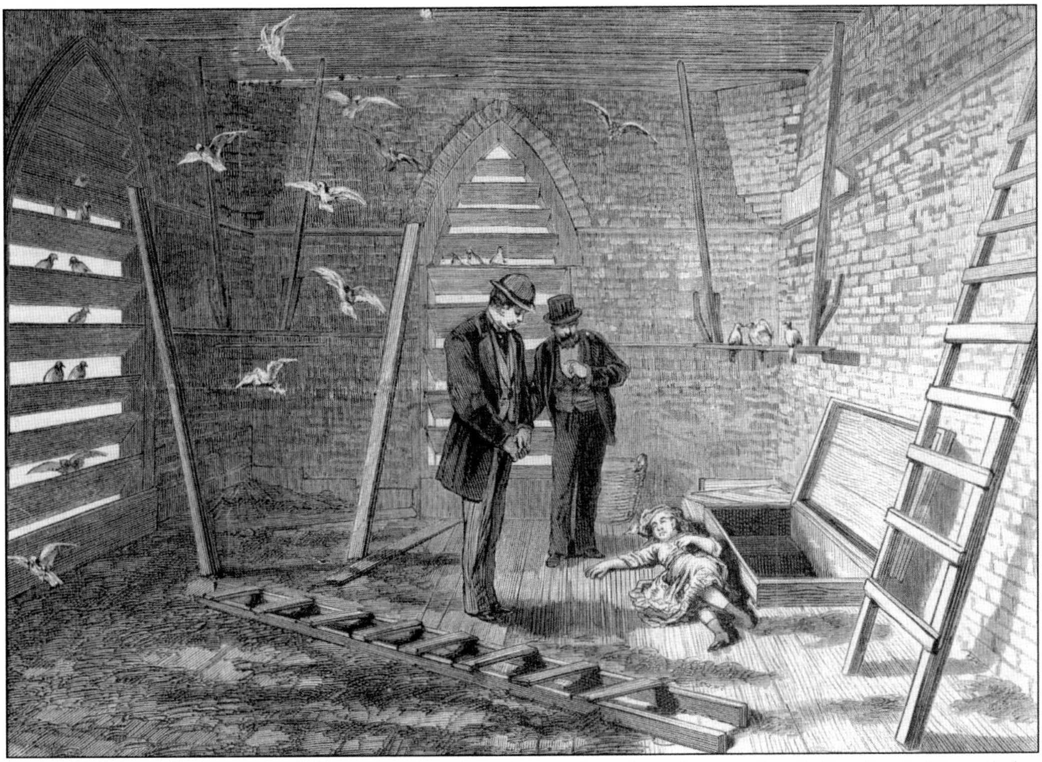

In 1872, five-year-old Mabel Young was found mutilated and near death in the belfry of the Warren Avenue Baptist Church in Boston. She died soon afterwards, and suspicion quickly turned to church sexton Thomas Piper, who later confessed to the murder, as well as to several other gruesome slayings. "The man appears to be a sort of Pomeroy, as he says he has no motive for these diabolical crimes but an unaccountable taste for blood," the papers reported, referring to his notorious contemporary.

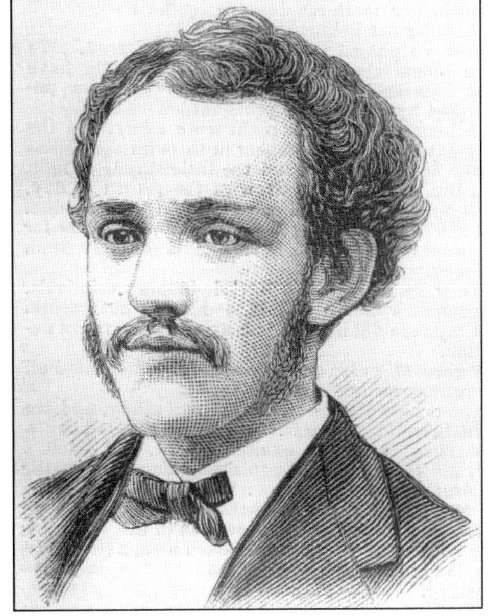

Thomas Piper was tried for the murder of Mabel Young in 1876. In an early example of forensic evidence in the courtroom, doctors used Young's crushed skull to demonstrate how blows to the head from a bat had caused her death, not being accidentally hit by the heavy trapdoor to the belfry, as the defense claimed. Piper was convicted and hanged in the rotunda of the Charles Street Jail. Young's fractured skull is still in the collection of the Harvard Medical School Library.

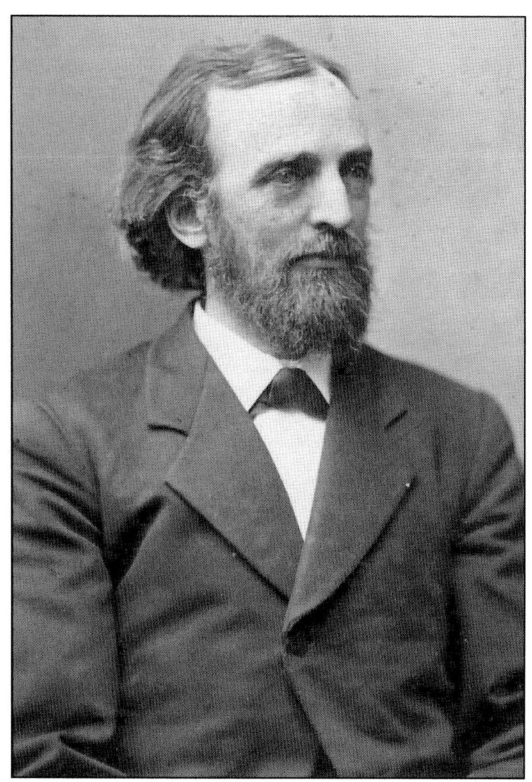

Ezra Heywood was an anarchist, abolitionist, and women's suffrage advocate. He was also an outspoken proponent of free love, a 19th-century movement that held matters such as sexual freedom, marriage, and birth control should not be subject to governmental regulation. Arrested in 1877 and convicted of violating obscenity laws for mailing his free love periodical through the US mail, he spent six months in jail, some of it at the Charles Street Jail, before receiving a pardon from Pres. Rutherford B. Hayes. (Courtesy of the Princeton [Massachusetts] Historical Society.)

In 1885, Rev. Horace Lorenzo Hastings was arrested and fined $10 for "preaching the Gospel on Boston Common" without a license in violation of a city ordinance. The following week, he returned and read passages of scripture, for which he was fined an additional $30 and ordered to pay or serve jail time. "Being a preacher without parish or salary," as he described himself, Hastings accepted the jail time at the Charles Street Jail, in part to shed light on an ordinance he felt restricted civil and religious liberties. (Courtesy of the Ellen G. White Estate, Inc.)

Rev. William F. Davis was arrested and fined along with Hastings for preaching on Boston Common without a license. He was taken to the Charles Street Jail and served 12 months. Davis continued to test the law over the coming years. In 1894, he took his case to the Massachusetts Supreme Court, claiming that not being allowed to preach freely on the Common violated his constitutional right to access public property. His claim was rejected in an opinion written by future US Supreme Court justice Oliver Wendell Holmes. (Courtesy of the Harvard University Archives.)

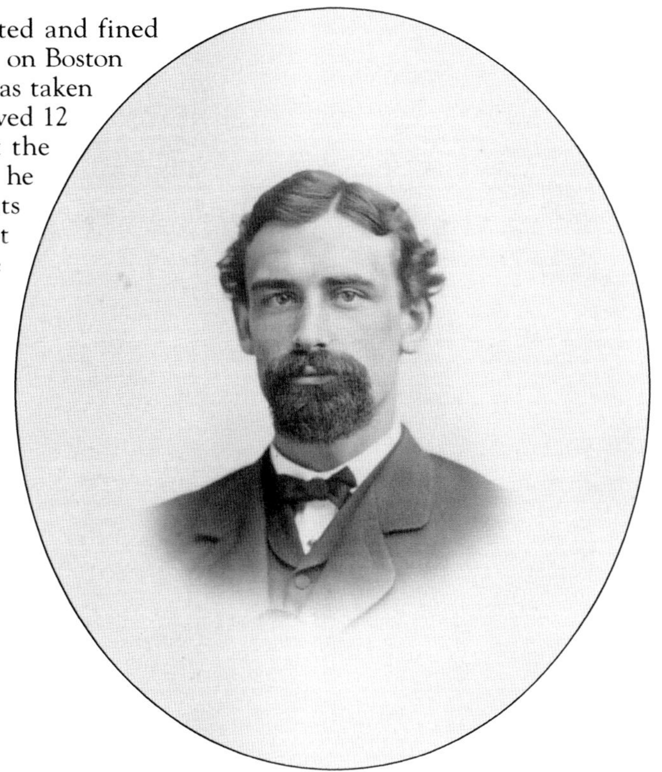

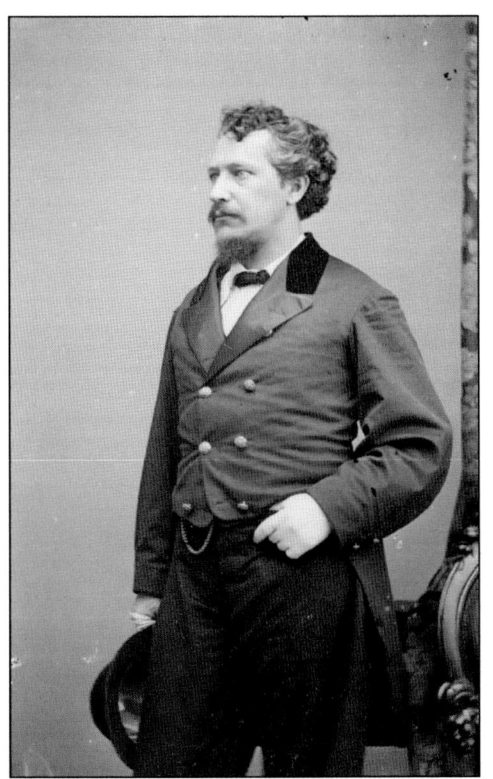

In 1888, George Francis Train was imprisoned at the Charles Street Jail for about a year for debt, though the case was eventually dismissed. A true eccentric, Train was many things in his life: orphaned at four, he became a wealthy real estate developer, newspaper man, shipping and railroad magnate, and presidential candidate. In 1870, he made a much publicized trip around the world in 80 days, possibly inspiring the character of Phileas Fogg in Jules Verne's famous novel *Around the World in 80 Days.* Train was jailed 15 times in his life and was said to have liked the food and lodging at the Charles Street Jail so much, he did not want to leave. (Courtesy of the Library of Congress.)

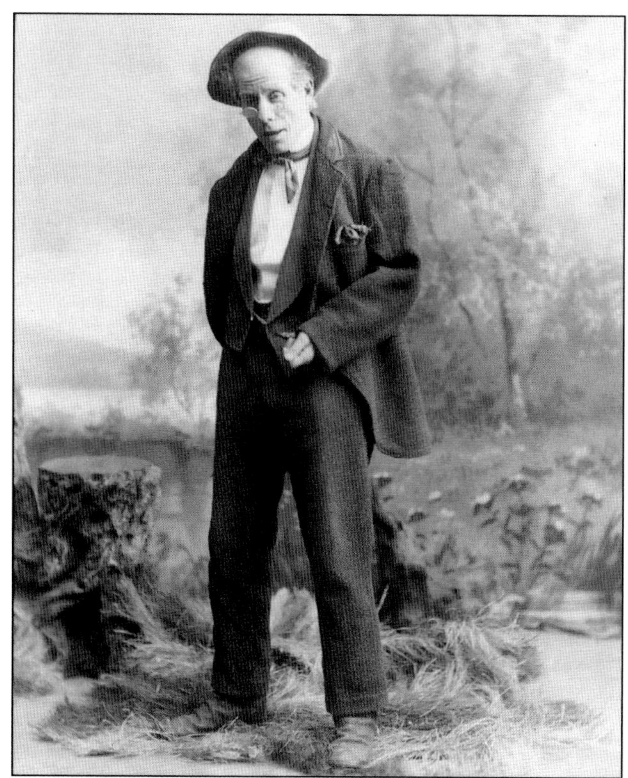

In 1894, famous stage actor Richard Golden was arrested in a Boston hotel for "alleged debt." According to newspapers, he spent a night at the Charles Street Jail in what the sheriff said was "the best cell in the institution"—the same one occupied by George Francis Train a few years before. Golden is seen here in character for his most famous role, Old Jed Prouty, in the long-running and now mostly forgotten play of the same name, which he wrote. (Courtesy of the Houghton Library, Harvard University.)

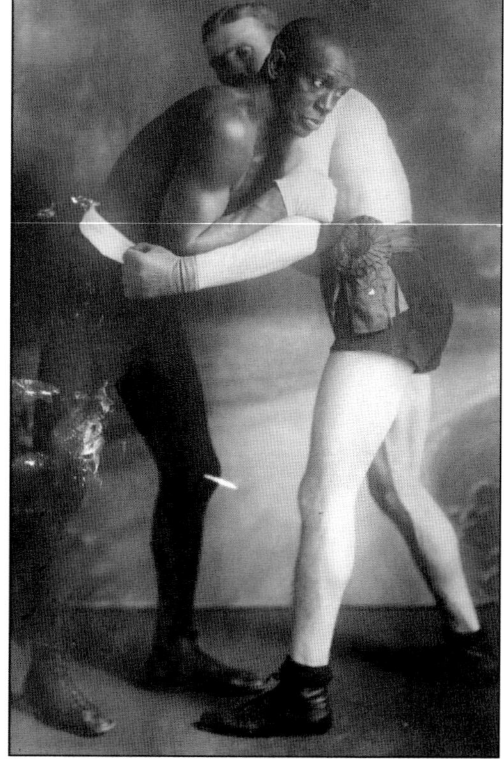

Bobby Dobbs (left) was a well-known boxer who was arrested and sent to the Charles Street Jail in 1894 on charges of evading a debt owed to his manager. His stay was brief. Seen here boxing in Germany in 1910, Dobbs racked up more than 180 prizefights in his career. He worked throughout the United States and all over Europe and even, according to some accounts, opened a boxing school in Budapest. (Courtesy of the Library of Congress.)

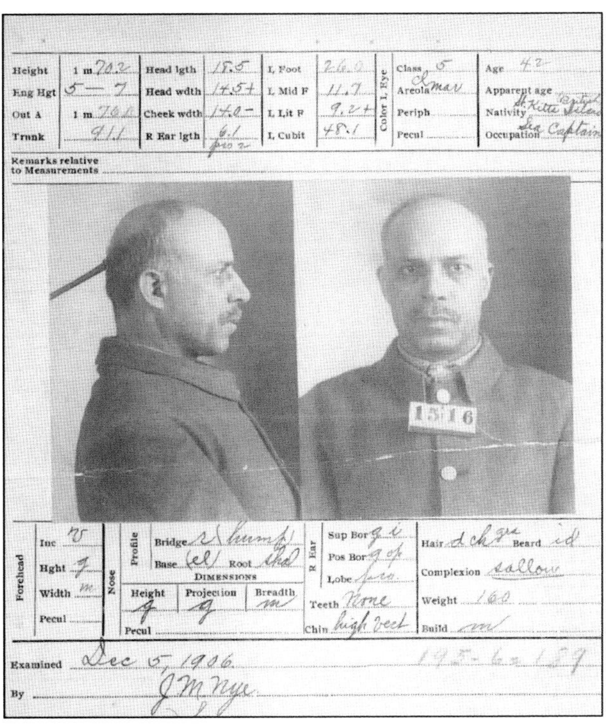

In July 1896, Thomas Bram, seen here on his Bertillon card, was charged with murder on the high seas. His alleged victims were the captain of the ship on which Bram was first mate, the captain's wife, and the second mate. Bram was sent to the Charles Street Jail, convicted, and sentenced to death, despite another man on the ship being recognized as the likely culprit. The Supreme Court overturned the conviction on grounds that the lower court erred in admitting some testimony. Tried and convicted again, Bram was sentenced to life in prison. After a popular novel based on the case raised significant doubt about his guilt, Pres. Woodrow Wilson granted him a full pardon. (Courtesy of the National Archives and Records Administration.)

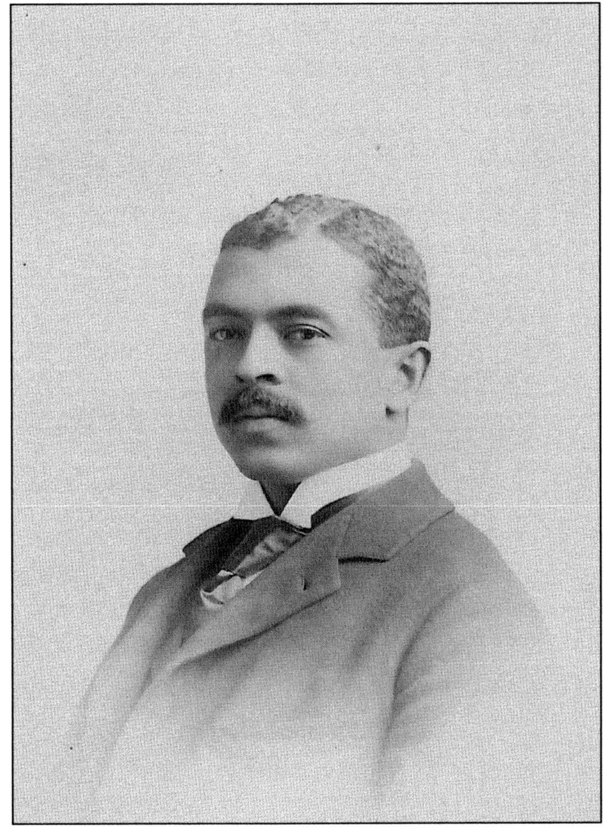

William Monroe Trotter spent 30 days at the Charles Street Jail in 1903 after being arrested for disturbing the peace at a speech by Booker T. Washington. Trotter earned his undergraduate and graduate degrees at Harvard, where this photograph was taken, and became a successful businessman and founder of the African American newspaper the *Guardian*. An outspoken critic of Booker T. Washington's policies, he was an early pioneer in the fight for civil rights and racial equality. (Courtesy of the Harvard University Archives.)

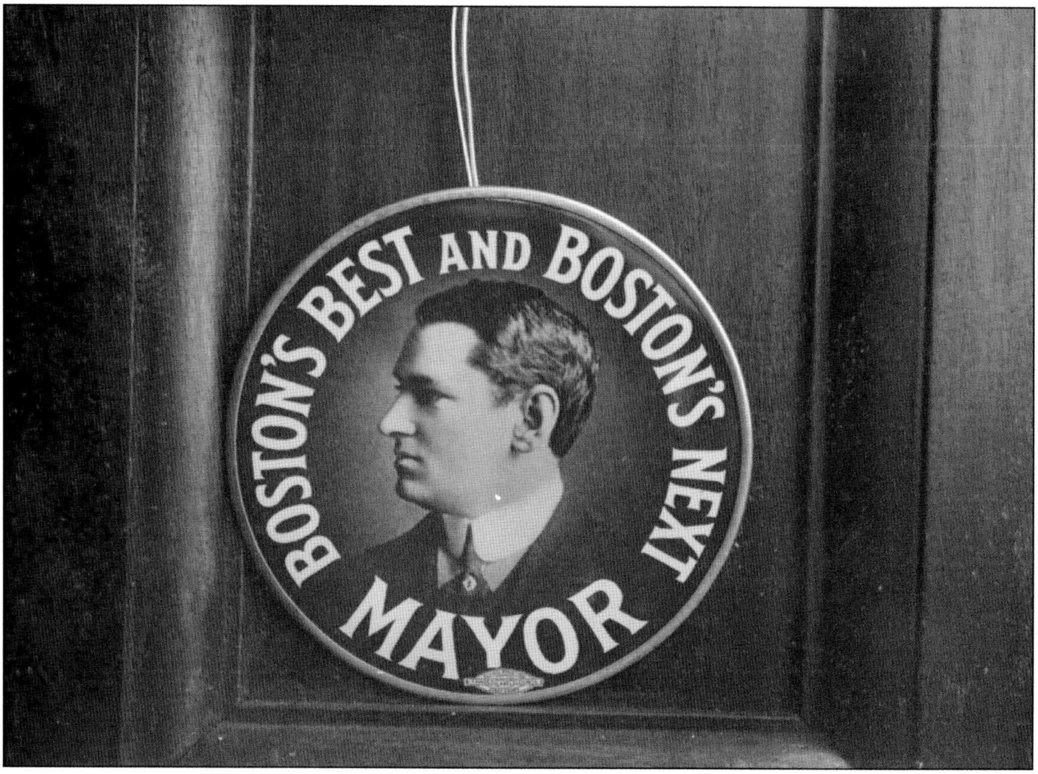

In 1903, Boston politician James Michael Curley was caught taking the civil service exam for a friend. He was sentenced to 60 days at the Charles Street Jail. Thanks in part to his slogan, "He did it for a friend," Curley was reelected to his seat from jail. He was sworn in less than seven hours after leaving his cell. Curley went on to serve four terms as mayor of Boston and one term as governor of Massachusetts. This photograph shows a campaign button from one of Curley's mayoral races. (Courtesy of the Boston Public Library, Leslie Jones Collection.)

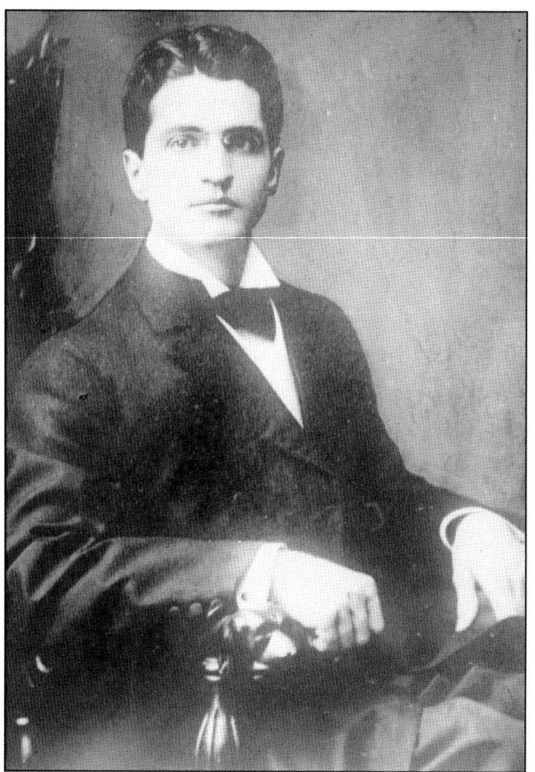

Rev. Clarence Richeson was charged with murder after his young fiancée, Avis Linnell, mysteriously turned up dead from cyanide poisoning. It turned out that Richeson had what the papers called a "continuous fondness for women," and wanted Avis out of the way so he could marry another woman to whom he was also engaged. Eventually, Richeson confessed to killing Linnell by slipping her the cyanide. He was sent to the electric chair in 1912. (Courtesy of the Library of Congress.)

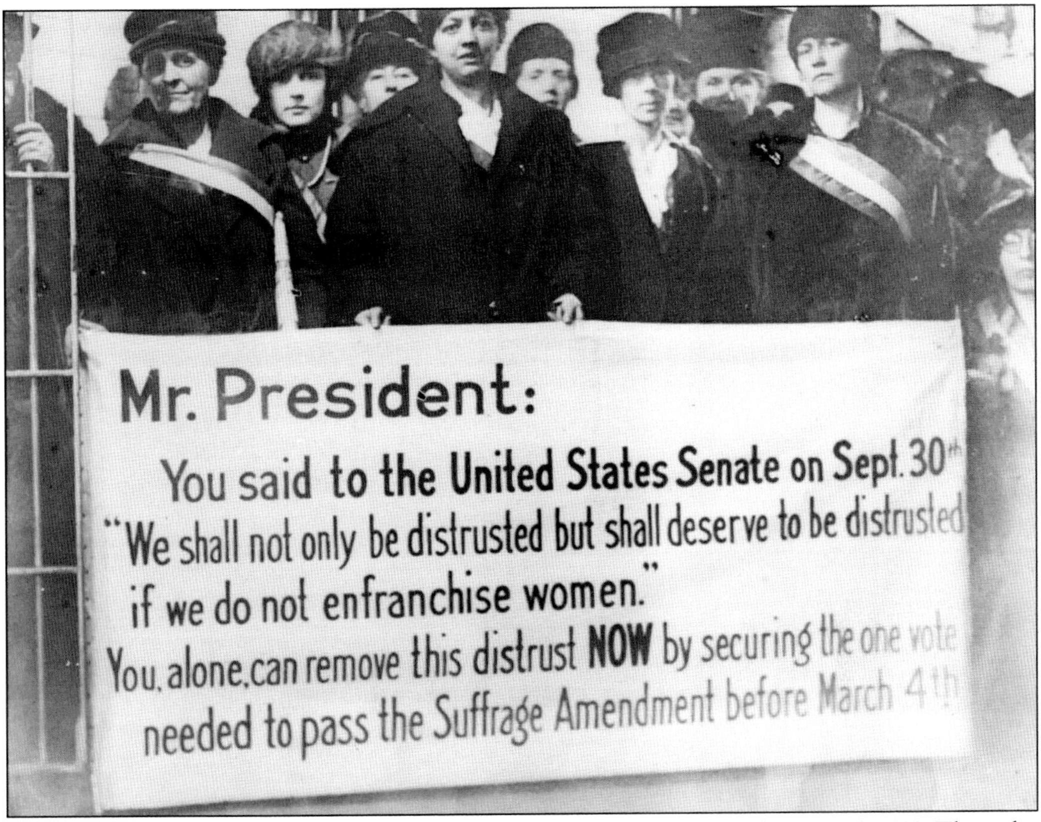

En route from Europe, Pres. Woodrow Wilson stopped in Boston on February 25, 1919. There, he was met with speeches, parades, and a group of what the press called "militant suffragists." Nineteen of the "suffs" were arrested and sent to the Charles Street Jail, where they were photographed holding this sign from the protest. (Courtesy of Maine Women Writers Collection, University of New England.)

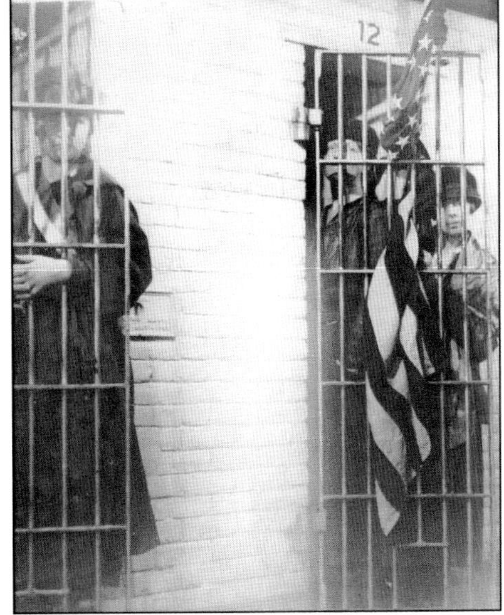

The women refused to pay their fines and were sentenced to serve up to eight days in jail. They are seen here outside their cells. The most trouble they made was refusing to give their names or answer to them, causing considerable confusion in court, and "talking cell to cell, although other prisoners wanted to sleep." The press reported their principal complaint was that they were not treated as "political prisoners." (Courtesy of the Maine Women Writers Collection, University of New England.)

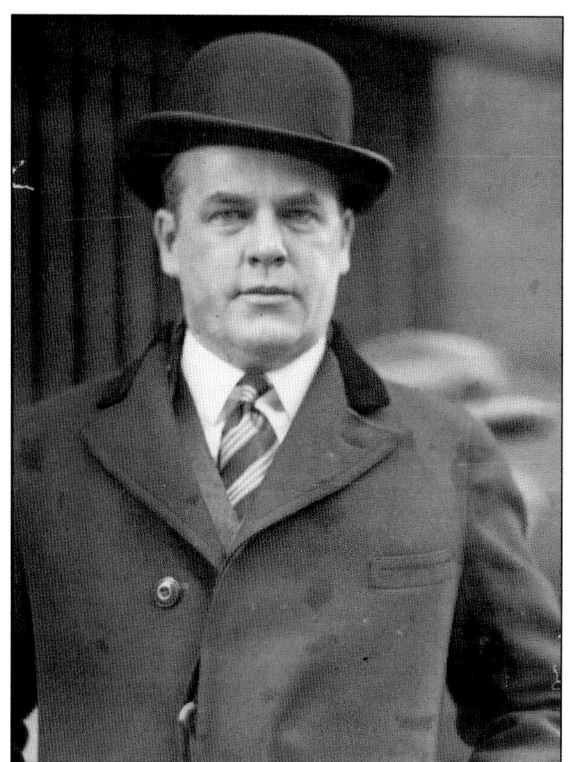

Frederick W. Enwright was the editor and publisher of the *Boston Telegraph* newspaper. Following a physical altercation with ex-mayor Curley in 1926, he was charged with "criminal libel" for printing a newspaper illustration of a man in a jail cell wearing prison clothes and a ball and chain with the words "Curley the Thug" above it. Enwright was found guilty, fined $500, and sentenced to eight months in the Charles Street Jail. (Photograph from the *Boston Herald-Traveler* Photo Morgue, courtesy of the Boston Public Library.)

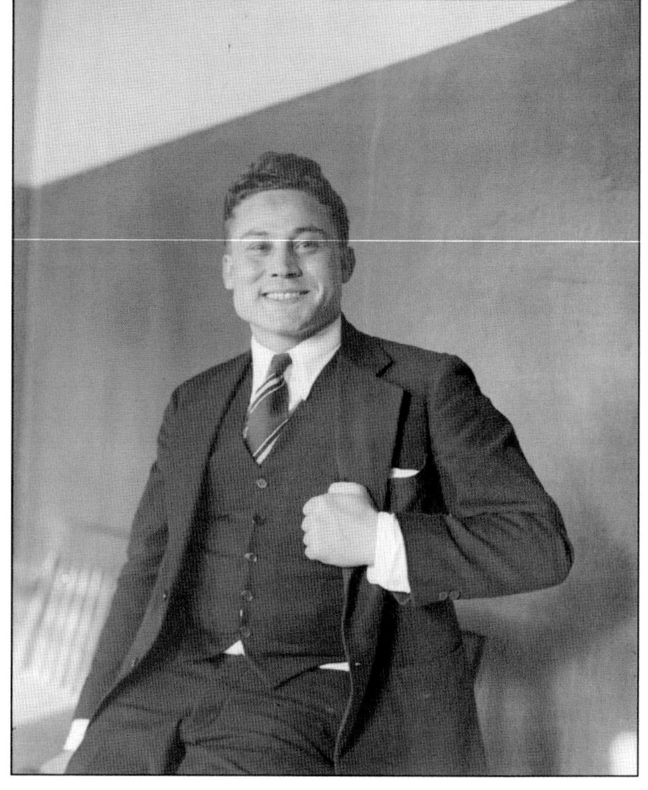

Gangi Cero was convicted of first-degree murder in 1927 and sentenced to die. Just hours before the execution, Cero's brother found a new witness who identified the true murderer. Cero was granted a second trial and acquitted. This photograph was taken after he received the good news. The case is often cited in arguments against capital punishment. (Courtesy of the Boston Public Library, Leslie Jones Collection.)

Anarchists Nicola Sacco and Bartolomeo Vanzetti, convicted of armed robbery and murder, are often said to have stayed at the Charles Street Jail. Some experts question whether they were ever housed there, though it is certain they were housed at two other jails designed by Gridley Bryant—Dedham and the Charlestown State Prison, where they were executed in 1927. Their case sparked worldwide controversy and protest, and many think the pair was wrongfully convicted due to the men's ethnicity and beliefs. On the 50th anniversary of their deaths in 1977, Massachusetts governor Michael Dukakis issued a proclamation stating, "Any stigma and disgrace should be forever removed from the names of Nicola Sacco and Bartolomeo Vanzetti." (Courtesy of the Boston Public Library, Leslie Jones Collection.)

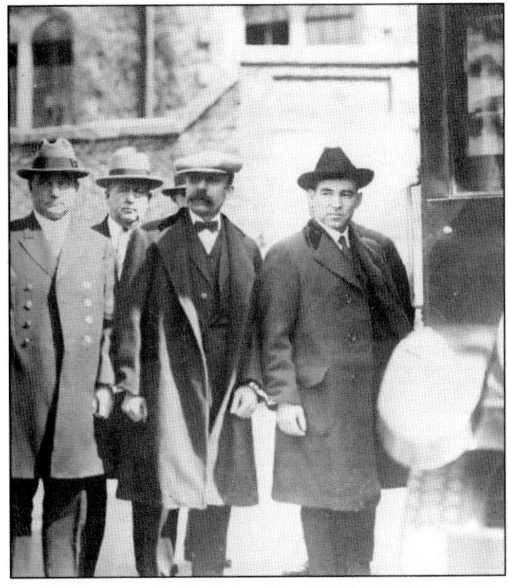

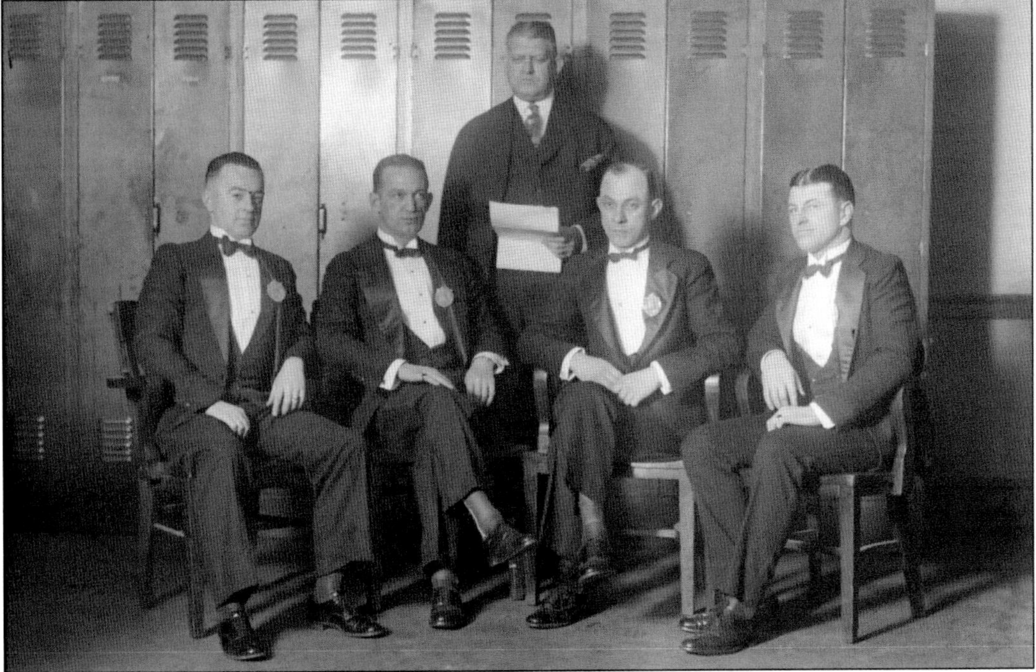

The 1920s were the height of Prohibition, and the men in this photograph were members of the Boston Police Department's so-called vice squad charged with enforcing the liquor ban. The squad's leader was Oliver Garrett, second from right. He and his colleagues are dressed up for visits to Boston hotels on New Year's Eve to ensure the laws are observed. Garrett lived a lavish lifestyle, owned several homes and race horses, and conducted himself with "the air of an English lord," the papers reported. The mystery of how he afforded such a standard of living on a policeman's salary was solved in 1930 when he was charged with extortion for taking payoffs from club and speakeasy owners to turn a blind eye to their illegal activities. Garrett stayed at the Charles Street Jail for months during his trial. He eventually pled guilty and was sentenced to two years in prison. (Courtesy of the Boston Public Library, Leslie Jones Collection.)

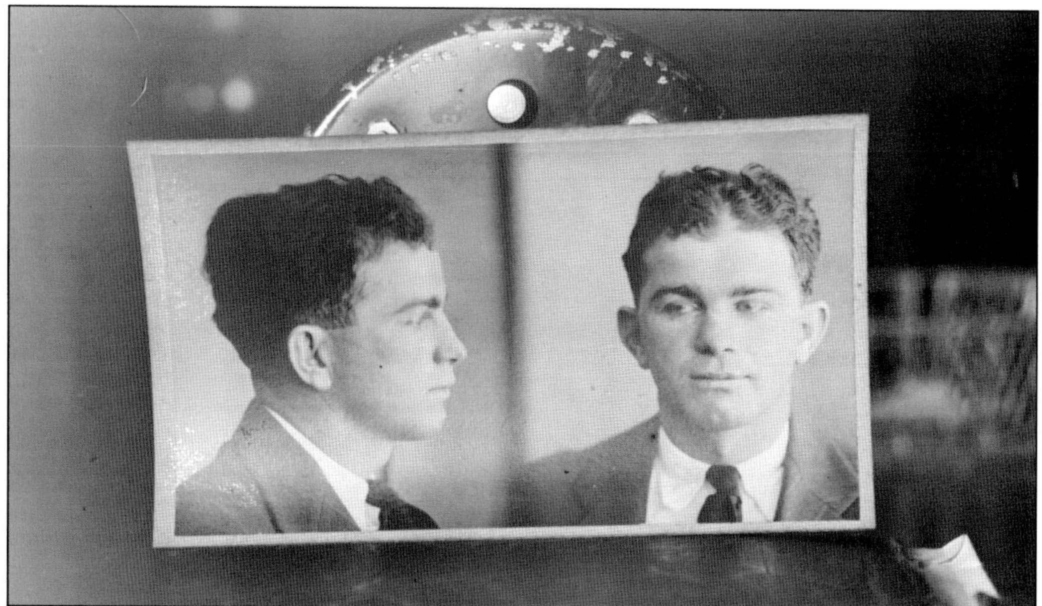

Frank Wallace was the leader of a Boston organized crime gang known as the "Gustin Gang." Among other things, they were bootleggers famous for hijacking rivals' trucks. Wallace was held at the Charles Street Jail in 1928 while Michigan authorities tried to have him extradited for participating in a robbery and the murder of a police officer there. He was acquitted in the case, but two days before Christmas in 1931, newspapers reported he was "rubbed out" in a "shower of lead" while on a visit to the "bootlegging and rum-running headquarters" of rival mob leader Joseph Lombardi. (Courtesy of the Boston Public Library, Leslie Jones Collection.)

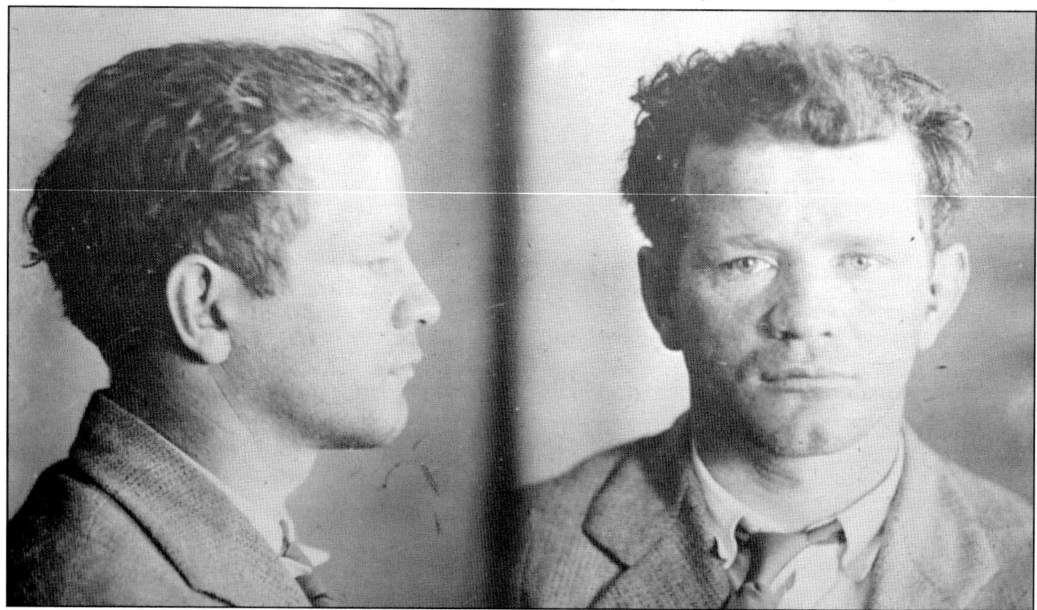

Stephen Wallace was Frank's brother and said to have been the enforcer in the gang. In 1937, he was charged with conspiracy to commit murder of a police officer and awaited trial at the Charles Street Jail. He was ultimately convicted and served two and a half years. (Courtesy of the Boston Public Library, Leslie Jones Collection.)

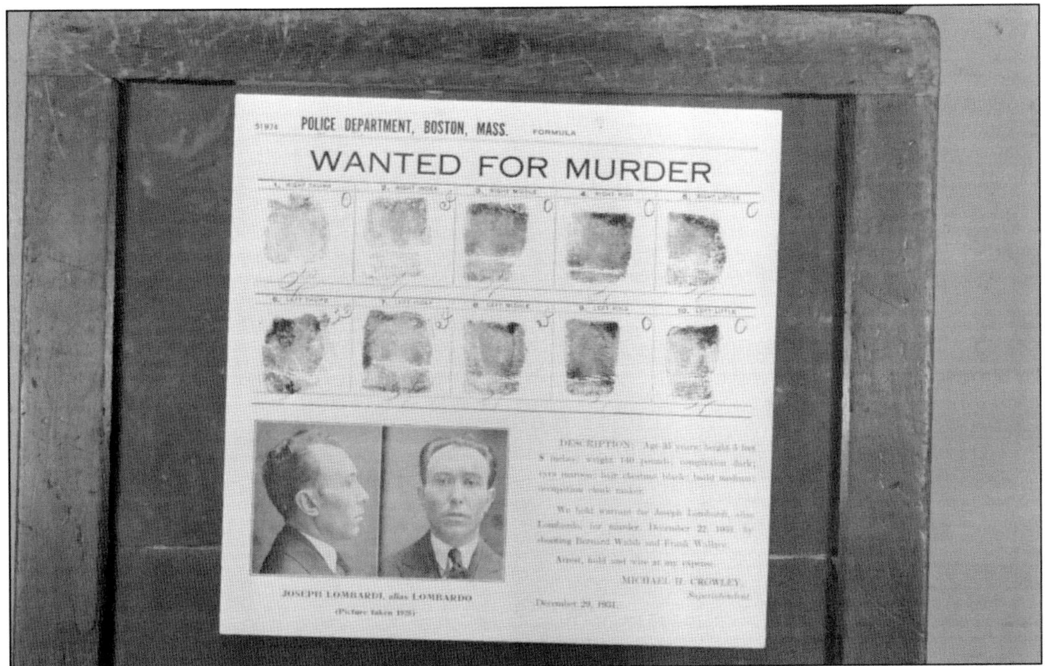

Known as "Big Joe L.," Joseph Lombardi ran a bootlegging gang that was a rival to the Gustin Gang. Charged with the murder of Frank Wallace and his "lieutenant" in 1931, he was held at the Charles Street Jail. Acquitted of those murders, he allegedly went on to oversee the growth of the Boston mafia in the coming decades. (Courtesy of the Boston Public Library, Leslie Jones Collection.)

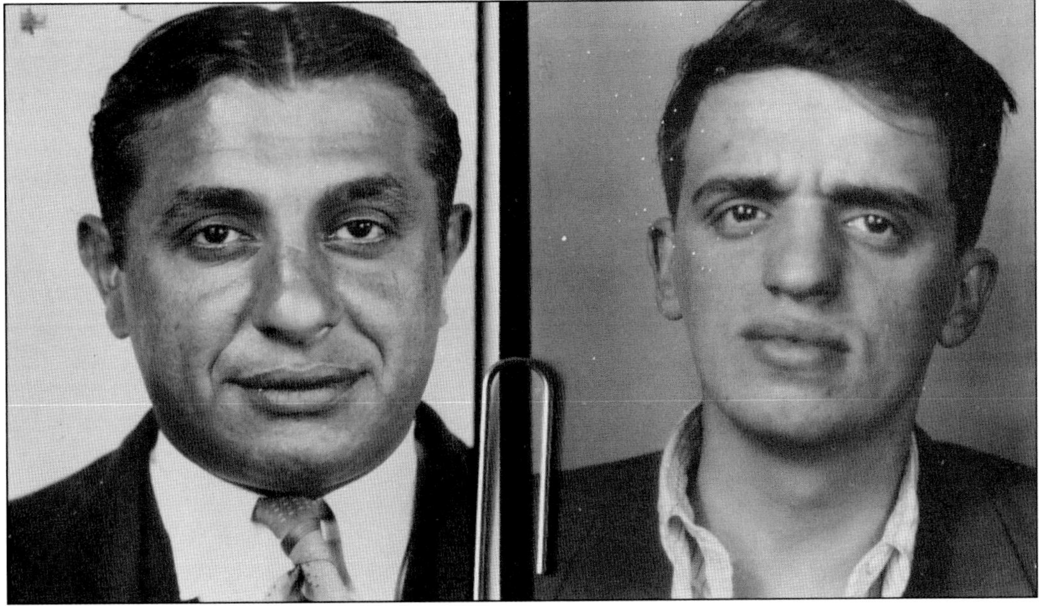

Henry Selvitelle (left) and Anthony "Bozo" Cortese were also charged with the murder of Gustin Gang leader Frank Wallace. They were held at the Charles Street Jail before charges against them were eventually dropped. A few years later, they were arrested for a Maine bank robbery, though they were never indicted. (Courtesy of the Boston Public Library, Leslie Jones Collection.)

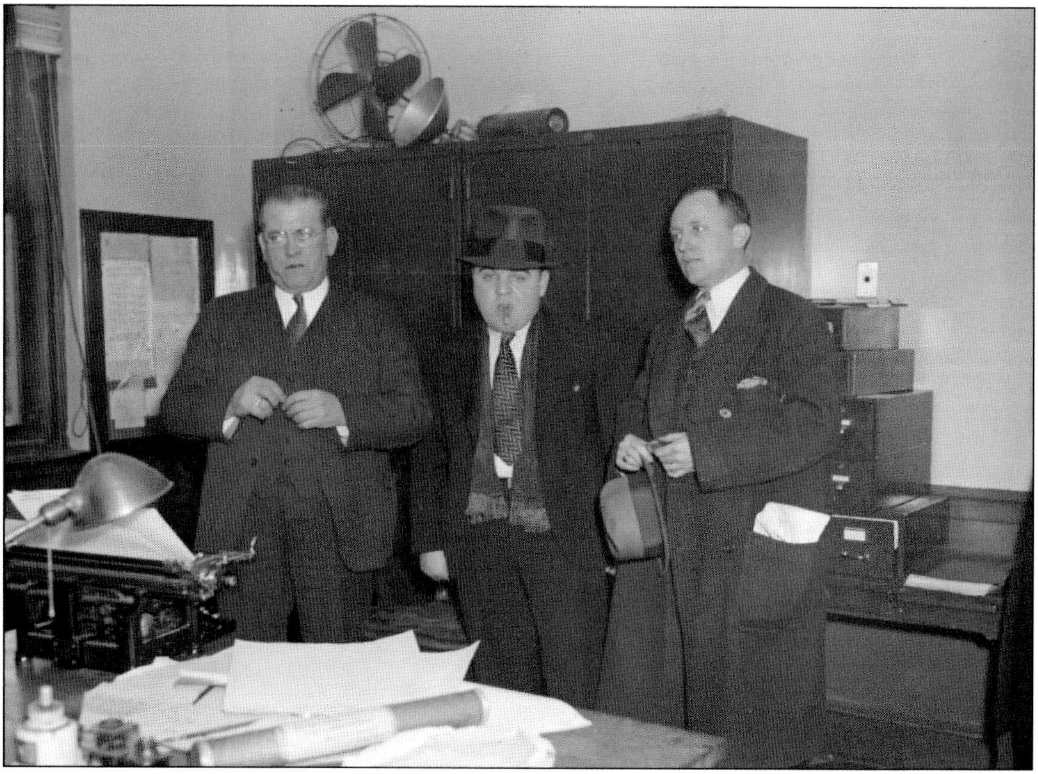

James "Skeets" Coyne (center) was sought in the 1933 murder of Boston crime boss Charles "King" Solomon in the men's room of the Cotton Club. Skeets was taken to the Charles Street Jail and eventually pleaded guilty to manslaughter. (Courtesy of the Boston Public Library, Leslie Jones Collection.)

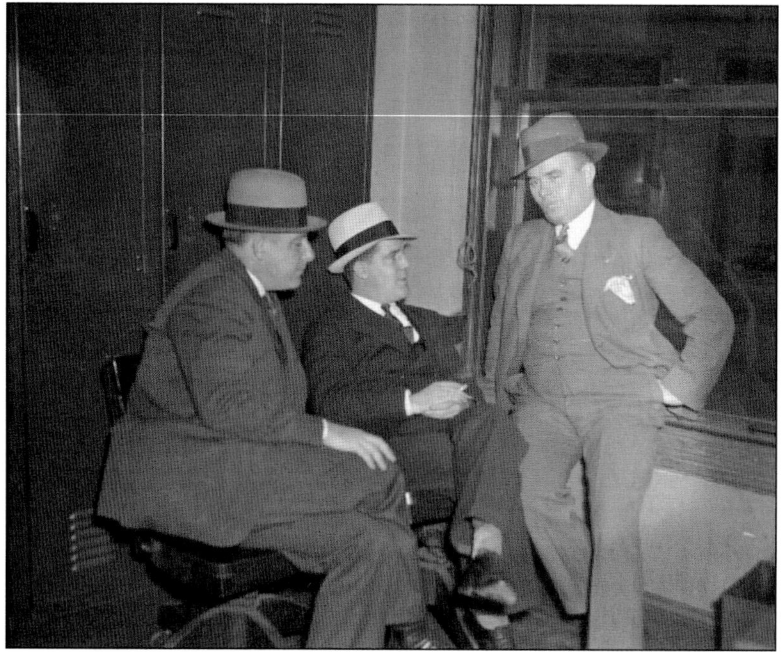

James Scully (right) was charged with the murder of Solomon and held at the Charles Street Jail in 1933. He was convicted of armed robbery in connection with the murder. (Courtesy of the Boston Public Library, Leslie Jones Collection.)

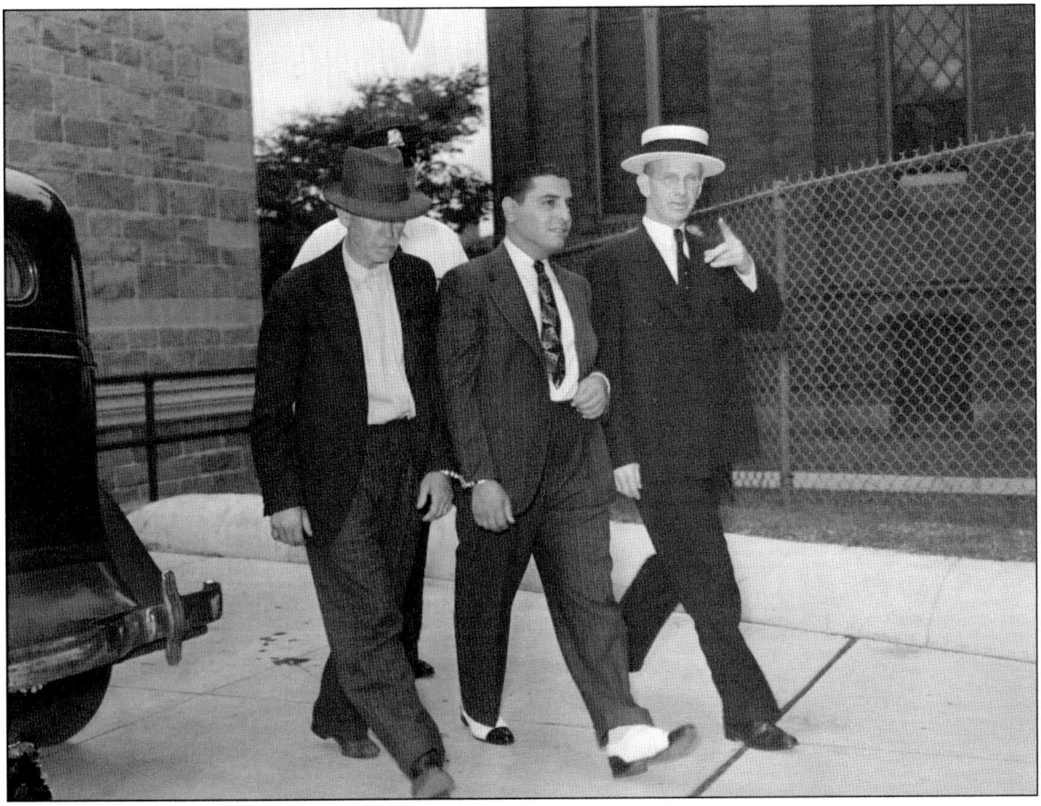

In 1939, Raymond Patriarca (center) was charged with armed robbery and assault with intent to murder. He is seen here handcuffed to another prisoner and being escorted to the Charles Street Jail by a court officer. Patriarca went on to become the reputed boss of organized crime in New England for decades. He was arrested more than 30 times in his career and was under indictment for two murders when he died at age 76. (Courtesy of the Boston Public Library , Leslie Jones Collection.)

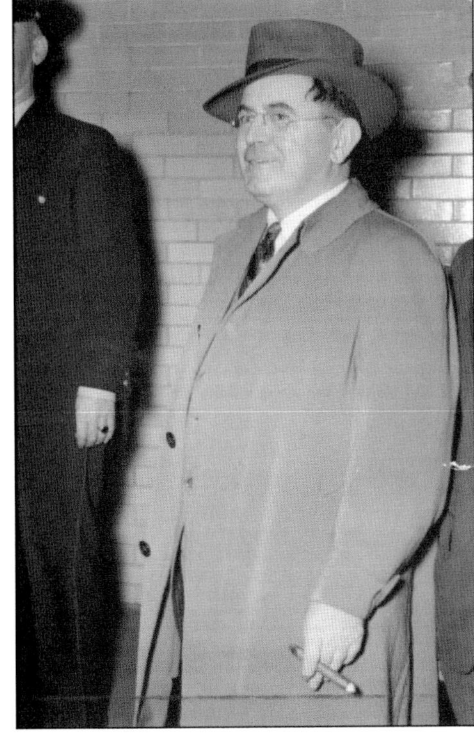

John Dowd became sheriff of Suffolk County and took charge of the Charles Street Jail in 1938. Soon accused of soliciting and accepting bribes from county employees, he resigned and fled Boston. Captured after 22 months on the run, he was held at the Charles Street Jail and then at Dedham Jail in cell no. 14, the same one where Nicola Sacco had spent many months. In this photograph, he is on his way to his arraignment. (Photograph from the *Boston Herald-Traveler* Photo Morgue, courtesy of the Boston Public Library.)

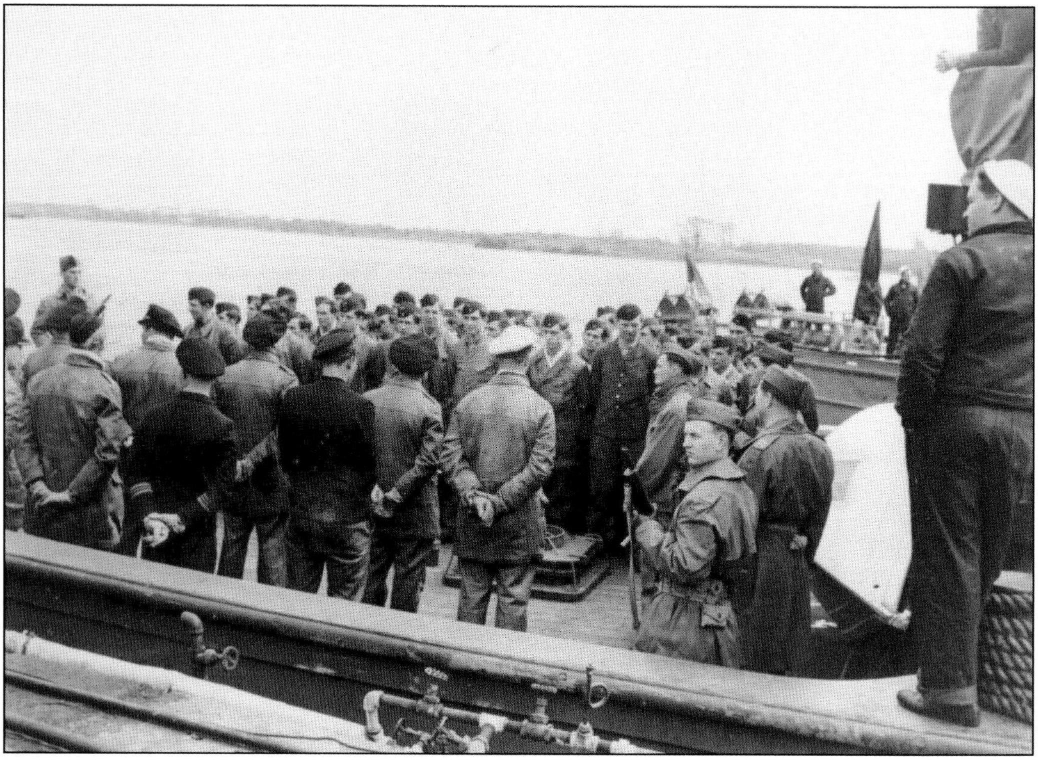

At the end of World War II, four surrendered U-boats were towed into New Hampshire's Portsmouth Naval Shipyard within a few days of each other. Here, the crew of one of those U-boats, U-873, stands on the deck of the tugboat that brought them to shore. The man in the white hat with his hands behind his back is the captain of U-873, Friedrich "Fritz" Steinhoff. (Courtesy of the National Archives and Records Administration)

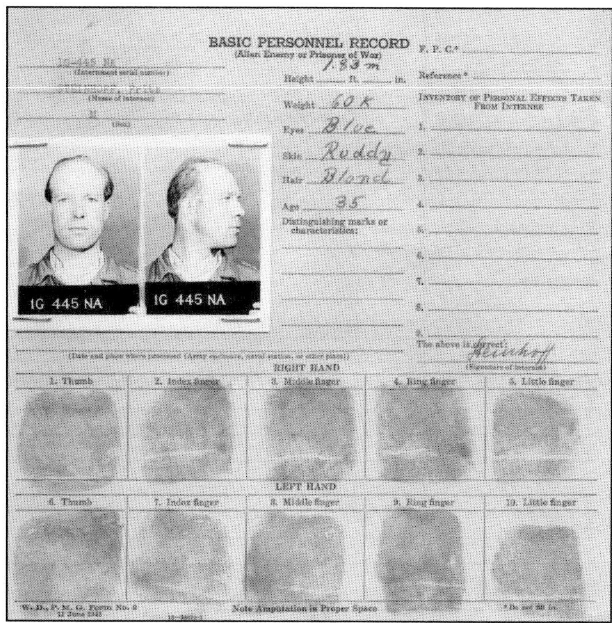

BASIC PERSONNEL RECORD
(Alien Enemy or Prisoner of War)

1G-445 NA
(Internment serial number)

(Name of internee)

M
(Sex)

Height 1.83 m ft. in.
Weight 60 K
Eyes Blue
Skin Ruddy
Hair Blond
Age 35
Distinguishing marks or characteristics:

1G 445 NA

1G 445 NA

(Date and place where processed (Army enclosure, naval station, or other place))

F. P. C.*
Reference*

INVENTORY OF PERSONAL EFFECTS TAKEN FROM INTERNEE
1.
2.
3.
4.
5.
6.
7.
8.
9.

The above is correct: Steinhoff
(Signature of internee)

RIGHT HAND

1. Thumb	2. Index finger	3. Middle finger	4. Ring finger	5. Little finger

LEFT HAND

6. Thumb	7. Index finger	8. Middle finger	9. Ring finger	10. Little finger

W. D., P. M. G. Form No. 2
12 June 1943
Note Amputation in Proper Space

Pictured here on his prisoner-of-war card, Steinhoff reportedly told his captors he did not understand English and refused to answer questions. He was sent to the Charles Street Jail to await transfer to a POW camp in Mississippi. Steinhoff never made it, though. He was reported to have committed suicide in his cell by slashing his wrists with the broken lenses of his glasses. A few months after Steinhoff's death, his brother, a rocket scientist, came to the Unites States as part of Operation Paperclip. (Courtesy of National Archives and Records Administration)

The crew of U-873—11 officers and 46 enlisted men—was also taken to the Charles Street Jail. This photograph shows the men at the submarine's commissioning ceremony, and each was given a copy before going to sea. Captain Steinhoff is on the lower deck with hands clasped at his waist and a book under his arm. This photograph is courtesy of the son of Peter Binnefeld, the fifth sailor from the left on the conning tower. (Courtesy of Peter Binnefeld.)

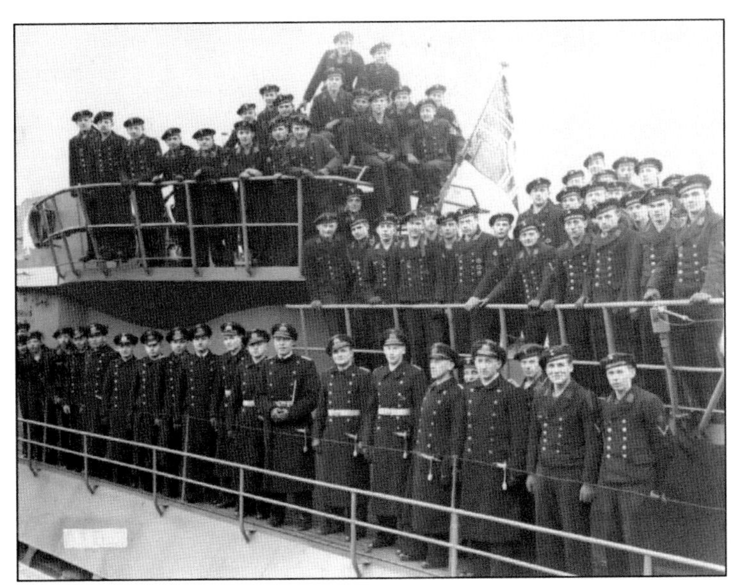

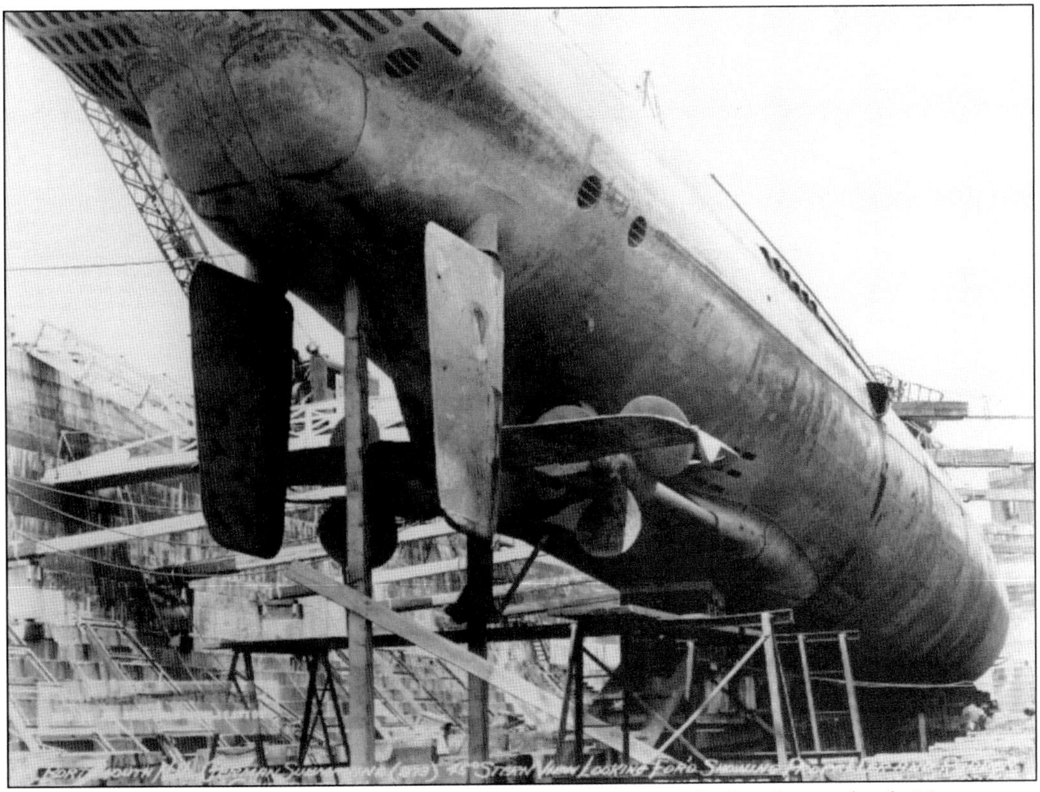

U-873 was placed in dry dock in Portsmouth, and US engineers studied its design closely. Newspapers reported that the U-boat was packed with food supplies and gallons of beer, cognac, and champagne for months at sea. U-873 was sold for scrap in 1948. (Courtesy of the National Archives and Records Administration.)

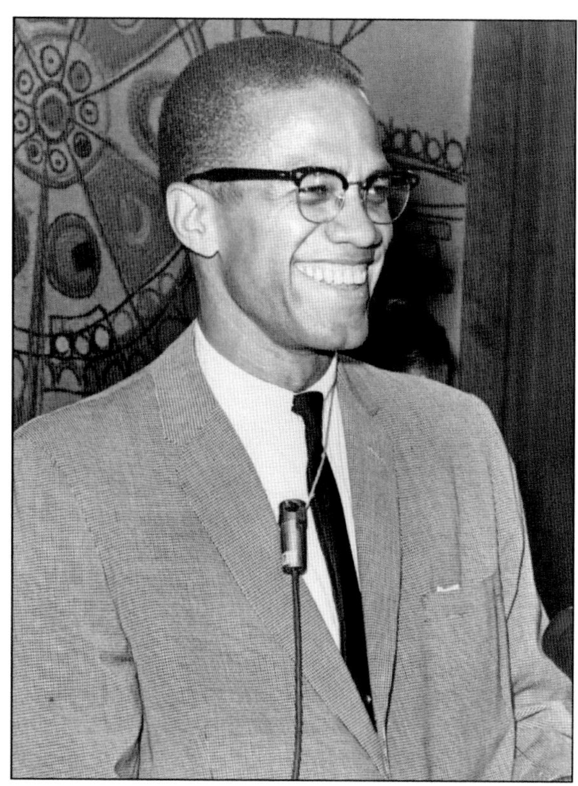

Malcolm X, born Malcolm Little, lived in Boston in the 1940s with his half sister. He had several run-ins with the law, and experts say it is possible he passed through the Charles Street Jail in connection with one of them. In 1946, he was sentenced to eight to ten years in prison and served time at Charlestown and several other area penitentiaries. He is seen here giving a speech in 1964. (Courtesy of the Library of Congress.)

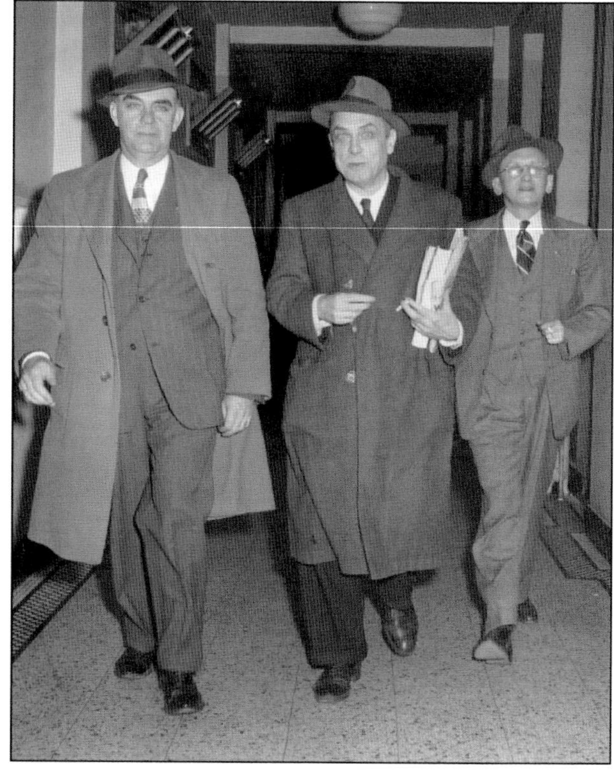

Robert Henry Best (center) was a noted American journalist and foreign correspondent in the years before World War II. When the war broke out, he chose to stay in Germany, where he became a broadcaster of Nazi propaganda. He was returned to the US in 1946 and convicted of treason in a Boston court. Best was held at the Charles Street Jail awaiting trial, at which he acted as his own attorney. Convicted on his 52nd birthday and sentenced to life in prison, he died a few years later. (Photograph from the *Boston Herald-Traveler* Photo Morgue, courtesy of the Boston Public Library.)

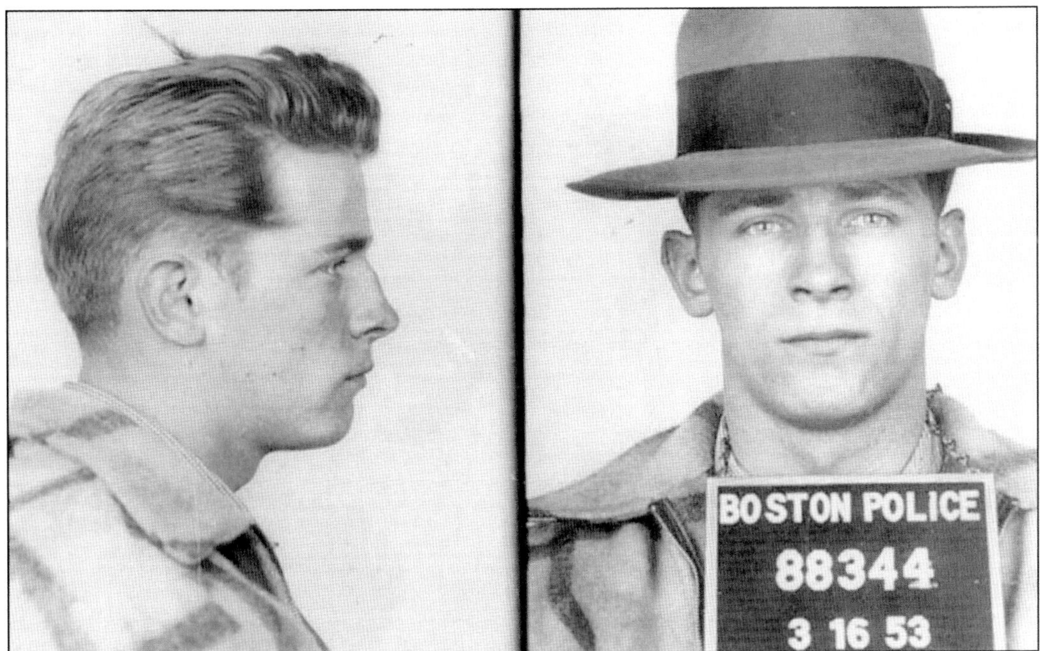

James "Whitey" Bulger was arrested when he was 26 years old in connection with a bank robbery. Held at the Charles Street Jail, he pleaded guilty and was sentenced to 20 years in prison. After his release, Bulger became a powerful organized crime figure and FBI informant. In 1995, he fled Boston and remained in hiding for 16 years. He was finally arrested at age 81 and sentenced to two life terms plus five years for his criminal activities, including involvement in multiple murders.

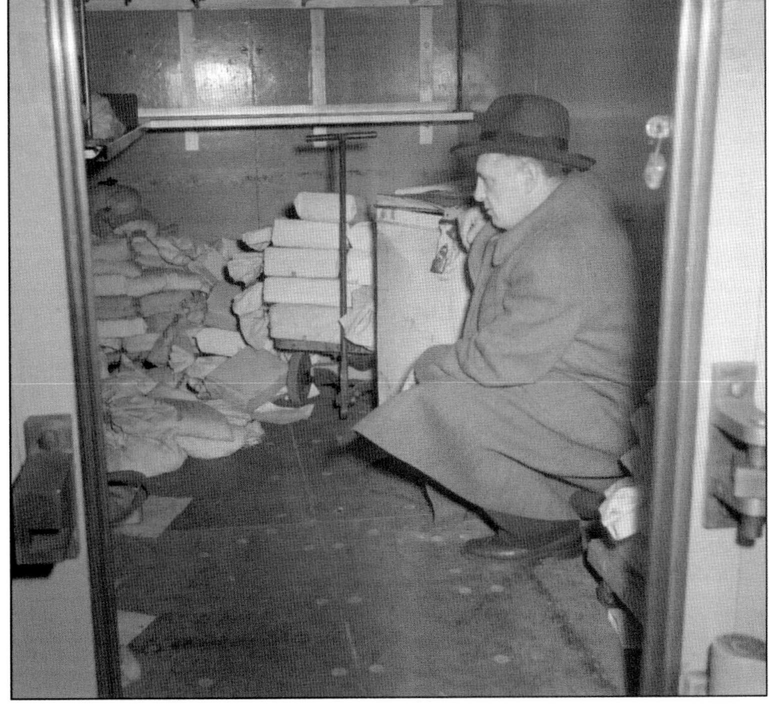

On January 17, 1950, about six men wearing Halloween masks invaded the headquarters of the Brinks armored car company in Boston. They stole $1,218,211.29 in cash and $1,557,183.83 in securities such as checks and money orders. In this photograph, a detective inspects the Brinks vault after the robbery. (Courtesy of the Boston Public Library, Leslie Jones Collection.)

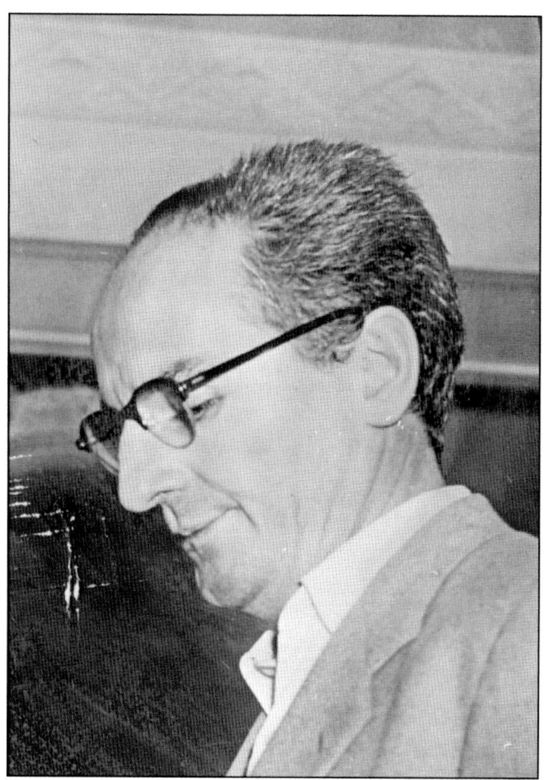

Joseph "Specs" O'Keefe was one of the Brinks robbers and turned government witness. He stayed at the Charles Street Jail while testifying before a grand jury in 1952. Eventually pleading guilty to the robbery, he spent four years behind bars in connection with the case and was released in 1960. (Courtesy of the Boston Public Library, Leslie Jones Collection.)

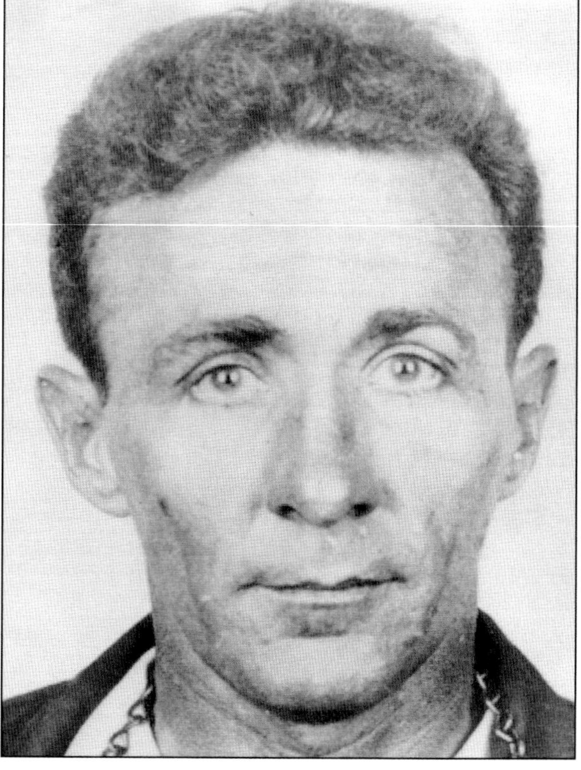

Elmer "Trigger" Burke, called a "slay-for-pay gunman" in the press, was hired to kill Specs O'Keefe in 1954. O'Keefe narrowly escaped a hail of bullets from Burke's machine gun on the streets of Boston. Captured and housed at the Charles Street Jail, Burke staged one of the most dramatic escapes in the jail's history. He was eventually convicted of murder in an unrelated case and executed.

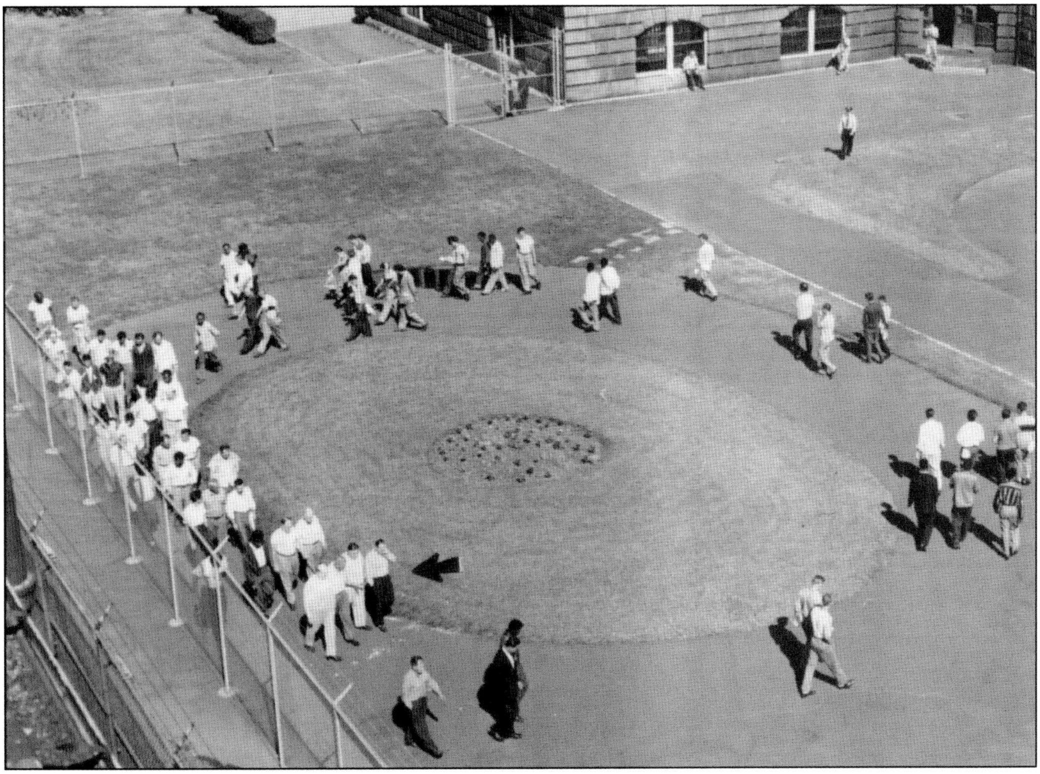

Six of the eight charged with the Brinks robbery were held at the Charles Street Jail while awaiting trial, and all of them were taken to the jail after a jury found them guilty. Here, several members of the gang are seen getting a bit of exercise in the jail yard. (Photograph from the *Boston Herald-Traveler* Photo Morgue, courtesy of the Boston Public Library.)

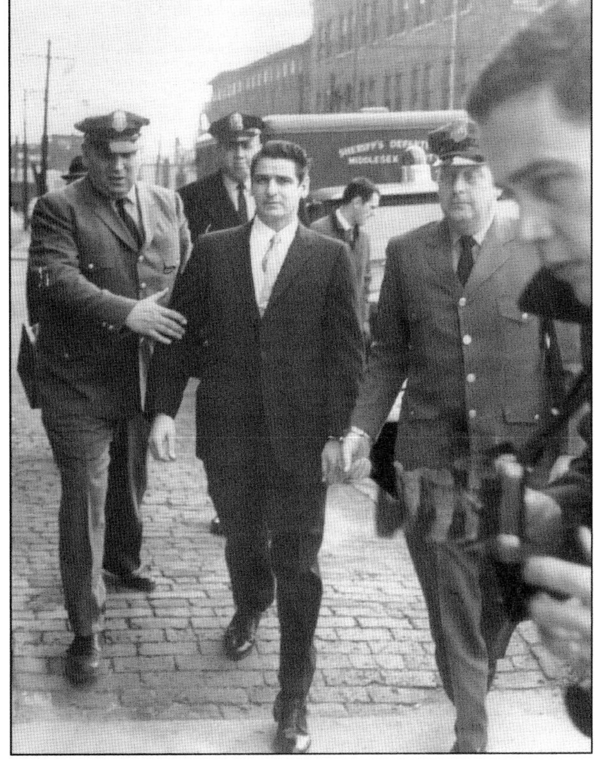

Albert DeSalvo, who claimed to be the Boston Strangler, responsible for the murders of multiple women in Boston between 1962 and 1964, is often said to have spent time at the Charles Street Jail. Over the course of his life, he had numerous run-ins with the law, and according to one newspaper story, a doctor who worked at the jail for decades recalled treating DeSalvo there. (Courtesy of the *Boston Herald*.)

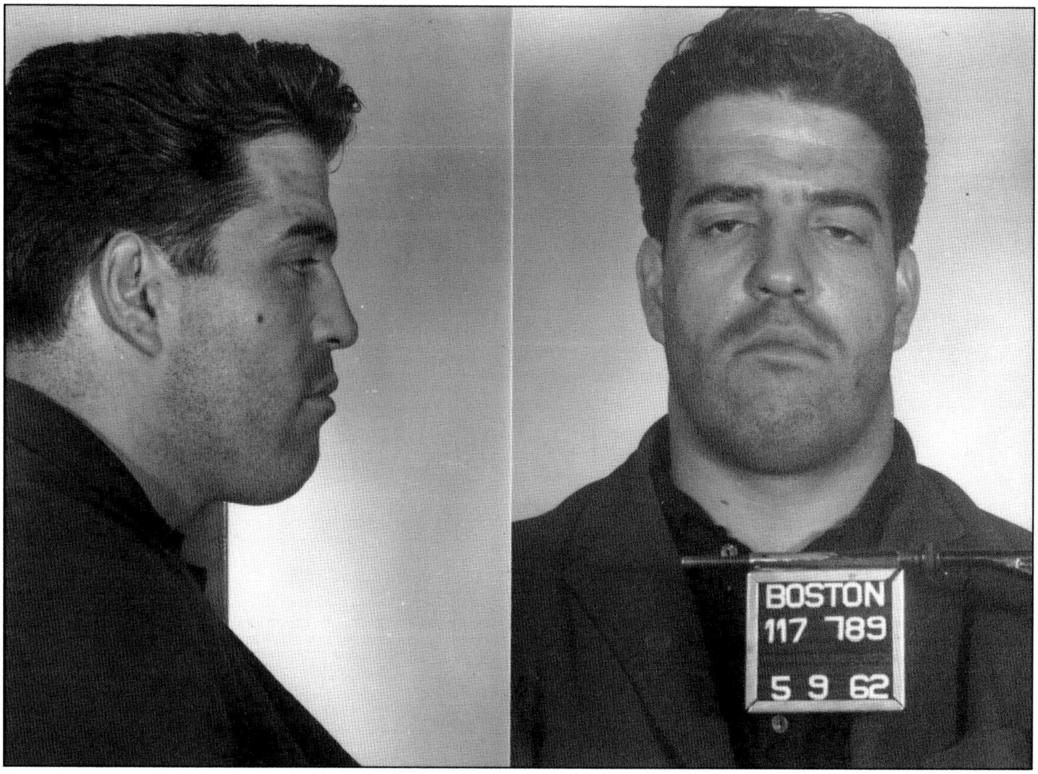

Joseph "The Animal" Barboza was a notorious mafia hit man active in Boston in the 1960s. While held at the Charles Street Jail in 1966, he had a falling out with his associates and became a government witness. His testimony—some of it later proven false—was instrumental in the convictions of many other underworld figures. In exchange for testifying, he entered the newly created Witness Protection Program. He came out of hiding, though, and was gunned down in San Francisco in 1976. (Courtesy of the Boston Police Department.)

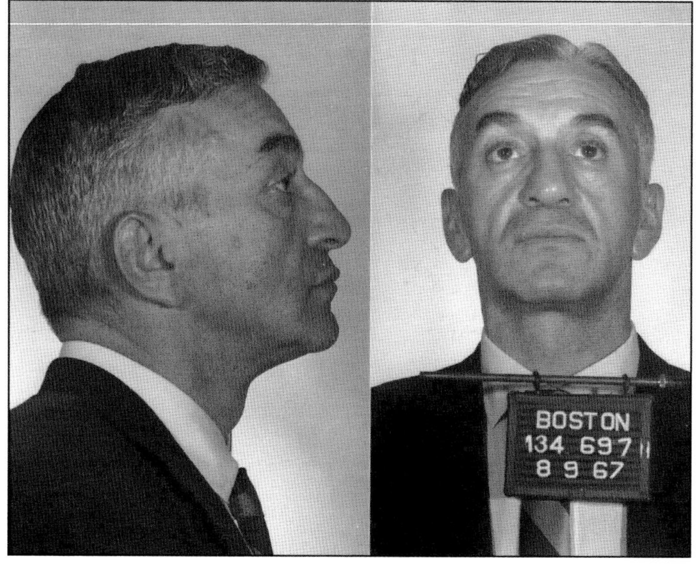

Reputed to have been the head of the mafia in Massachusetts, Gennaro Angiulo did time at the Charles Street Jail in 1967. Accustomed to more refined fare than the cuisine at the jail, Angiulo complained vociferously when served fried bologna as his first meal behind bars. He was later transferred to another facility after being seen sending hand signals from the jail's top-floor barbershop to a woman on a street corner. (Courtesy of the Boston Police Department.)

In the spring of 1970, Vietnam War opponents staged nonviolent protests at the Boston Army Base, where they blocked busloads of draftees. One hundred eight were arrested, and 23 were sent to the Charles Street Jail after they pleaded guilty and refused to pay their $20 fines. (Courtesy of the *Boston Herald.*)

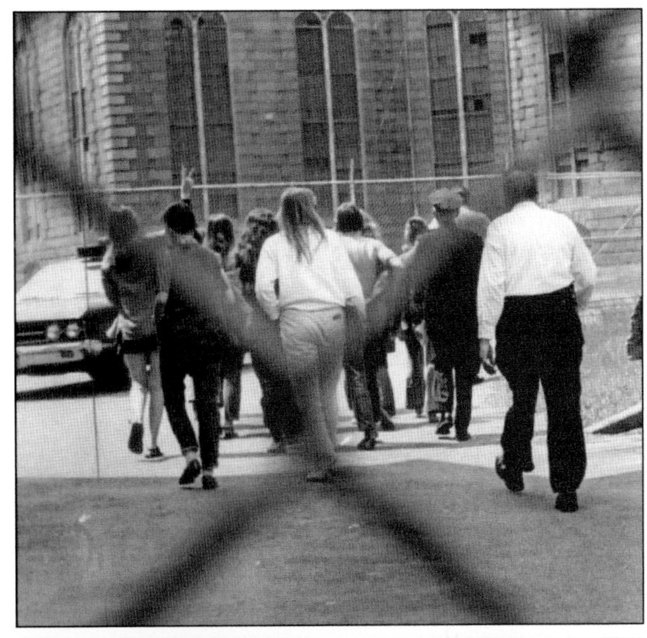

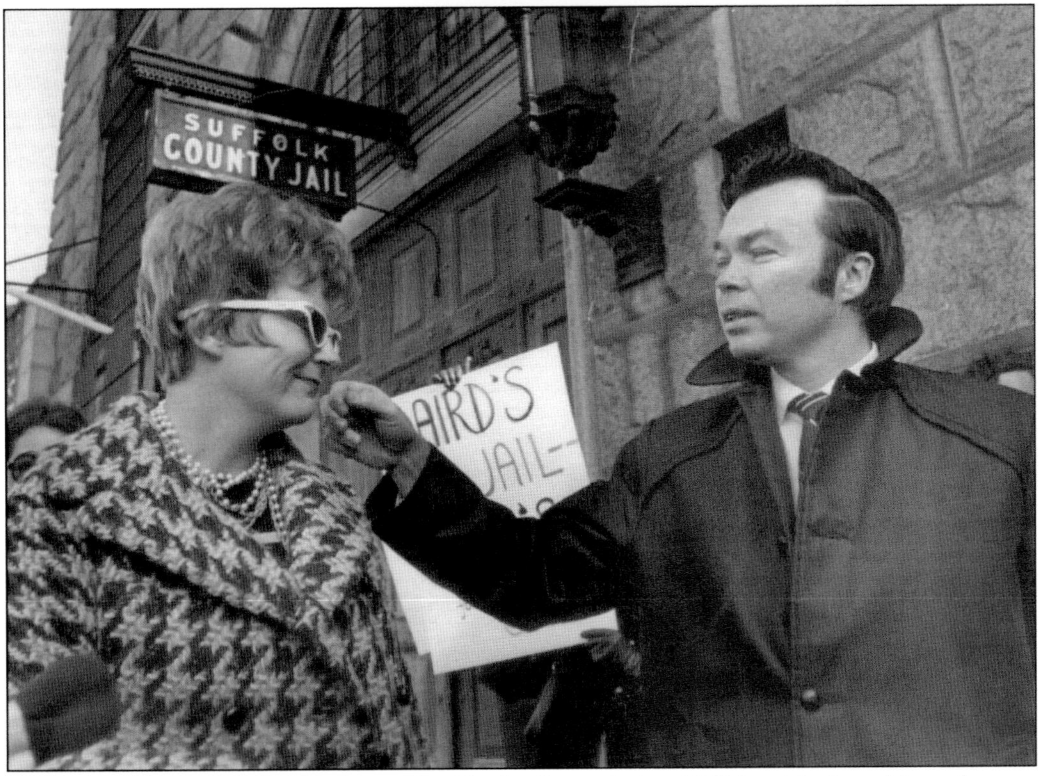

Bill Baird was sentenced to 90 days at the Charles Street Jail in 1967 for violating a Massachusetts law forbidding distribution of birth control to unmarried individuals. Here, Baird holds a news conference with his wife, Eve, outside the jail before starting to serve his sentence for this act of civil disobedience. The case eventually went to the Supreme Court, which struck down the state law in a landmark ruling. (Courtesy of the *Boston Herald.*)

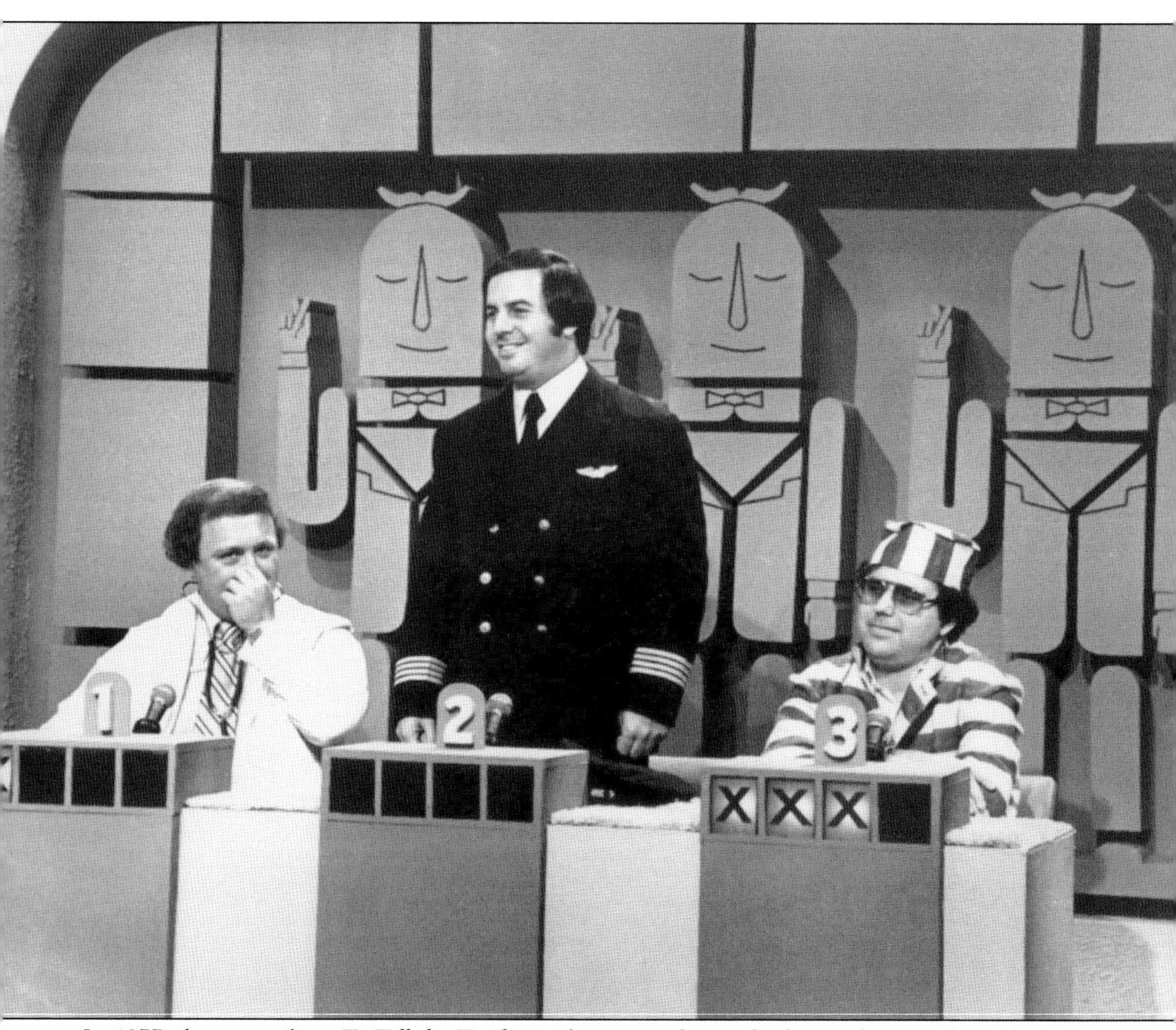

In 1977, the game show *To Tell the Truth* aired an episode in which panelists tried to identify a man the announcer called "the most outrageous imposter we've ever come across on this show." Frank Abagnale (center) had successfully posed as a doctor and airline pilot before being sent to federal prison. Years before, Abagnale spent a few hours as a prisoner at the Charles Street Jail after being detained on suspicion of impersonating a pilot. Though he called the place "a rat hole," he says it was "a lucky place" for him because a bail bondsman appeared and he slipped out before the FBI could pick him up in the morning. Eventually, Abagnale went straight. Since then, he has worked with the FBI for more than three decades and runs a successful fraud prevention consulting company. He wrote a book about his experiences, *Catch Me If You Can*, which was turned into a hit movie of the same name with Leonardo DiCaprio playing Abagnale. (Courtesy of Frank Abagnale.)

Five

Escapes

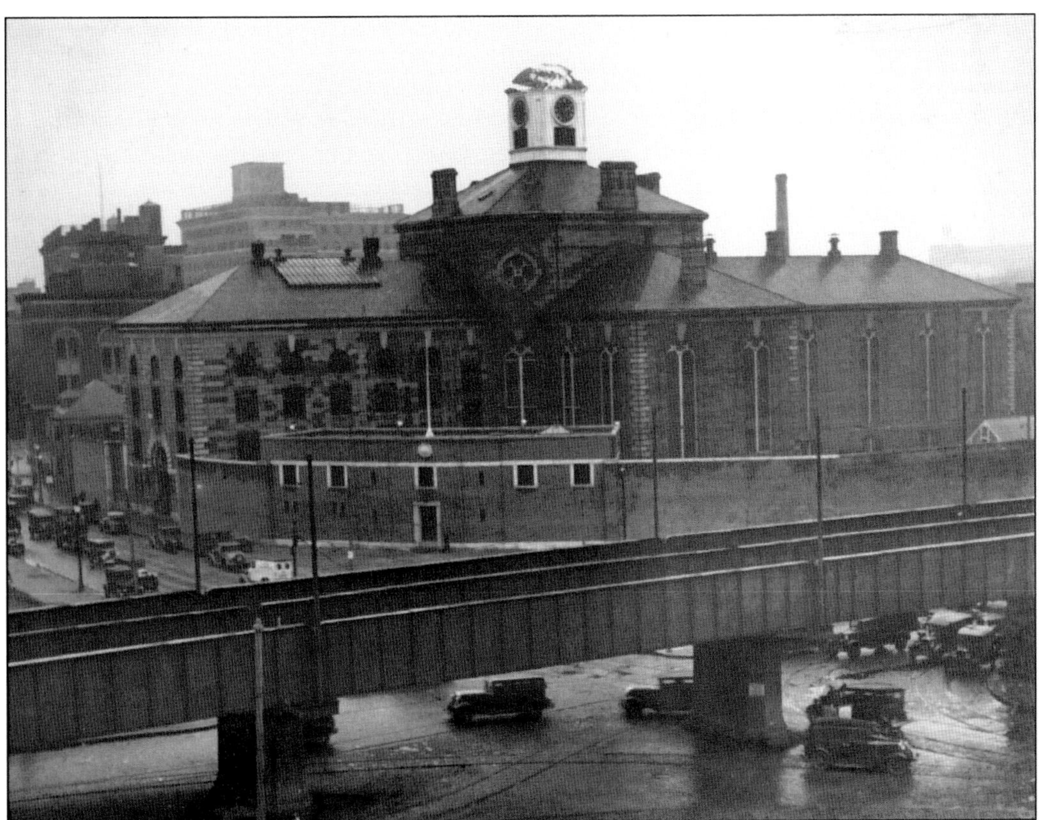

When it was built, the Charles Street Jail was thought to be extremely secure. Over the years, its reputation changed drastically as the jail became the scene of spectacular and brazen escapes. (Courtesy of the *Boston Herald*.)

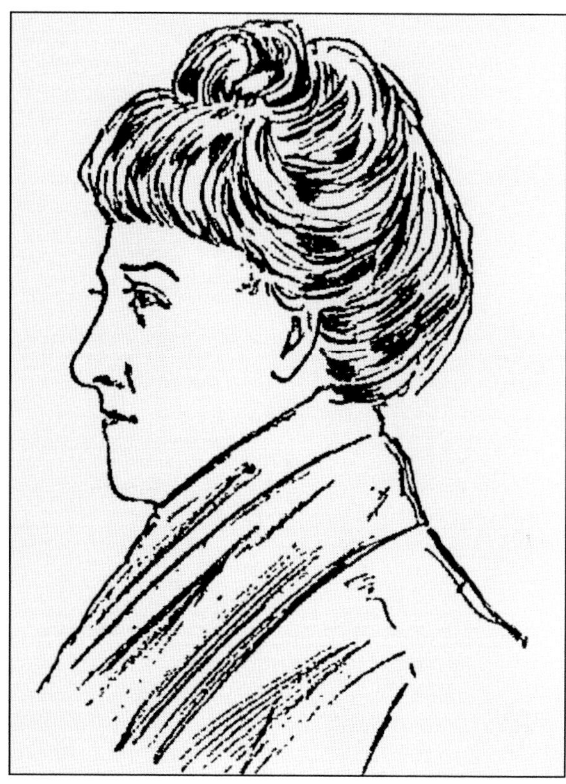

In 1894, a convicted shoplifter named Carrie Wheeler escaped from the Charles Street Jail; she was the only woman to have done so up to that point. She gave jailers the slip when she ducked into the sheriff's office and claimed to be a friend of the sheriff's family, then calmly walked out of the jail. She was recaptured the next day. Wheeler returned to the Charles Street Jail years later on shoplifting charges; 49 pairs of stolen men's trousers had been found in her rooms.

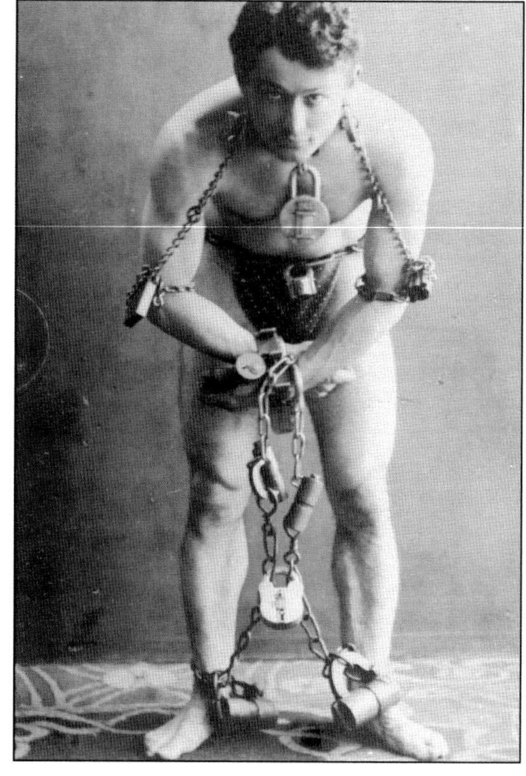

According to a newspaper reminiscence in 1930, Harry Houdini was locked up at the Charles Street Jail in a publicity stunt in the early 1900s. "[The] Superintendent of Police . . . locked him in a cell in the second tier of the city jail after he had been stripped, searched, manacled and leg-ironed and his clothes locked in a cell in the first tier," the report states. In 16 minutes, he "slipped out of his cell, recovered his clothes, dashed up to the third tier and released a prisoner, whom he locked in his own second-tier cell, let himself through two steel doors into the prison yard, climbed the wall and jumped into a waiting automobile." A few minutes later, he called the superintendent of police from a nearby theater. In a book Houdini wrote about his career, he places this event not at the Charles Street Jail but at "the Tombs"—probably referring to the jail at the nearby courthouse. (Courtesy of the Library of Congress.)

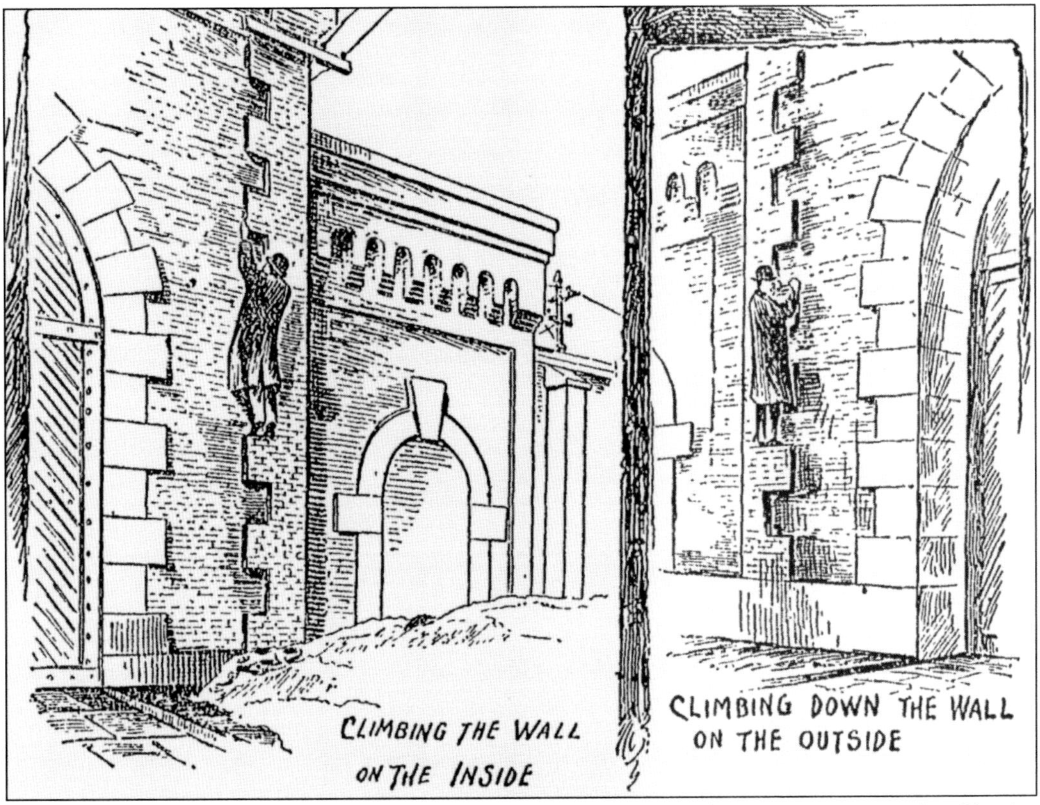

CLIMBING THE WALL ON THE INSIDE

CLIMBING DOWN THE WALL ON THE OUTSIDE

A tipster contacted a Boston newspaper in 1897 claiming that the "trimming" on the Charles Street Jail's wall was built in such a way that the stones effectively formed a ladder on both sides, making it possible for prisoners to escape. Alerted to the situation, the sheriff ordered more bricks added to the trim to fill up the spaces and prevent anyone climbing the wall.

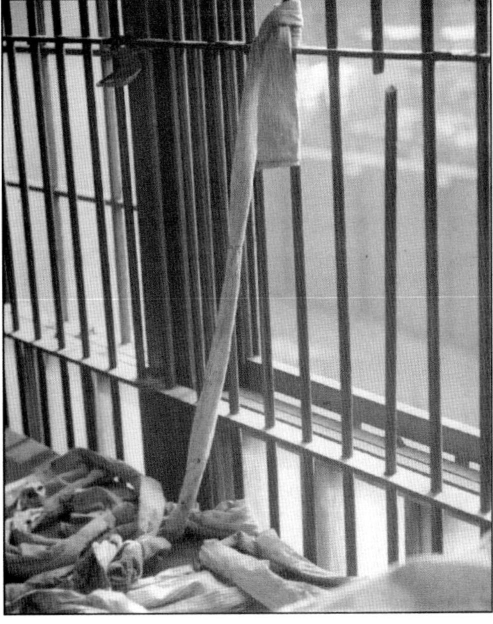

Three men reported to be "dope fiends" escaped from the Charles Street Jail on December 30, 1913, when they sawed through the bars with a file and let themselves down with a 40-foot rope made of ticking from eight mattresses. Two were recaptured within a few days, and the third, who had only nine days left on his sentence, was returned to the Charles Street Jail a few months later. (Courtesy of the *Boston Herald*.)

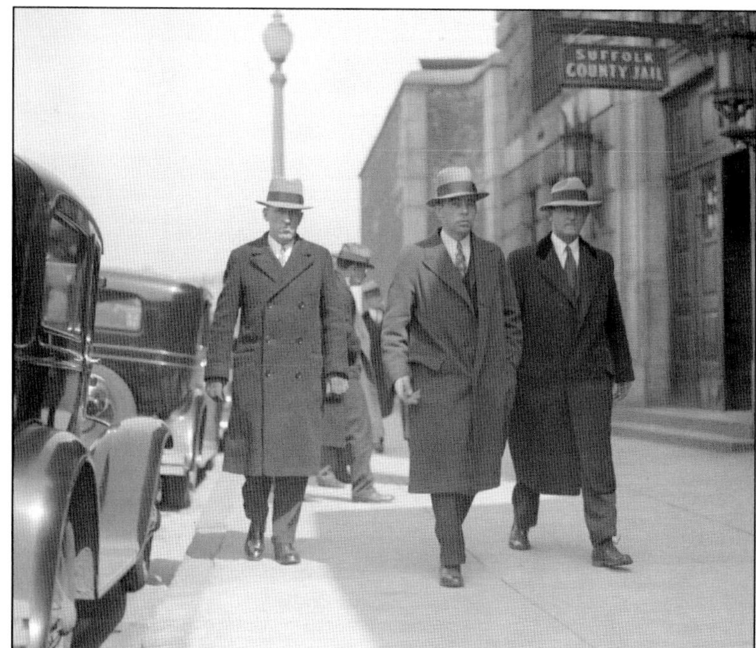

Between 4:00 a.m. and 5:00 a.m. on March 30, 1932, William "Bad Willie" Gray and Vincent Zamotel escaped from the Charles Street Jail by sawing through bars and sliding down bedsheets. Almost immediately, inspectors (pictured from left to right) Warren Liese, George Augusta, and William LeBlanc were on the case. (Courtesy of the Boston Public Library, Leslie Jones Collection.)

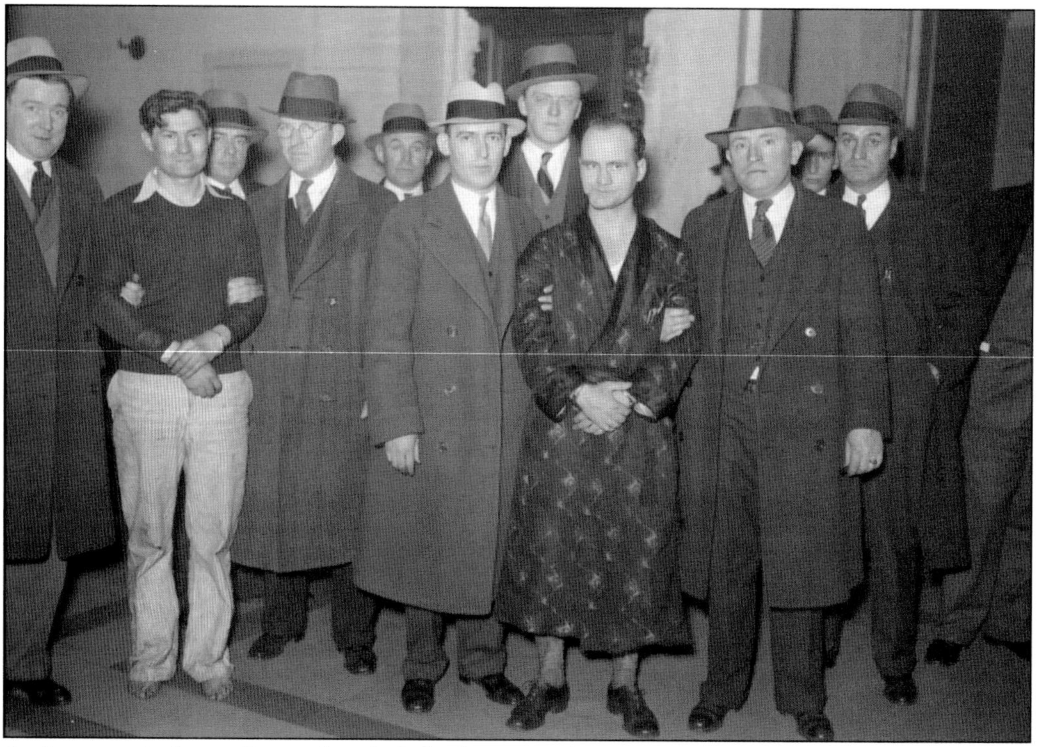

Acting on a tip from a Boston hotel clerk who noticed two suspicious guests, police captured and returned the pair to jail within 17 hours. Bad Willie Gray was expecting accomplices to drop clothing for him at the hotel where he and Zamotel were hiding. The clothing never arrived, and Gray was hauled back to jail in a bathrobe, as seen in this photograph. (Courtesy of the Boston Public Library, Leslie Jones Collection.)

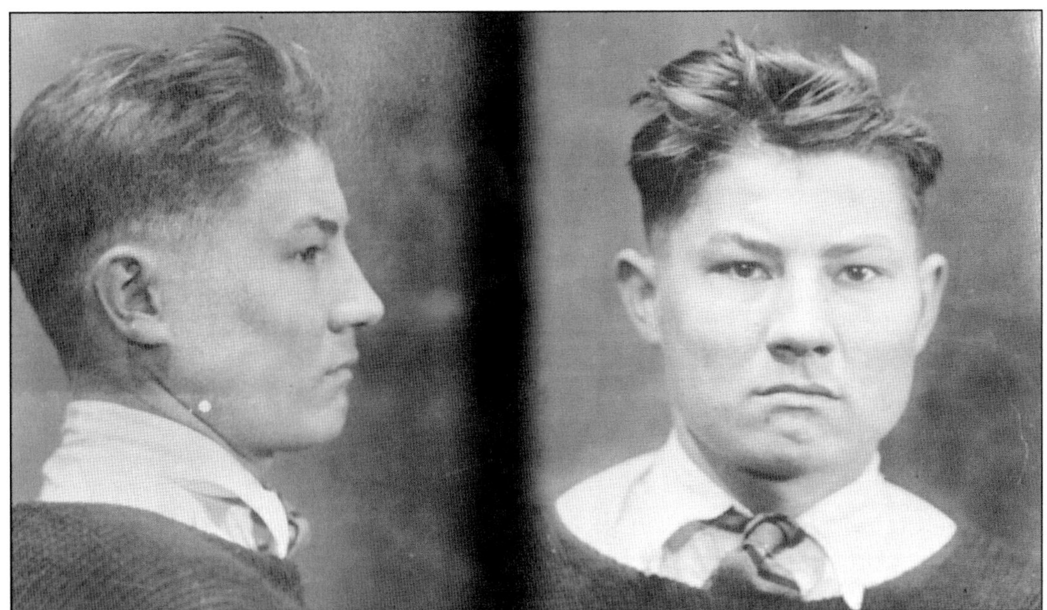

Zamotel was a trusty, a prisoner who had earned more freedom and responsibility at the jail. Information obtained from what newspaper reports called "underworld channels" indicated that someone on the outside had hidden metal files in the car of an unsuspecting jail employee. Unbeknownst to the employee, Zamotel retrieved them when the car arrived at the jail and delivered them to Gray. Zamotel had been eligible for parole in a few months. (Courtesy of the Boston Public Library, Leslie Jones Collection.)

Elmer "Trigger" Burke—the hitman who had been hired to kill Specs O'Keefe, the Brinks robber turned informant—made one of the most dramatic escapes in the history of the Charles Street Jail on August 28, 1954. While exercising in the jail yard, he suddenly made a mad dash for the steel door in the solitary confinement cell block—the building adjoining the brick wall. The door opened, and an accomplice held off guards at gunpoint while Burke escaped through three more supposedly locked doors and was whisked away by a car waiting just outside. Burke was recaptured exactly one year later. He was convicted of an unrelated murder and executed at Sing Sing. (Courtesy of the *Boston Herald*.)

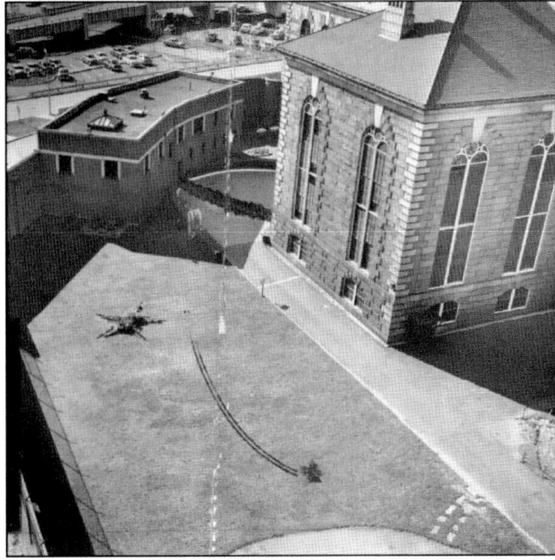

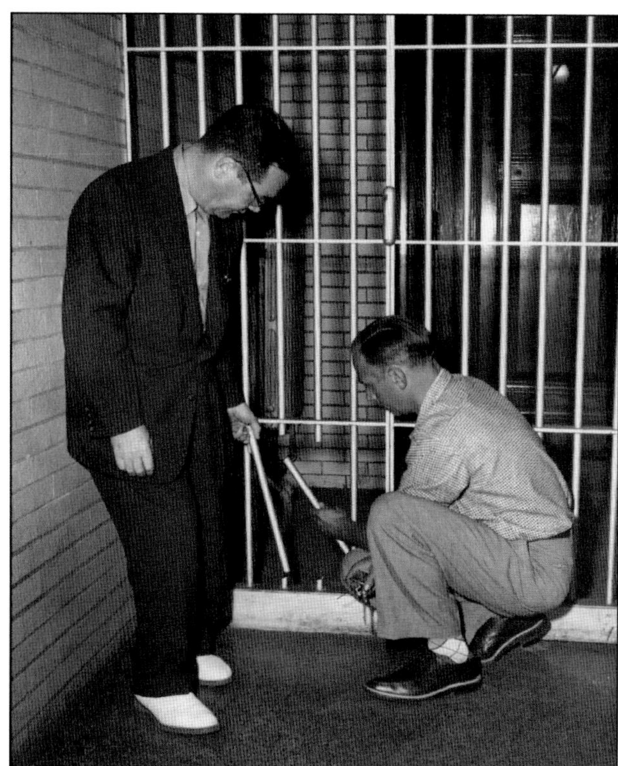

Burke's escaped had been carefully planned with help from the inside. Here, officials inspect some of the bars along the escape route that had been sawed ahead of time and held in place with chewing gum. Several guards were indicted for assisting Burke, and the sheriff was tried for negligence. (Courtesy of the *Boston Herald*.)

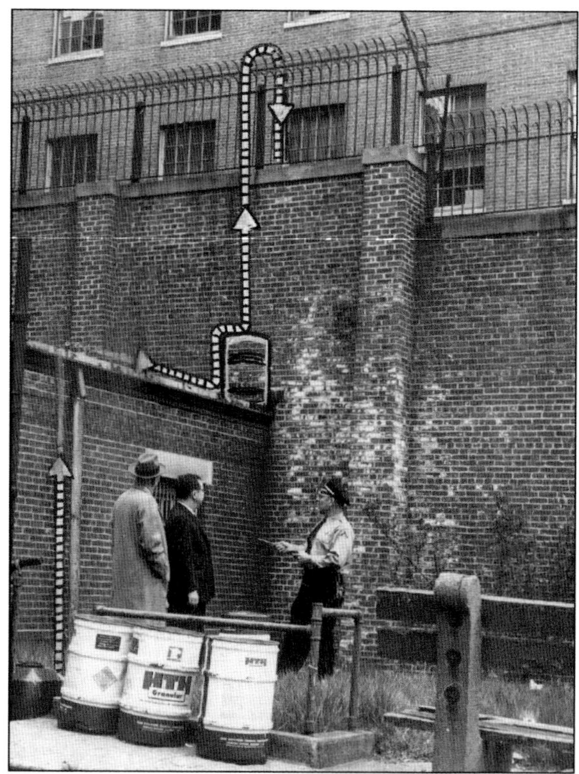

In this 1962 photograph, officials inspect the escape route of a man who apparently used empty barrels to scale the 25-foot wall. (Courtesy of the *Boston Herald*.)

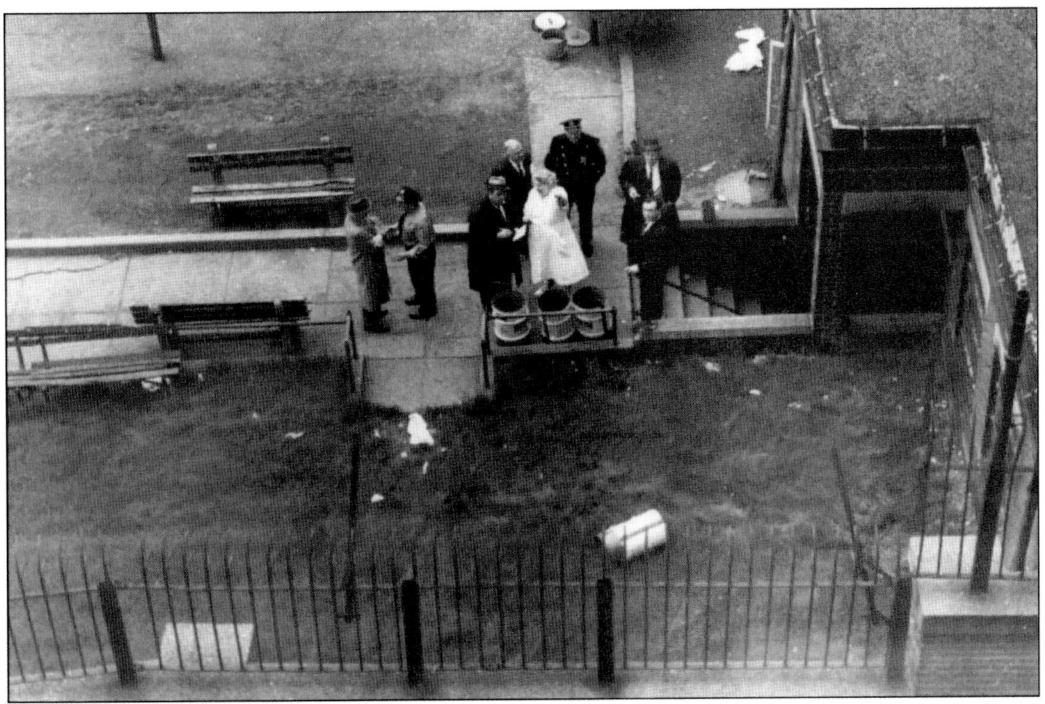

Gathering on the street, witnesses to the jailbreak point out the route taken by the escapee. (Courtesy of the *Boston Herald.*)

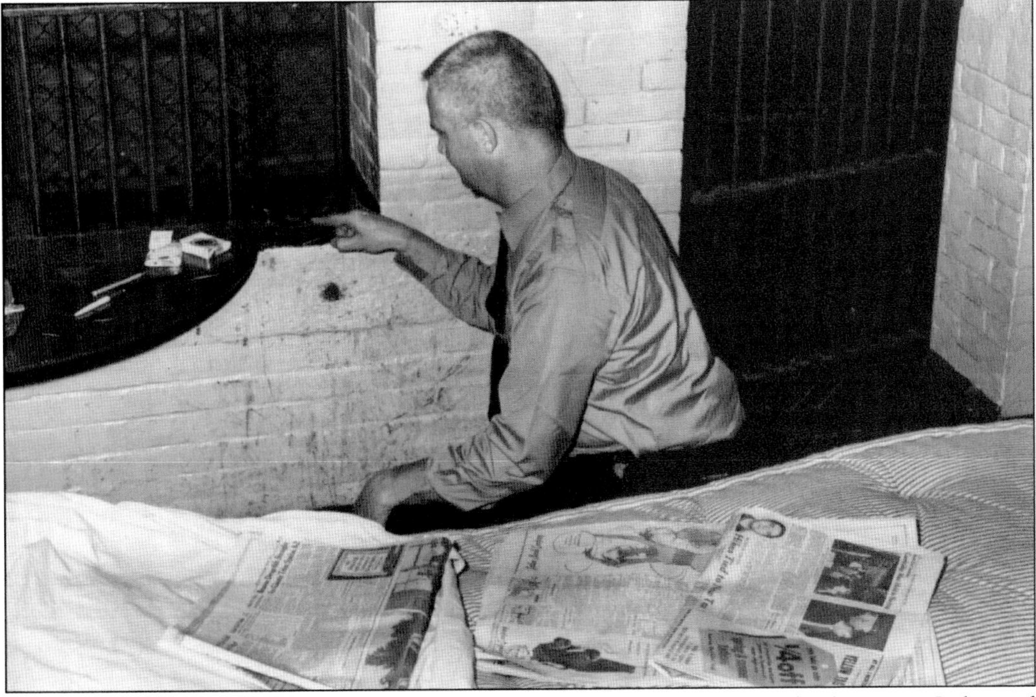

In 1963, an accused murderer made a daring escape at 1:45 a.m. Here, a Charles Street Jail guard points to two metal bars the prisoner sawed though, allowing him to climb out of his cell into the corridor. (Courtesy of the *Boston Herald.*)

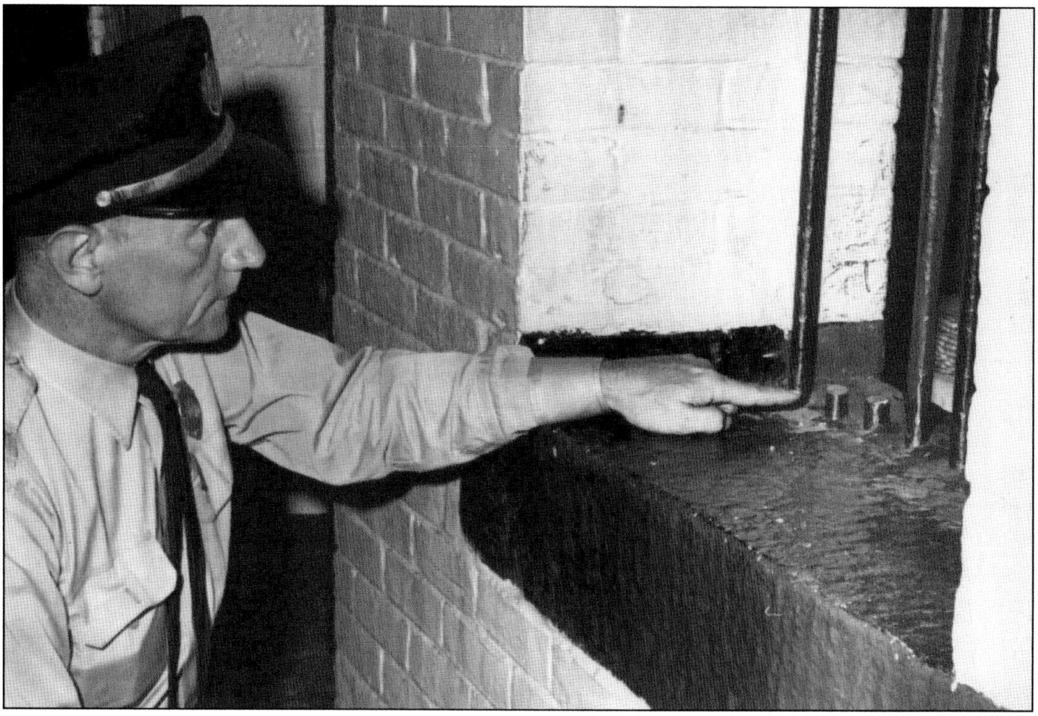

In this photograph, a guard points to the sawed-off bars from the corridor outside the cell. (Courtesy of the *Boston Herald.*)

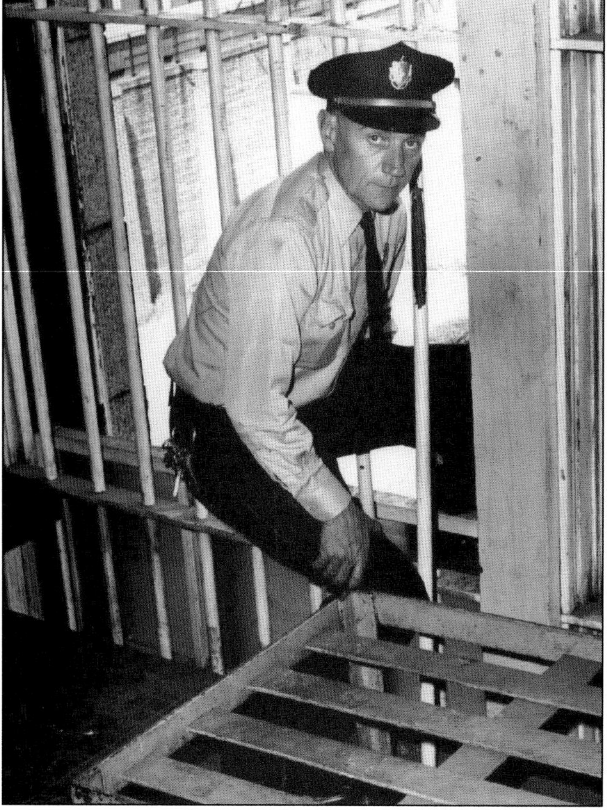

The jail guard in this photograph demonstrates how the escaped inmate squeezed through the window bars in a nearby vacant cell. From there, he dropped to the roof of the kitchen below. (Courtesy of the *Boston Herald.*)

Spectators gathered on the street outside the jail walls where the prisoner used knotted blankets, seen in the right of this photograph, to lower himself close enough to the sidewalk that he could drop safely. As a result of the escape, Sheriff Frederick Sullivan sent a letter to the mayor asking that a commission be set up to study the possibility of building a new jail or renovating the old one. (Courtesy of the *Boston Herald*.)

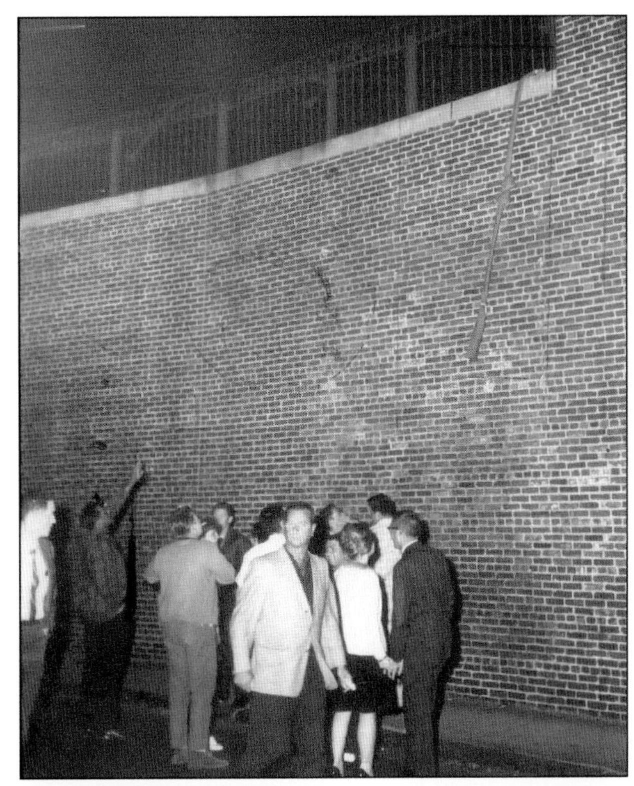

In 1964, an accused bank robber and two others escaped from the jail medical clinic. Here, police and detectives plunge into bushes on the grounds of the Massachusetts General Hospital in the search. Two of the escapees were captured quickly, but the third remained at large. (Courtesy of the *Boston Herald*.)

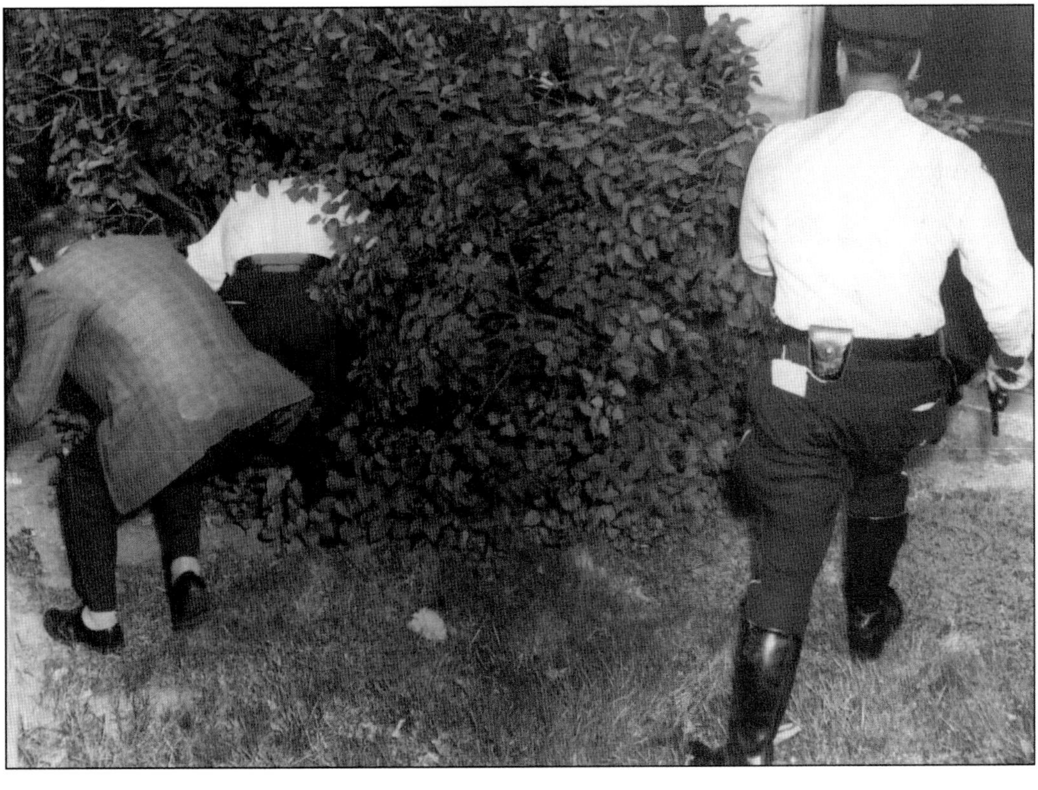

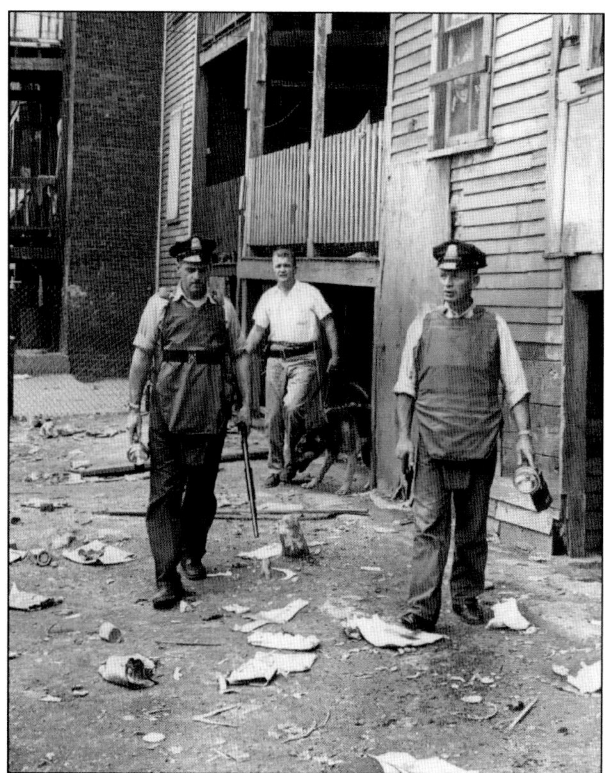

The escape sparked what was called one of the biggest manhunts in Boston history. Police officers wearing bulletproof vests and accompanied by a police dog conducted a house-to-house search for the man. (Courtesy of the *Boston Herald*.)

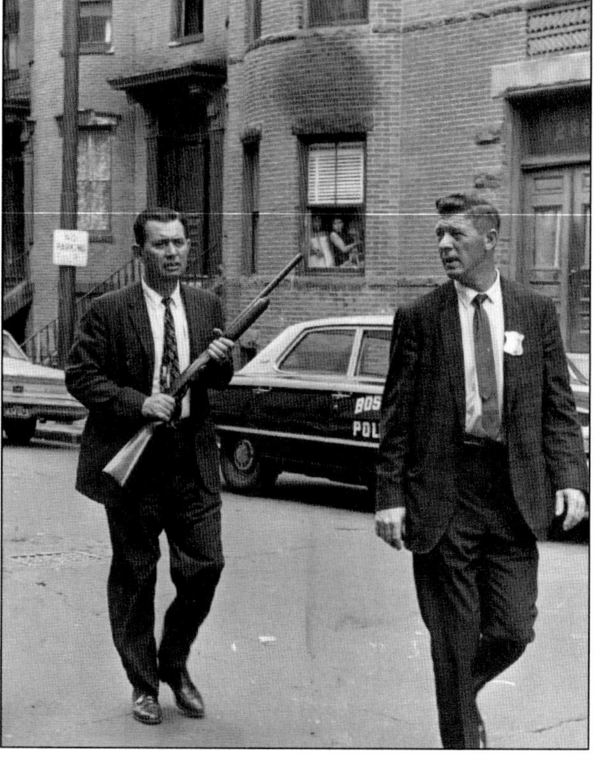

Heavily armed, Boston police, federal agents, and state police joined together in the search, scouring various neighborhoods of Boston. A week later, it was reported that all the locks at the jail were being replaced because a complete set of keys had been stolen in the escape. (Courtesy of the *Boston Herald*.)

Officials searched the neighborhood near the Charles Street Jail. Nineteen days after escaping, the last suspect was captured. The escape prompted a report on the jail that alleged, among other things, that the recent escapes (six in 15 months) "could not have been effected without collusion." (Courtesy of the *Boston Herald*.)

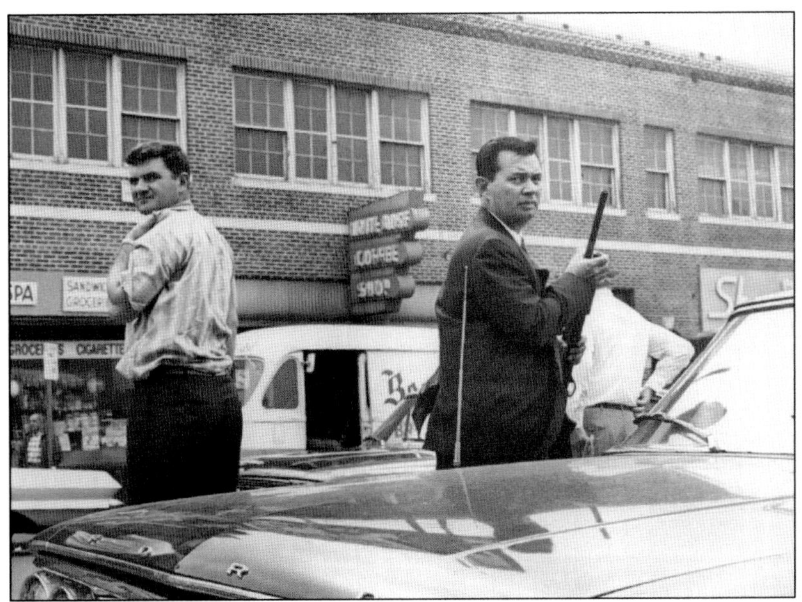

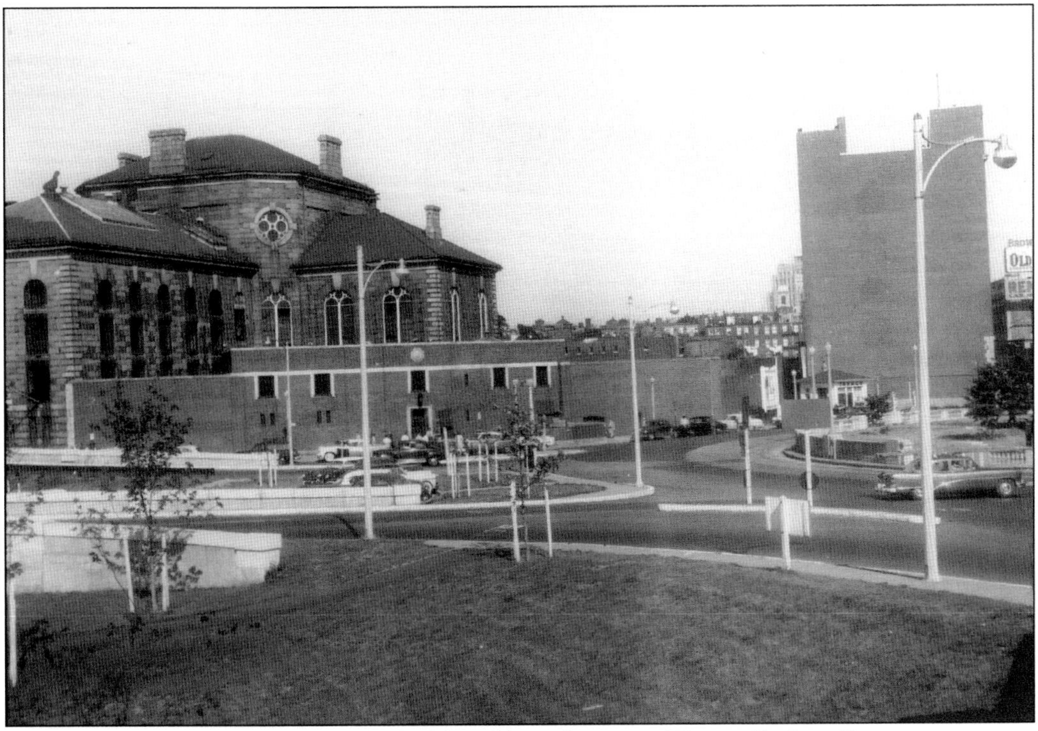

Following these escapes, and with the highly publicized escape of Trigger Burke still a recent memory, calls mounted for the Charles Street Jail to be torn down. "It's been investigated, denounced, and ridiculed for years," said the press. "But it's still there; a gray ghost of granite in Boston's West End. For decades it has been a cancer." Another report calls it "a depressing and inefficient relic of the past," "antiquated," "dilapidated," and "obsolete." The criticisms notwithstanding, the Charles Street Jail continued to pass inspections by the Federal Bureau of Prisons twice a year. (Courtesy of the *Boston Herald*.)

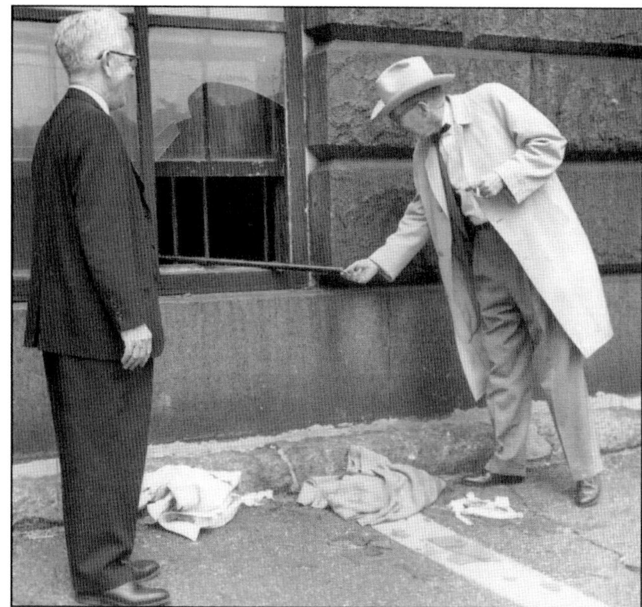

In 1968, two more inmates sawed their way out of their cell. Here, Jail Master Vincent Rice and a newspaper reporter inspect the sawed-off bars on the ground floor. (Courtesy of the *Boston Herald.*)

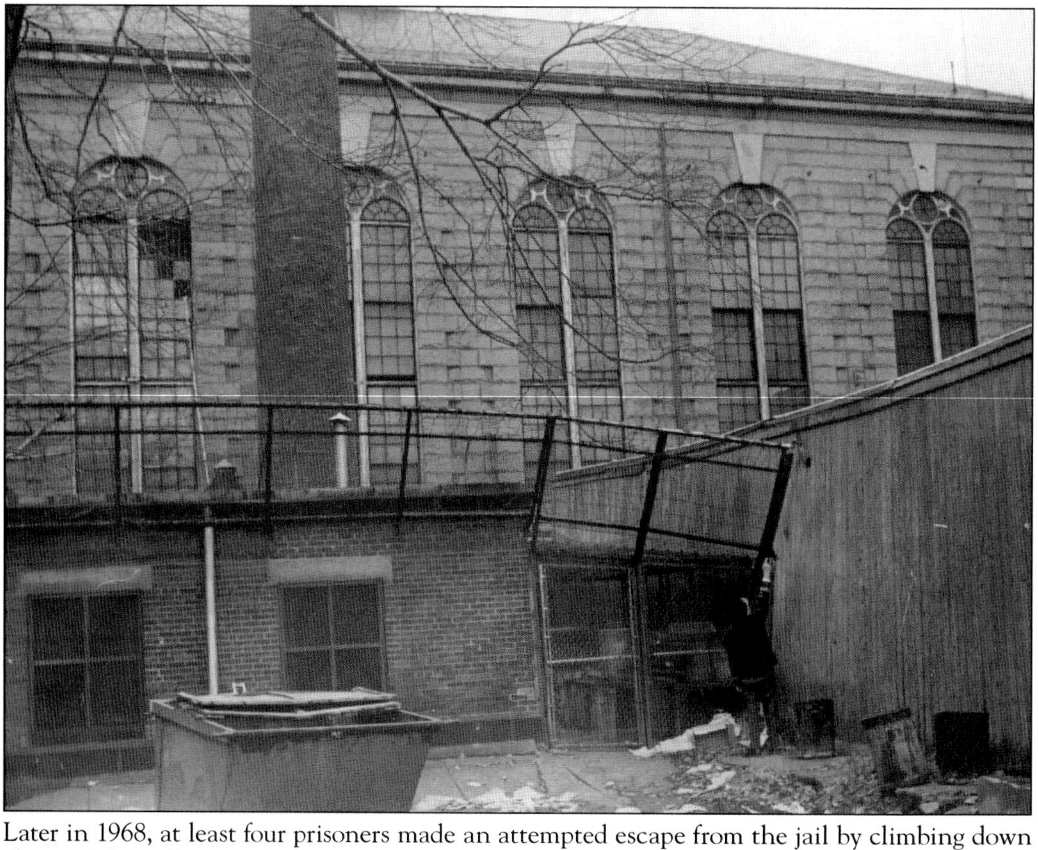

Later in 1968, at least four prisoners made an attempted escape from the jail by climbing down about 40 feet of knotted bedsheets. This image shows the sheets hanging out of the fourth-floor window on the left. Scrambling across the roof of the laundry building, the escapees took off in the direction the official on the right is pointing. (Courtesy of the *Boston Herald.*)

One of the prisoners made it over the wall but was captured after breaking both ankles when he dropped 30 feet to the ground on the other side. (Courtesy of the *Boston Herald.*)

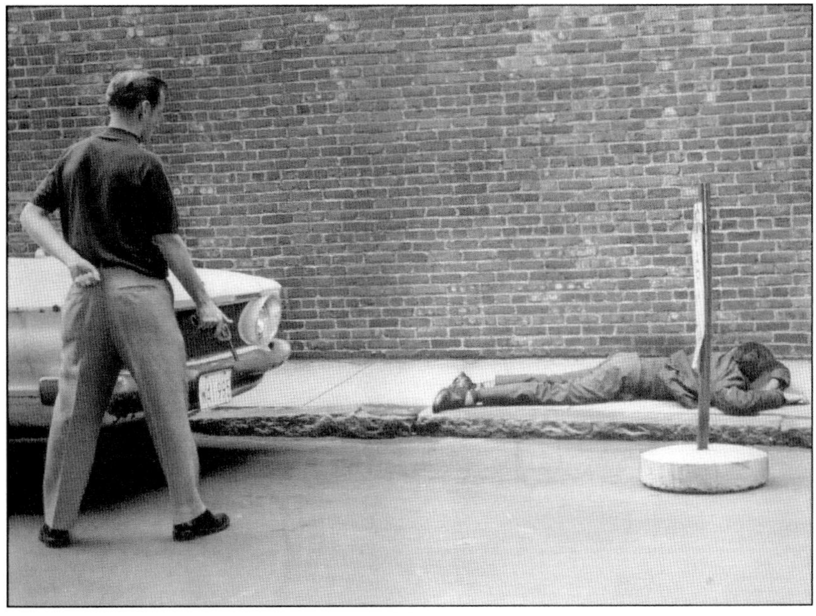

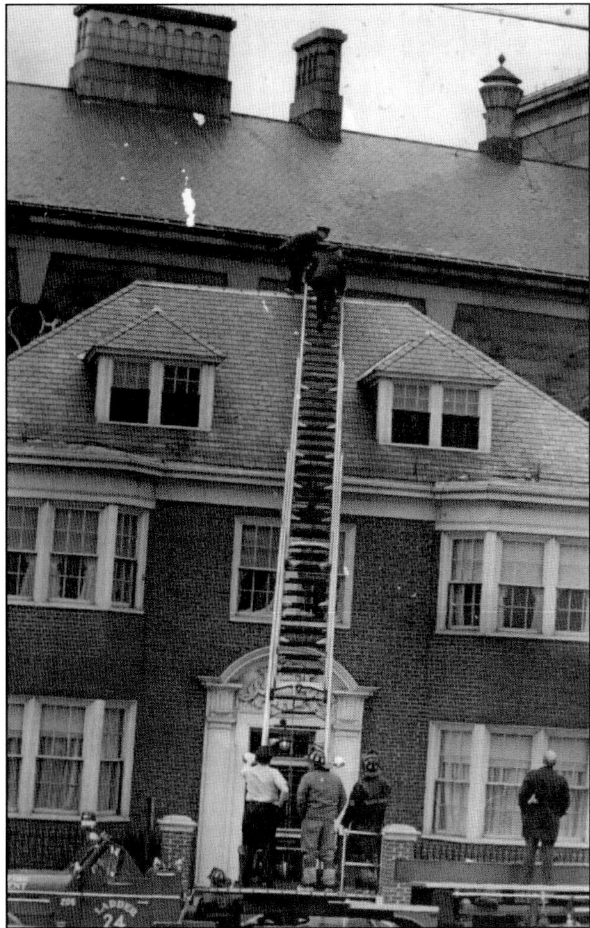

Looking for one of the other escapees, police surrounded the jail and swarmed over the buildings with the help of a Boston Fire Department ladder truck. (Courtesy of the *Boston Herald.*)

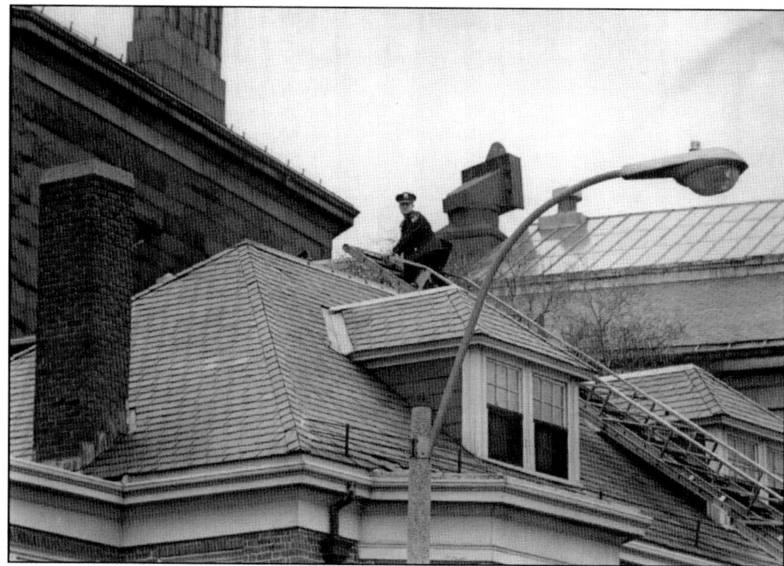

Here, one policeman searches the roof of the sheriff's house. (Courtesy of the *Boston Herald.*)

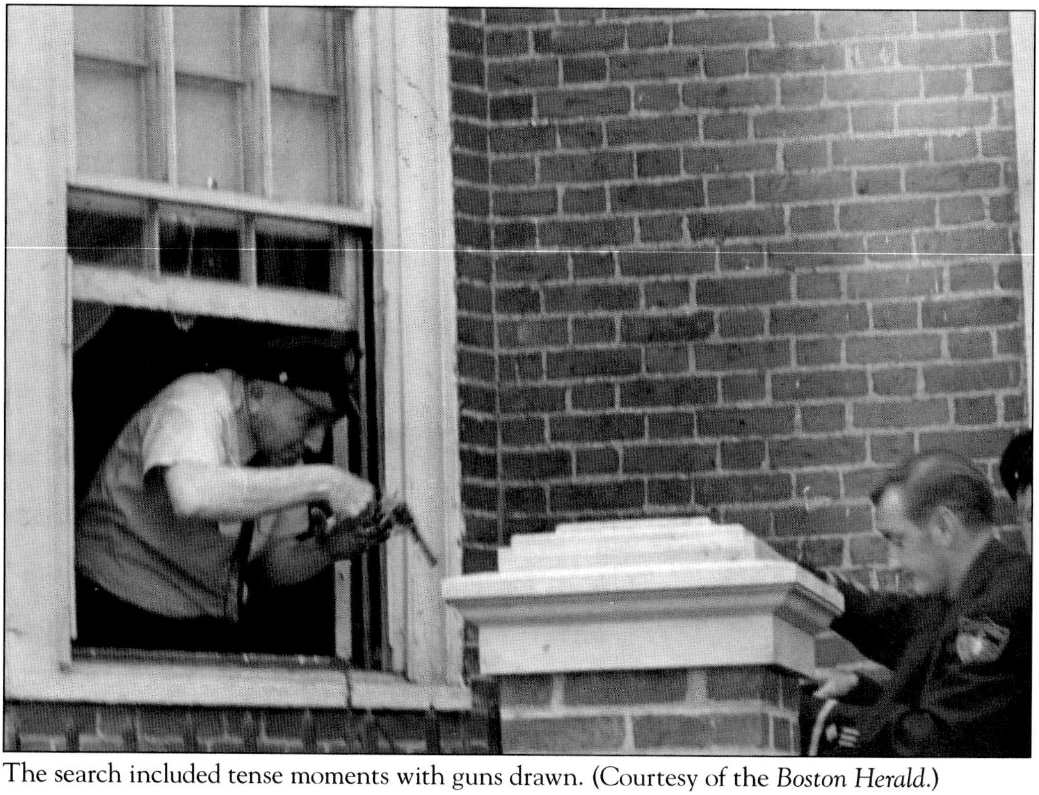

The search included tense moments with guns drawn. (Courtesy of the *Boston Herald.*)

Suffolk County sheriff Thomas Eisenstadt examines bars that were bent by two inmates who escaped from the chapel section of the jail in 1969. (Courtesy of the *Boston Herald*.)

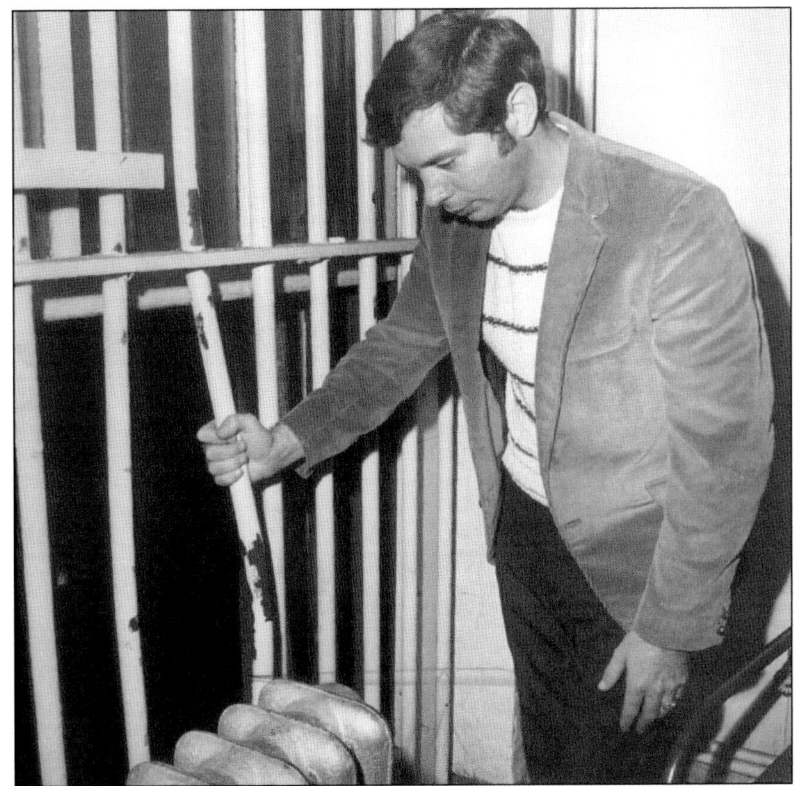

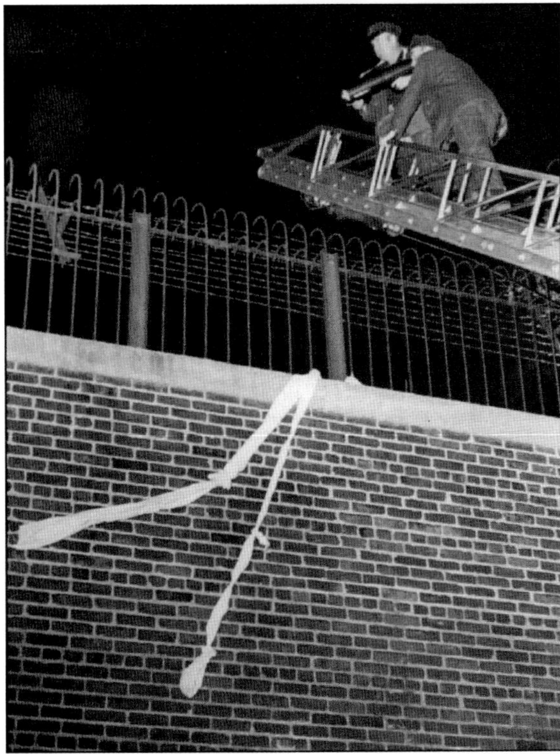

These knotted bedsheets, hanging from the wall of the jail in October 1969, caught the attention of a doctor at the Massachusetts General Hospital who notified the police. Two men had escaped; reportedly, the sixth and seventh in four months. Here, Boston police use a searchlight at the scene of the escape. (Courtesy of the *Boston Herald*.)

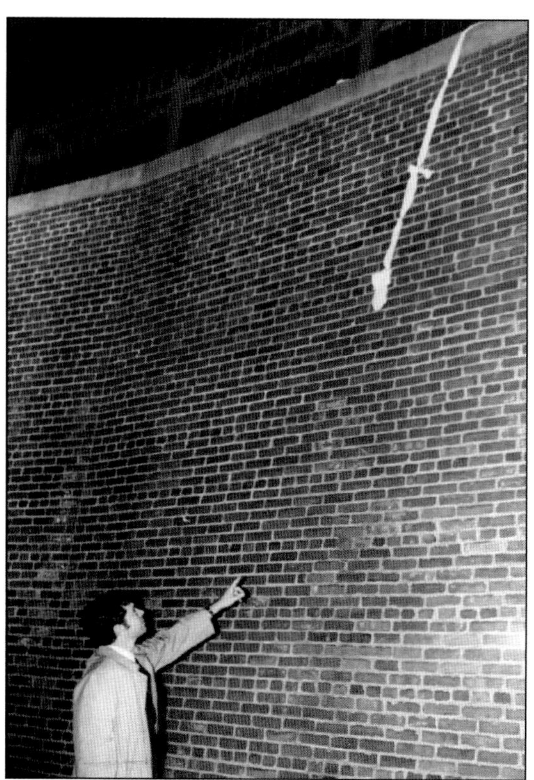

Suffolk County sheriff Thomas Eisenstadt points to the sheets used in the escape. (Courtesy of the *Boston Herald.*)

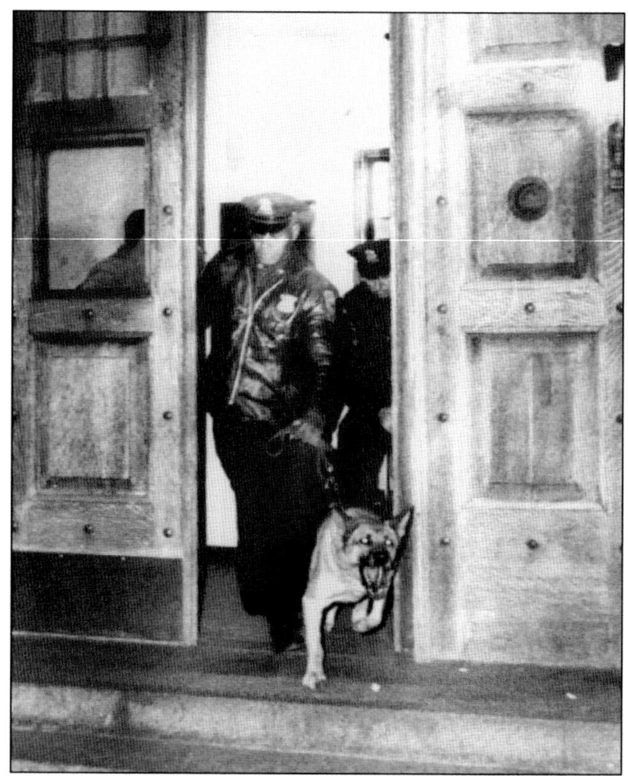

This officer and police dog set out in search of the October 1969 escapees. (Courtesy of the *Boston Herald.*)

Amid the multiple escapes and attempted escapes, Sheriff Eisenstadt (right) and the jail keeper (left) give a tour of the Charles Street Jail to a city councilor. (Courtesy of the *Boston Herald*.)

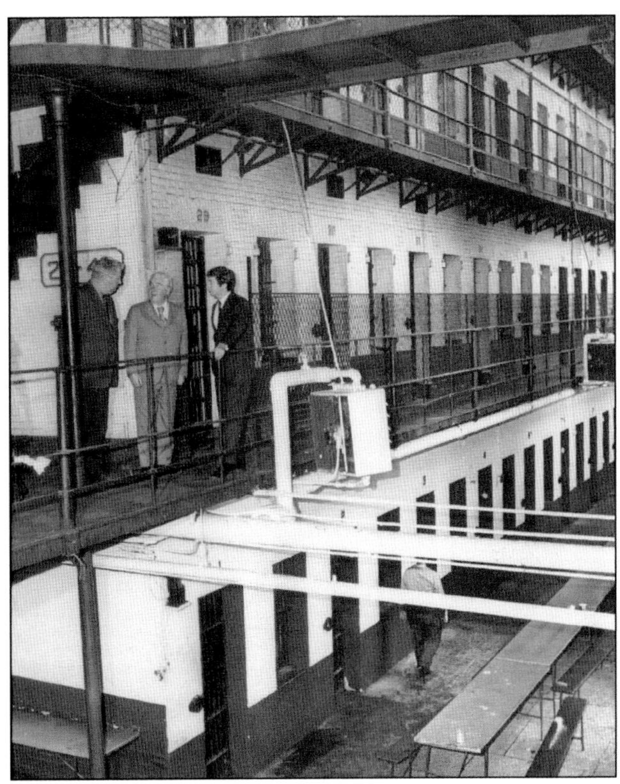

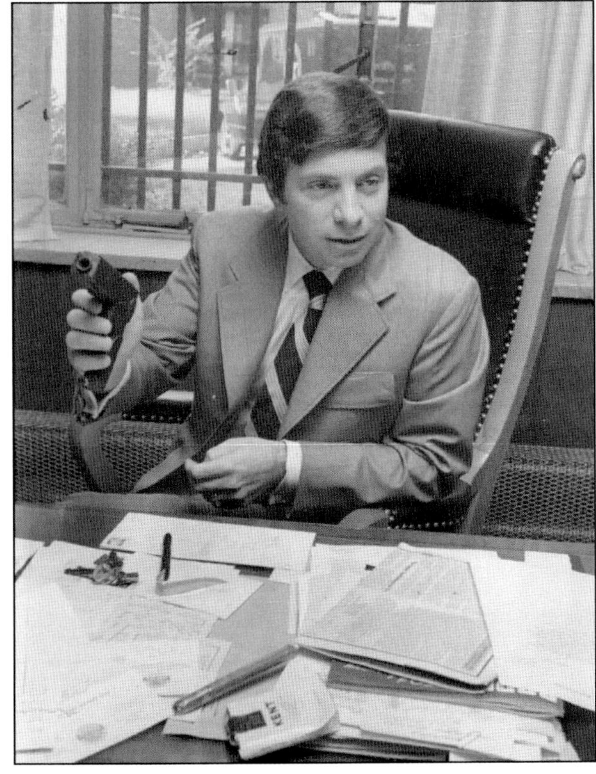

In 1972, guards foiled another escape. Here, Sheriff Eisenstadt shows a pistol that was to be used in the break. (Courtesy of the *Boston Herald*.)

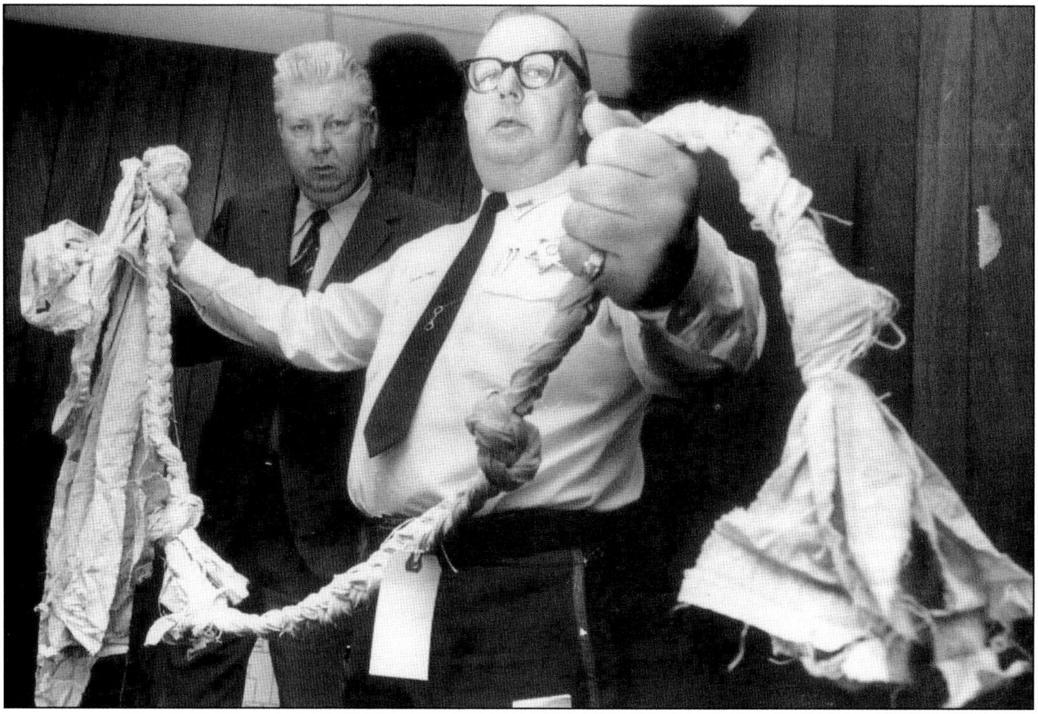

The jail master (left) and deputy master display ropes made from bedsheets from another thwarted escape in 1972. (Courtesy of the *Boston Herald*.)

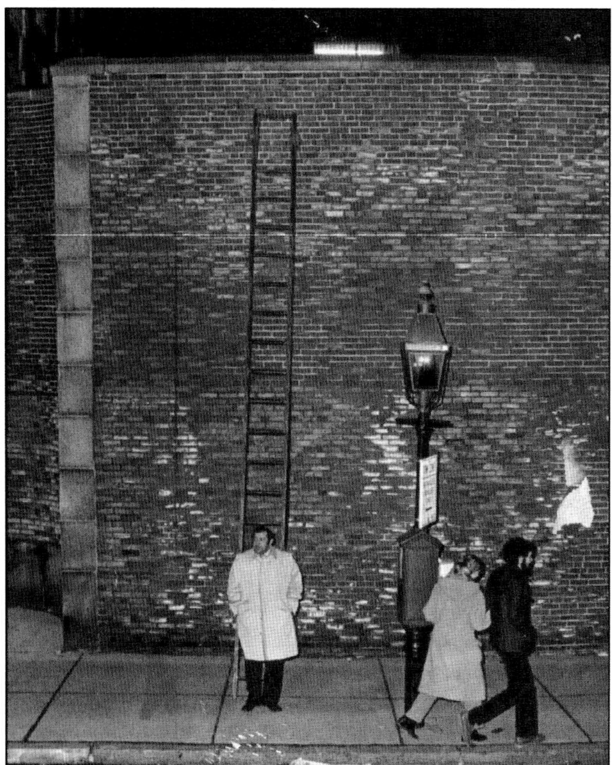

In 1973, two men successfully escaped from the Charles Street Jail by breaking into the cellar below the kitchen, taking a ladder, and using it to scale the jail yard wall. Once atop the wall, they pulled the ladder up and used it to climb down the other side. They were in such a hurry to get away that they apparently left the ladder standing against the wall. (Courtesy of the *Boston Herald*.)

Six

Last Days of the Charles Street Jail

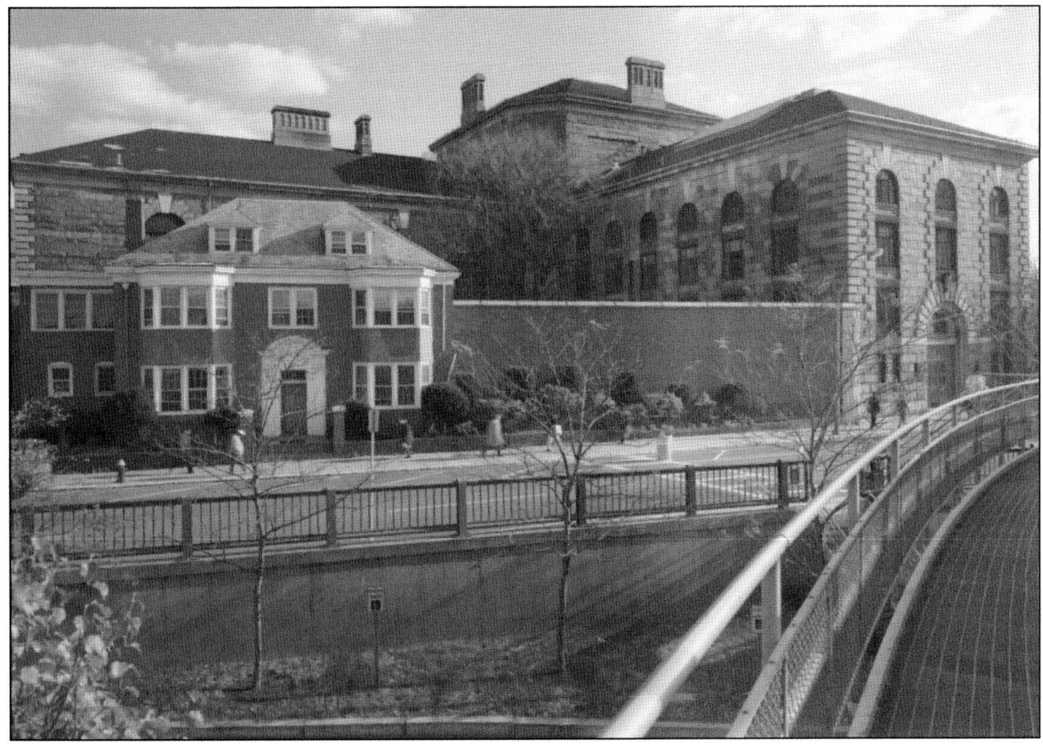

In January 1971, inmates filed a lawsuit alleging that conditions at the Charles Street Jail were so bad, they amounted to cruel and unusual punishment and were therefore unconstitutional. Over the next several years, momentum built for the closure of the jail as conditions prompted riots and demonstrations. (Courtesy of the Library of Congress.)

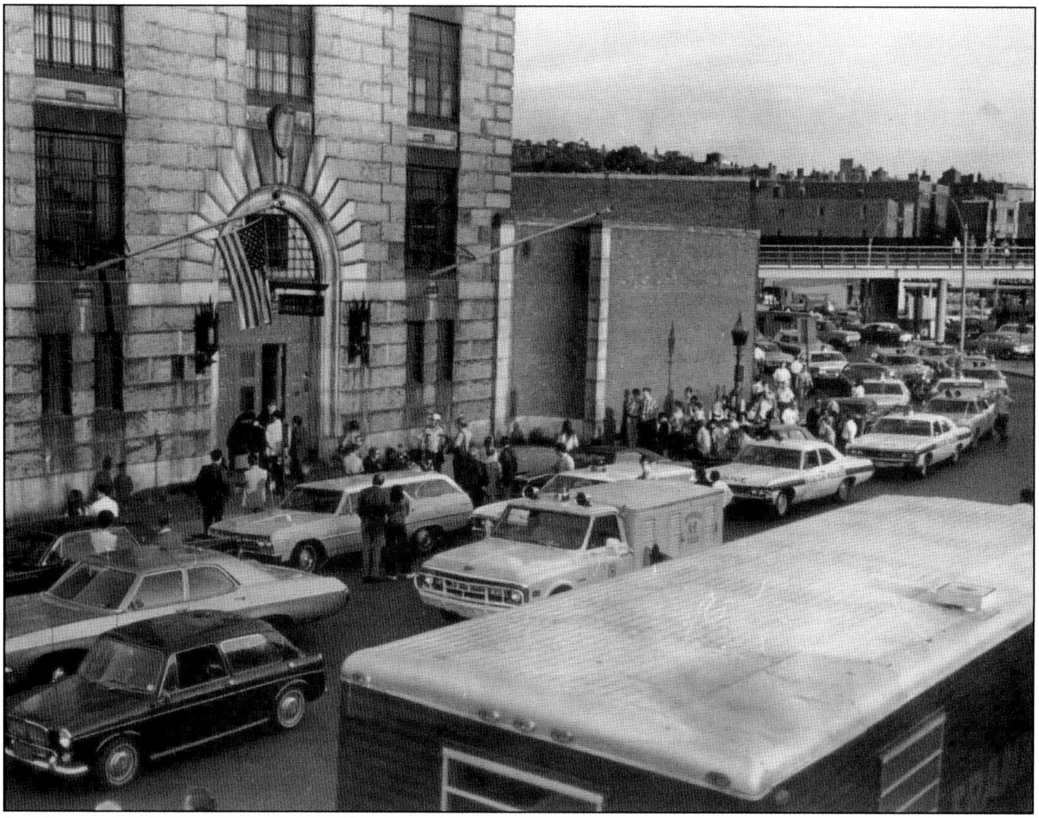

In August 1970, inmates staged a two-hour demonstration protesting conditions at the jail. When the demonstration grew unruly, police officers were called in to help guards restore order. (Courtesy of the *Boston Herald.*)

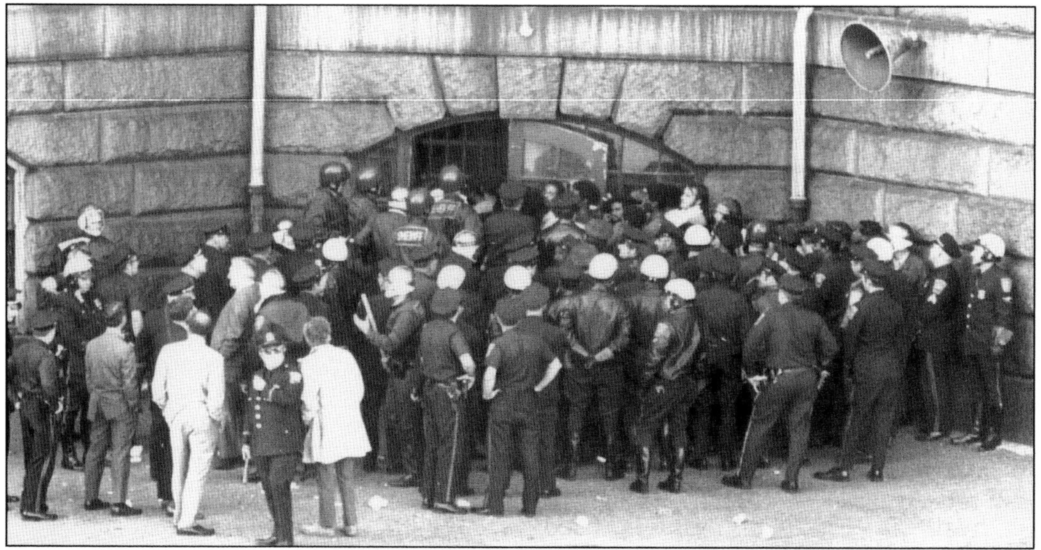

A little more than a year later, about 90 inmates refused to return to their cells after exercise period. Chanting "we want the press" and "we need help," they staged a four-hour demonstration that ended peacefully. (Courtesy of the *Boston Herald.*)

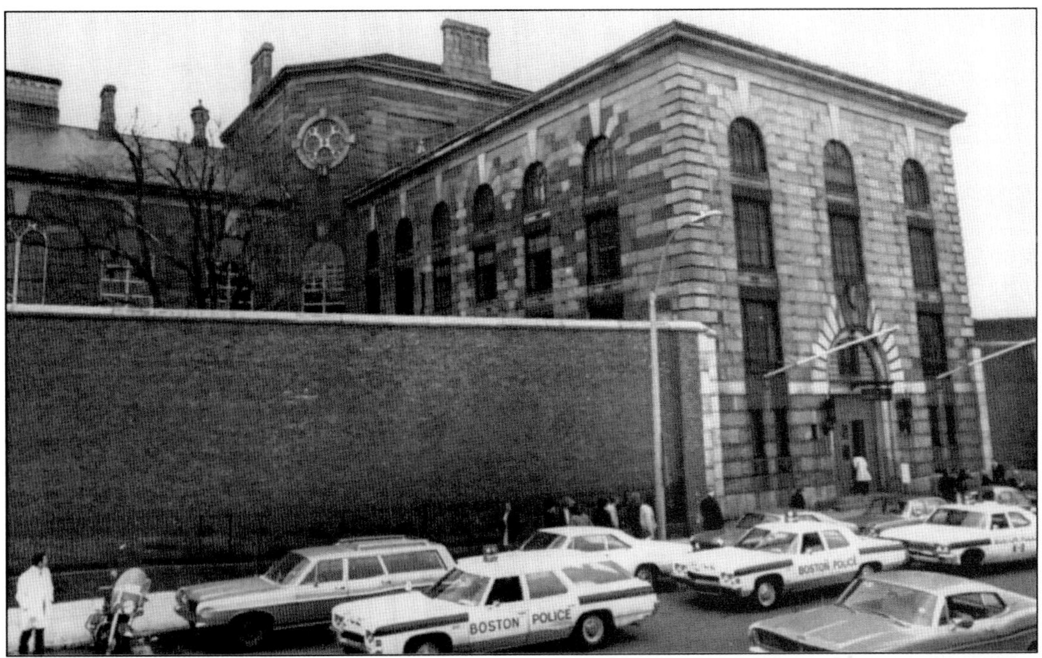

In November 1972, a riot started when prisoners reportedly found bugs in their pea soup at lunch. Police equipped with riot gear were summoned. (Courtesy of the *Boston Herald*.)

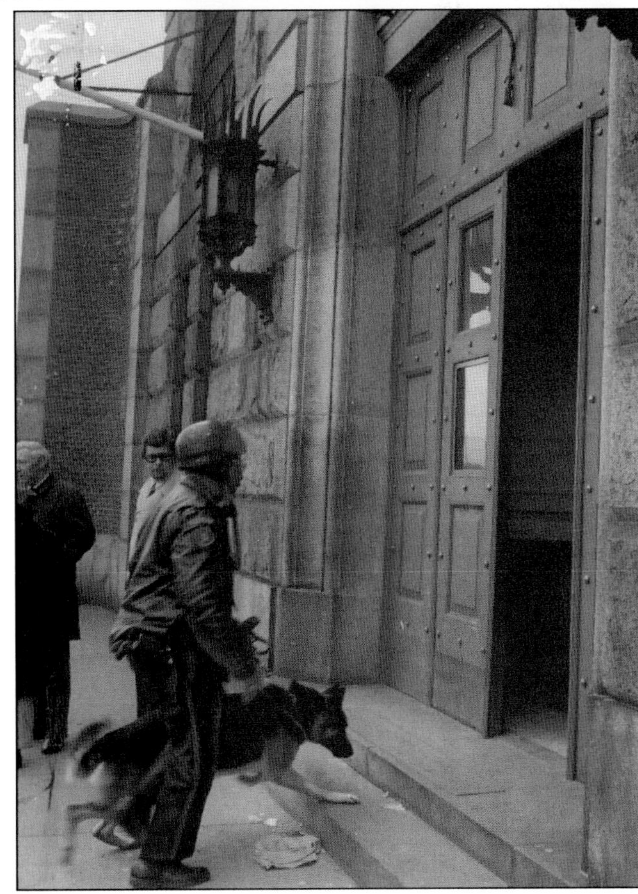

To help quell the riot, police dogs were brought in. (Courtesy of the *Boston Herald*.)

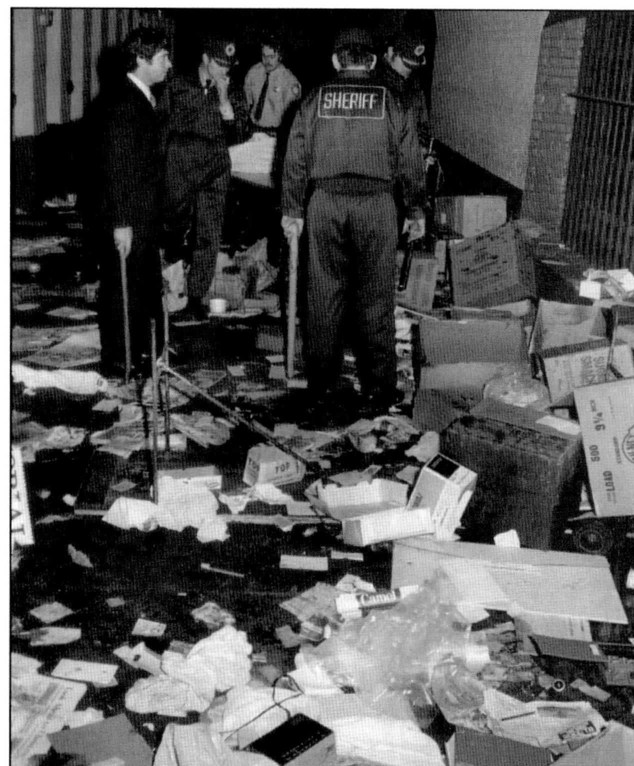

Once the riot was put down, Sheriff Eisenstadt and jail employees assessed the damage, which was estimated at about $250,000. (Courtesy of the *Boston Herald.)*

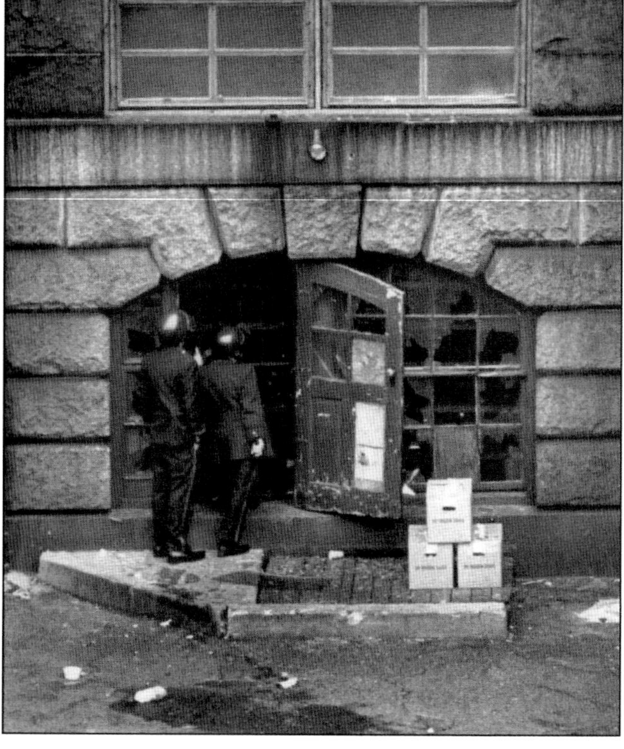

Here, policemen inspect the destruction from the riot. The incident prompted a scathing newspaper editorial entitled "Boston's ugly scar." It called the jail an "embarrassment" and declared, "Boston can no longer tolerate Charles Street Jail on her conscience." (Courtesy of the *Boston Herald.*)

On June 20, 1973, Judge W. Arthur Garrity (right) issued his ruling in the 1971 lawsuit. As part of his research, Garrity and a law clerk spent a night at the jail. He found conditions there so bad that he wrote in his opinion, "the Charles Street Jail stands in violation of plaintiffs' rights under the Constitution" because they violated the Eighth Amendment prohibition of cruel and unusual punishment. He ruled that after November 30, 1973, no inmates awaiting trial could be held in a cell with any other inmates and that after June 30, 1976, no inmates awaiting trail could be held at the Charles Street Jail. Since most of those held at Charles Street were awaiting trial, the ruling effectively set a timetable for permanently closing the jail. Garrity added, "Both the testimony and our own personal observations lead us to conclude that constitutional requirements cannot be satisfied without construction of a new jail." This photograph was taken several years earlier when Garrity was sworn in as US Attorney for the District of Massachusetts. (Photograph from the *Boston Herald-Traveler* Photo Morgue, courtesy of the Boston Public Library.)

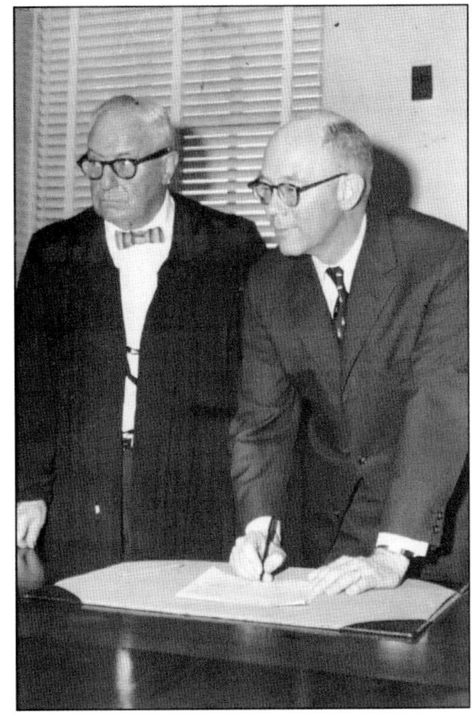

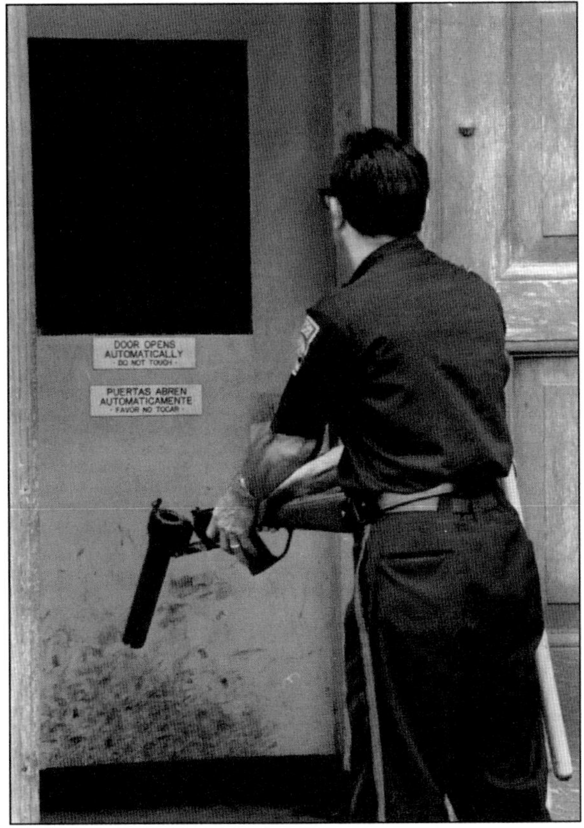

In June 1975, police were again called to the Charles Street Jail to help restore order when about 200 of the approximately 240 prisoners refused to return to their cells. In this photograph, a police officer readies tear gas in case it is needed. (Courtesy of the *Boston Herald*.)

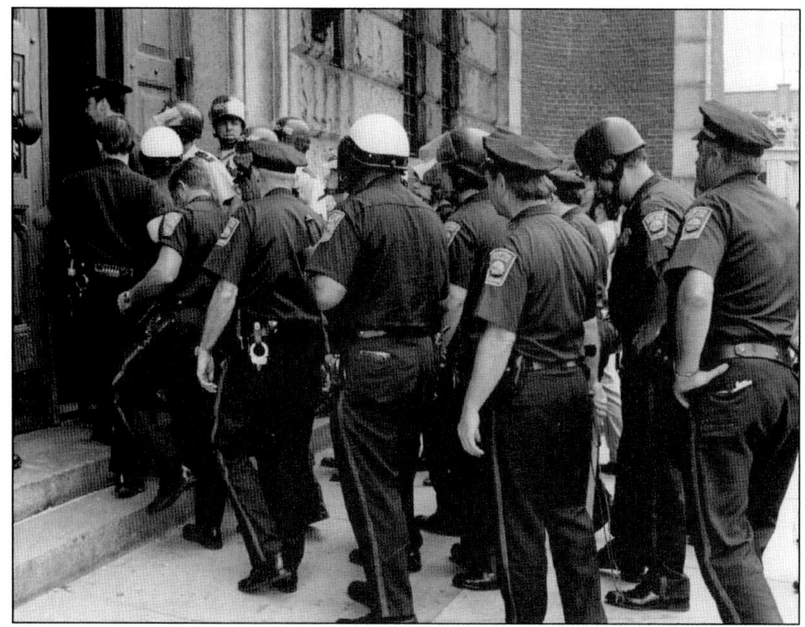

In the summer of 1975, police were summoned to the jail yet again when about 150 inmates refused to reenter their cells for a noon head count. "They were running wild in there, going from tier to tier throwing missiles," said one officer. (Courtesy of the *Boston Herald*.)

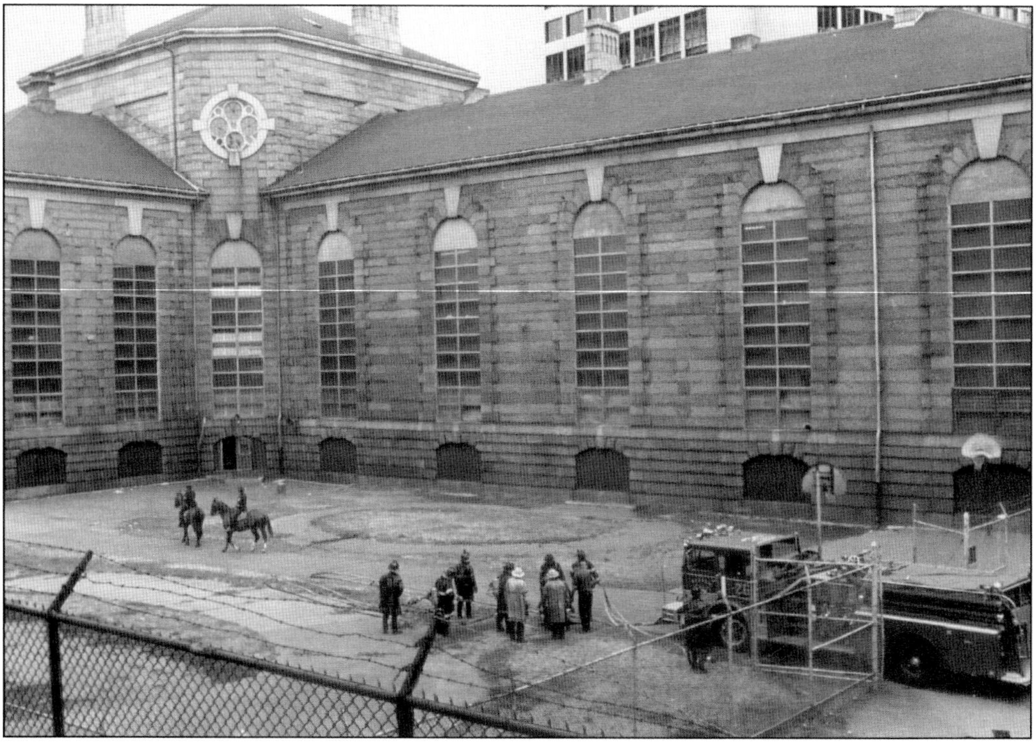

Mounted police and Boston firefighters entered the exercise yard to assist jail officials. Papers reported it was at least the fifth disturbance in five years that required police intervention at the jail. (Courtesy of the *Boston Herald*.)

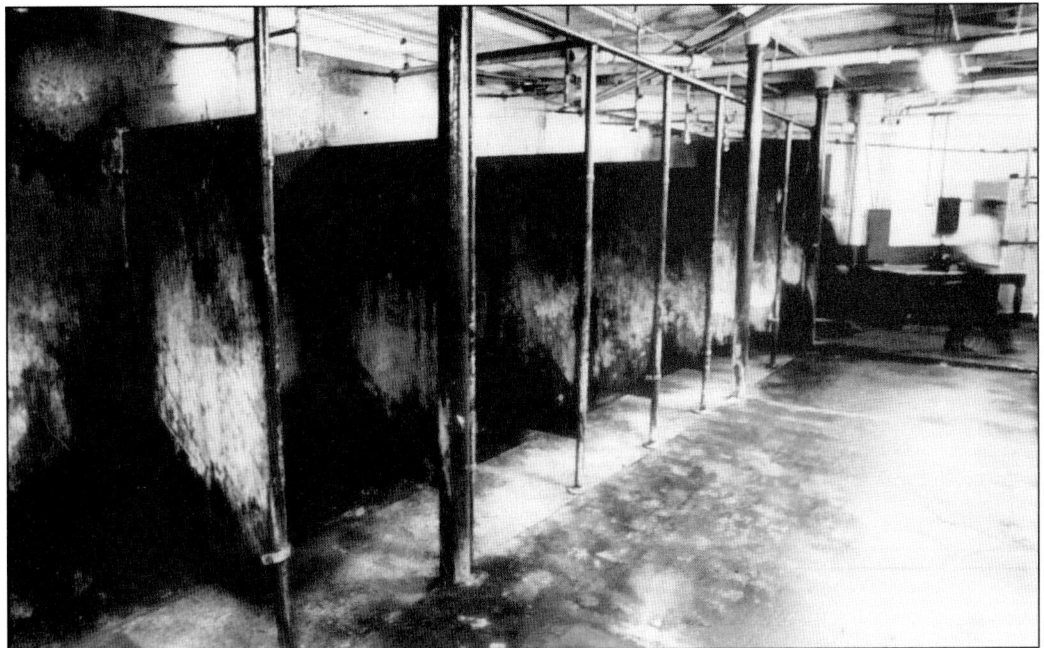

The causes of the disturbances and riots were many. Among the issues was the condition of the jail. This photograph from 1975 shows the decrepit shower room. At the time, the Charles Street Jail was reported to be one of the oldest such facilities still in use in the United States. (Courtesy of the *Boston Herald*.)

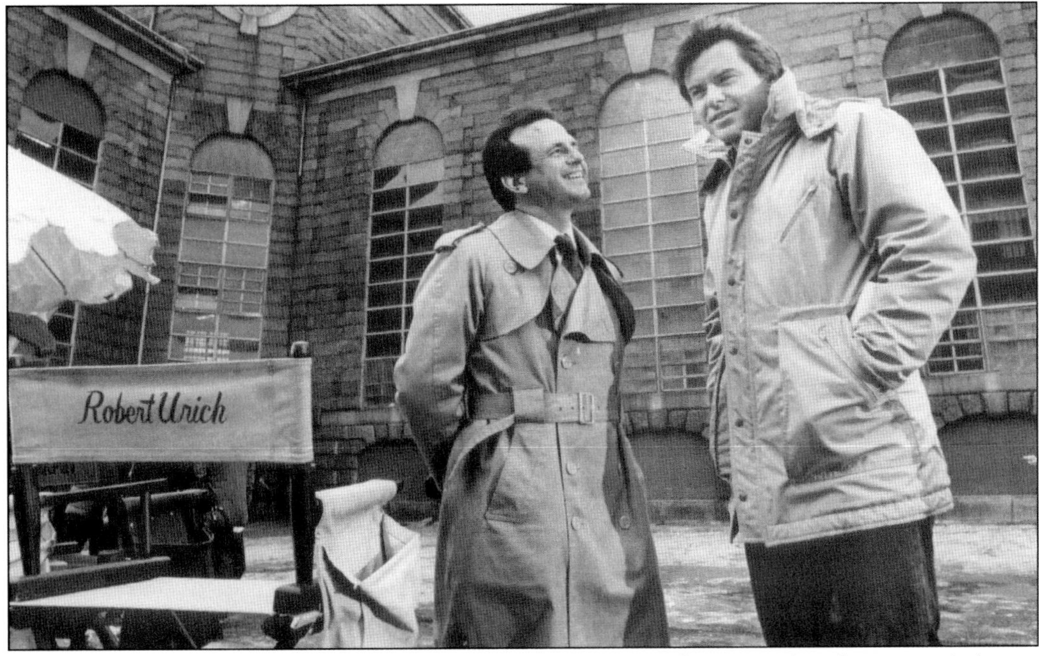

Courts allowed the Charles Street Jail to continue operating for years after the original closing deadline in 1976. Still in use in 1986, it served as the set for an episode of the television series *Spenser: For Hire*, filmed largely in Boston. Here, Dennis Kearney (left), the Suffolk County sheriff at the time, chats with series star Robert Urich on the set. (Courtesy of the *Boston Herald*.)

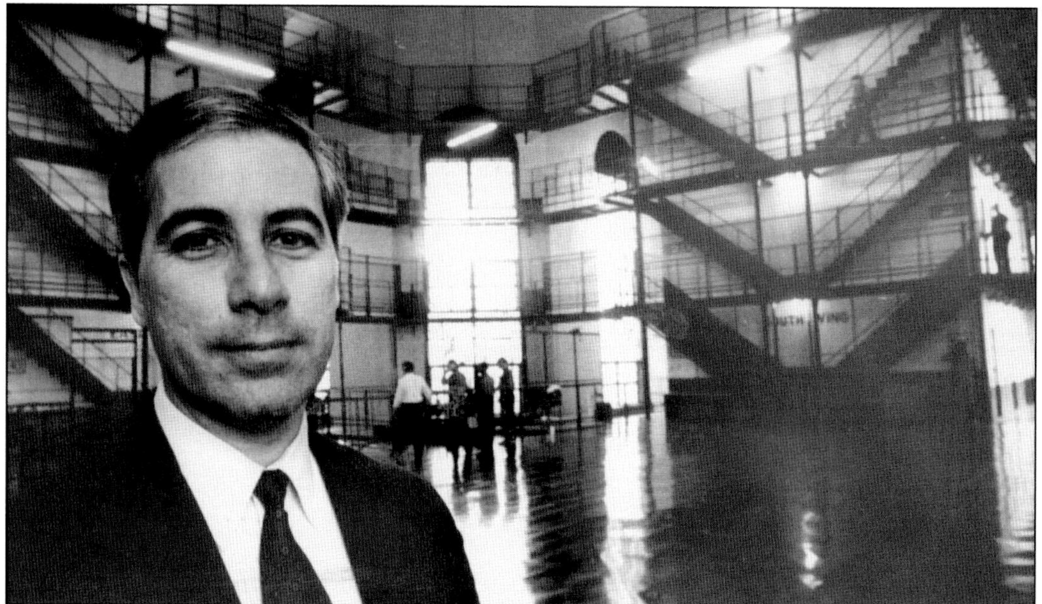

Robert Rufo, the last Suffolk County sheriff to serve with jurisdiction over the old jail, poses in the rotunda of the building in March 1990, shortly before the jail closed. (Courtesy of the *Boston Herald*.)

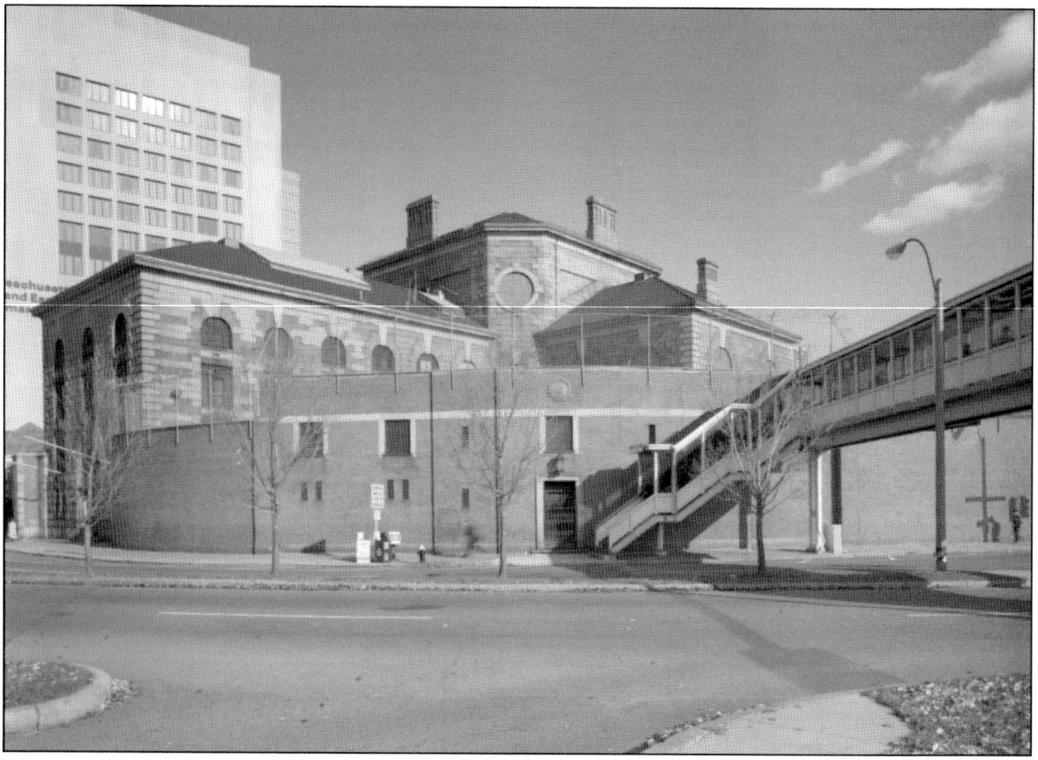

In operation continuously for nearly 140 years, the Charles Street Jail officially closed after the last prisoner left in May 1990. A new jail for Suffolk County, Massachusetts, opened a few blocks away. (Courtesy of the Library of Congress.)

Seven

ABANDONED

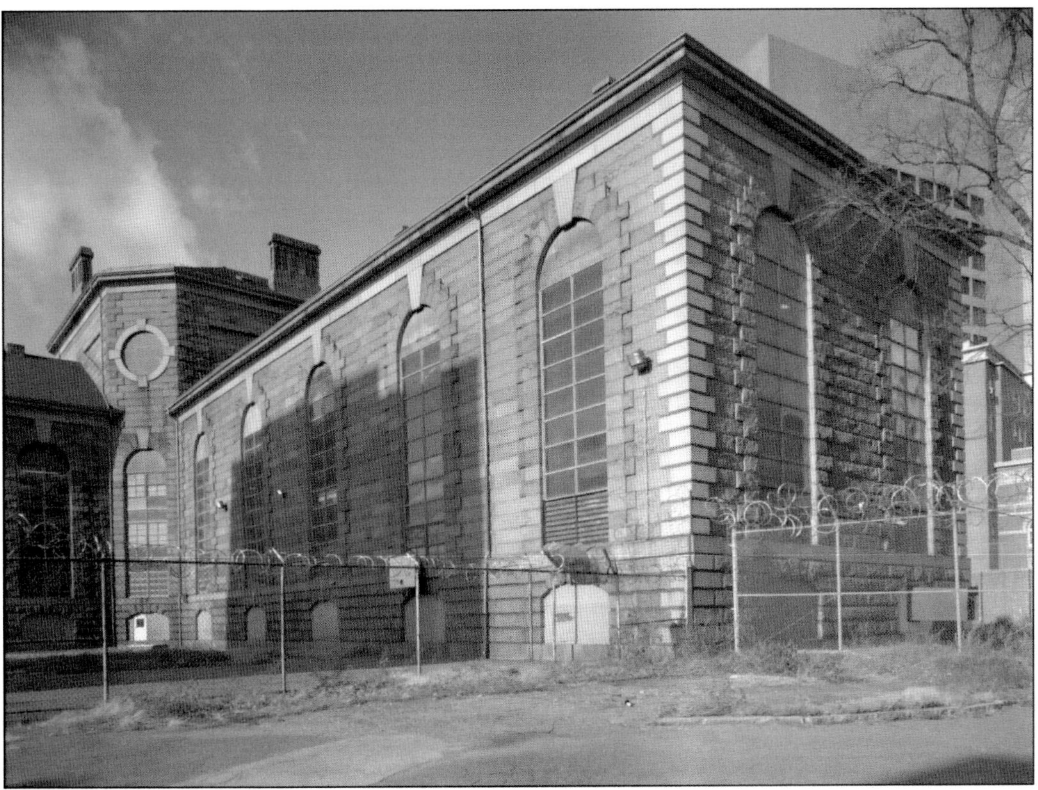

Massachusetts General Hospital bought the jail building and acquired the land in a swap for a site where the new jail was built. In an ironic twist, fences topped with razor wire were put up to keep people out of the building rather than in. (Courtesy of the Library of Congress.)

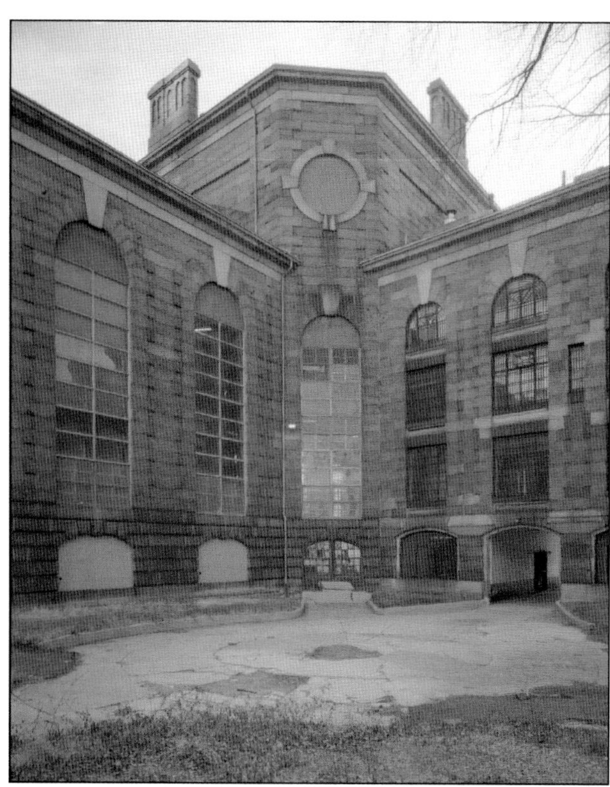

Many of the building's windows were boarded up while hospital officials considered what to do with the property. (Courtesy of the Library of Congress.)

This image shows the exterior of the jail with some of its disused outbuildings. (Courtesy of the Library of Congress.)

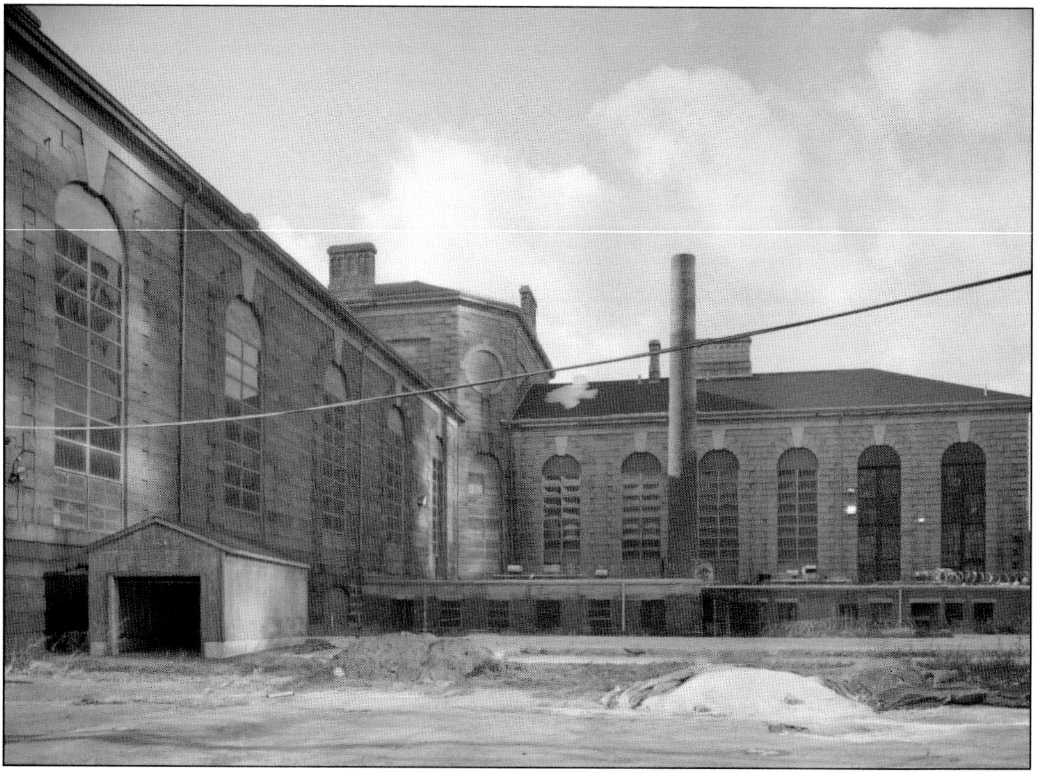

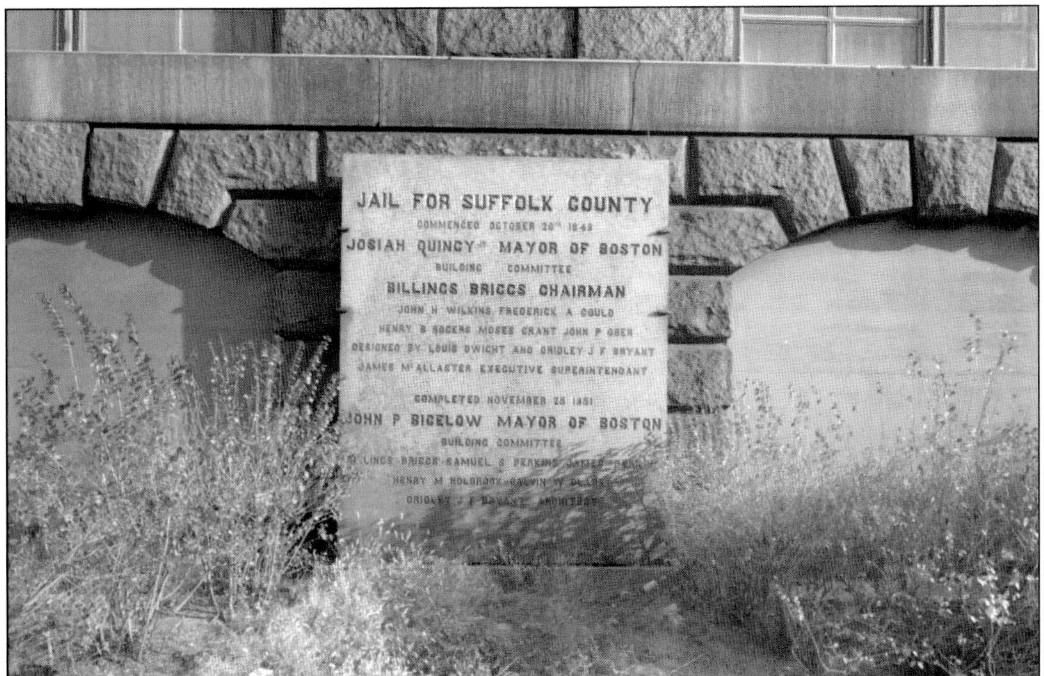

Looking like a relic of a bygone era, this inscribed stone had been placed on site to commemorate those responsible for commissioning, designing, and constructing the jail. (Courtesy of the Library of Congress.)

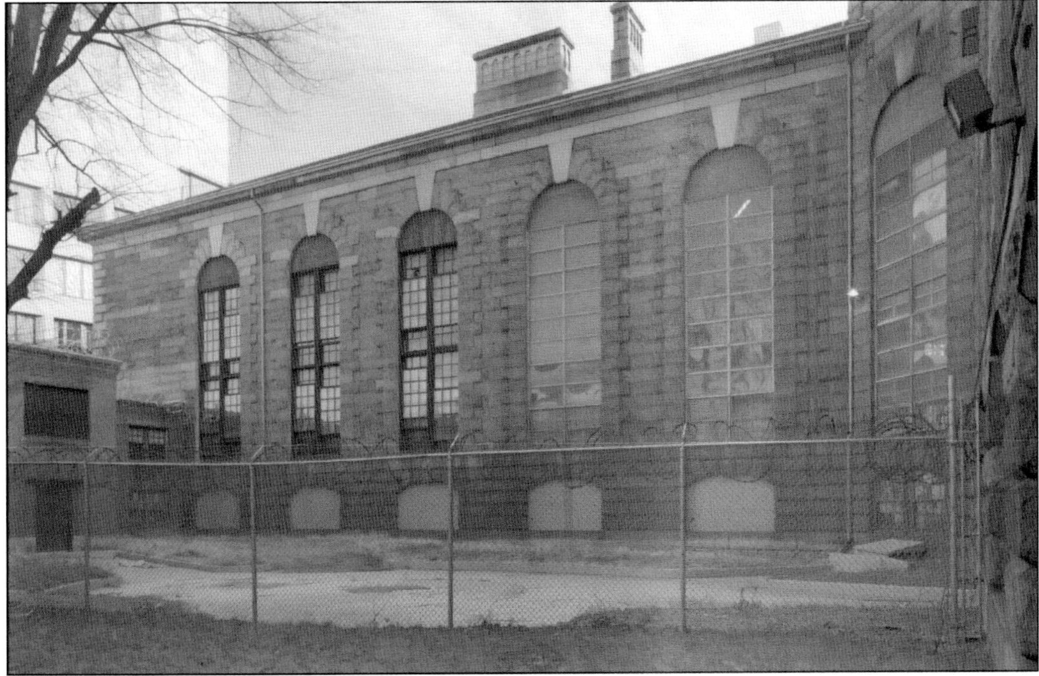

Judge Garrity pulled no punches in his ruling when it came to describing the condition of the jail. "During the past quarter century, seven separate governmental commissions studied Charles Street and condemned it," he noted. (Courtesy of the Library of Congress.)

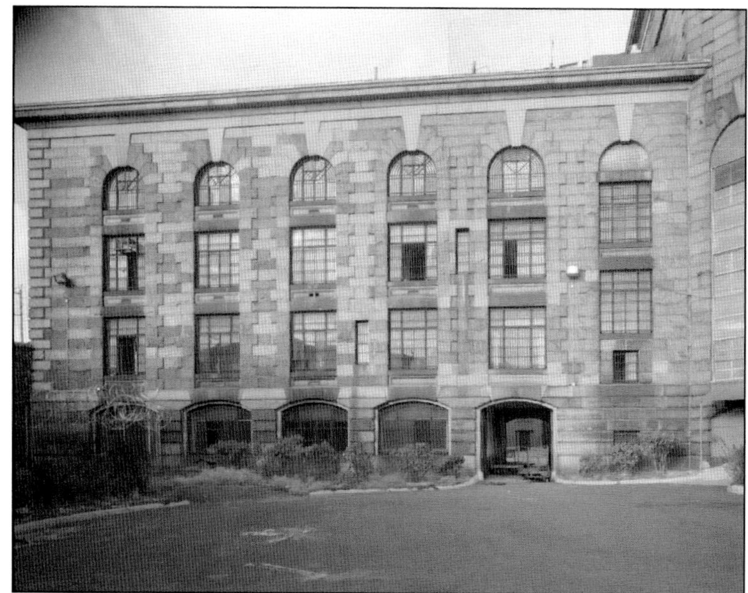

"Mosquitoes are a serious year-round problem. Roaches and waterbugs are prevalent. Rats are a serious, continuing problem. There is a recurrent problem of pigeons roosting inside the main jail, although programs of extermination and window repair periodically eliminate them," Garrity writes in his 1973 opinion. (Courtesy of the Library of Congress.)

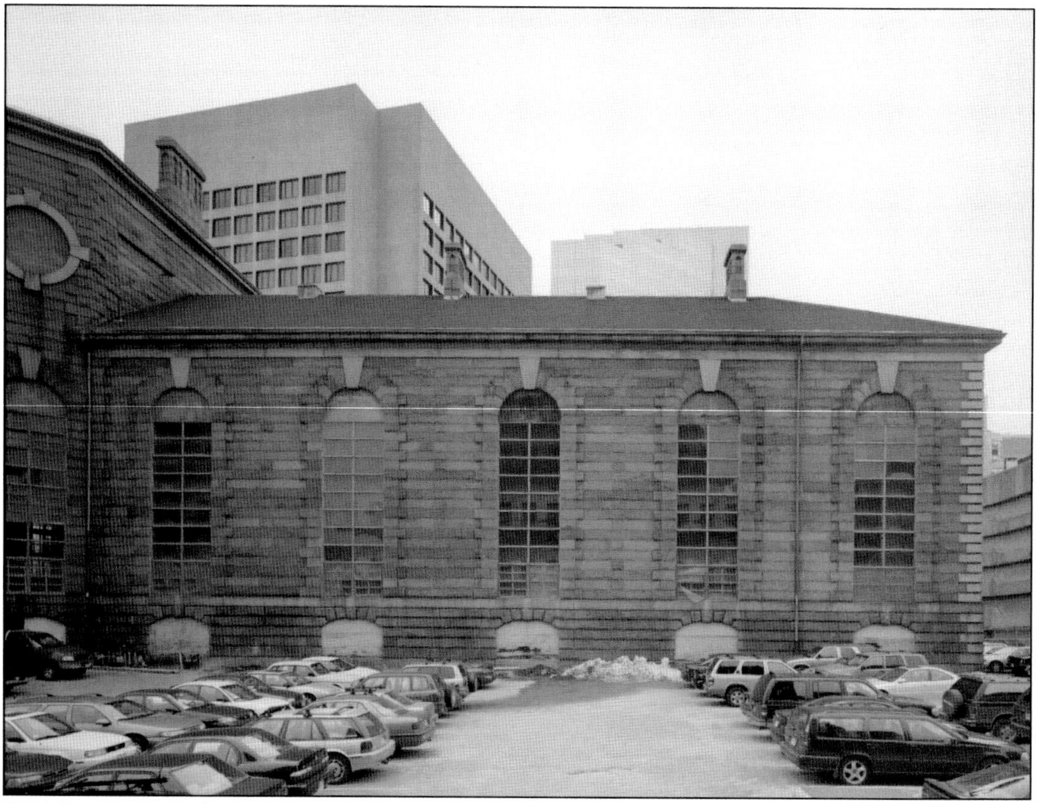

A 1968 report proclaims, "the physical plant of the Suffolk County Jail is antiquated, insufficiently secure for high risk prisoners and does not provide decent housing arrangements for any of its prisoners. The facility is a relic of the past. It cannot be remodeled to provide a modern adult detention program." After taking possession of the jail, Massachusetts General Hospital used the jail grounds as a temporary parking lot. (Courtesy of the Library of Congress.)

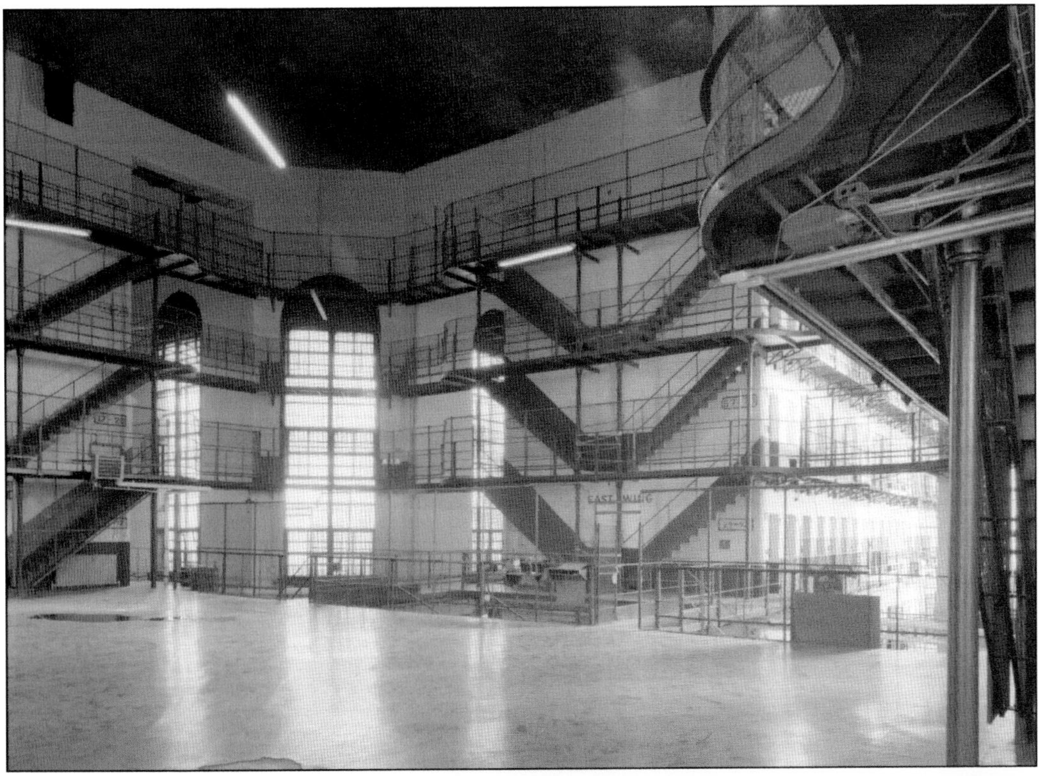

Despite the deteriorated condition, the open rotunda appeared to have changed little since it was built almost 150 years earlier. (Courtesy of the Library of Congress.)

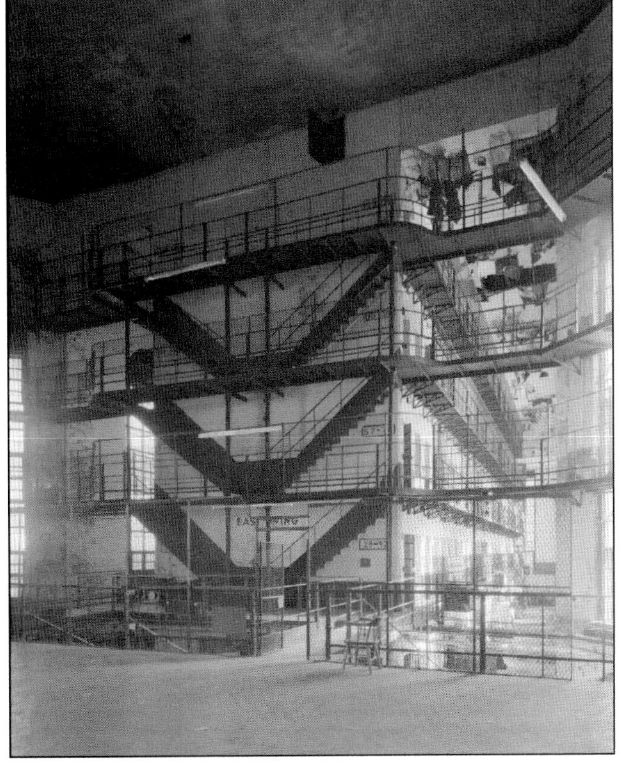

Recalling the night he spent in the jail as part of his research for the court case, Garrity wrote, "There is a din which persists 24 hours a day which includes noise from radios, noise made by drug addicts and alcoholics during withdrawal and steam pipes banging during cold weather. Since the cells are open, save for bars and sometimes screens, and there are so many stone and metal surfaces, noise made in any part of the main jail can be heard throughout the tiers. This makes sleeping extremely difficult." (Courtesy of the Library of Congress.)

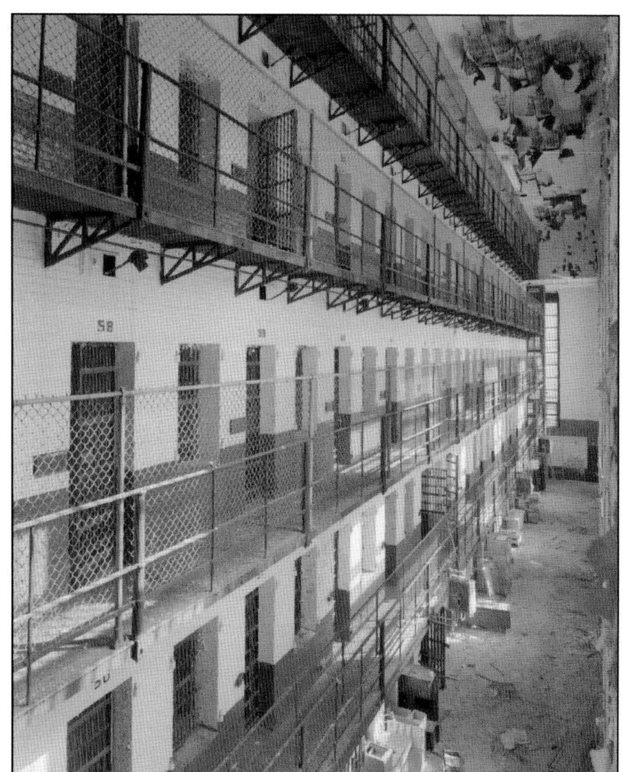

Regarding safety conditions, the court opinion notes, "The jail as a whole poses a serious fire hazard. In case of fire, removal of inmates can only be accomplished by unlocking each cell door individually." (Courtesy of the Library of Congress.)

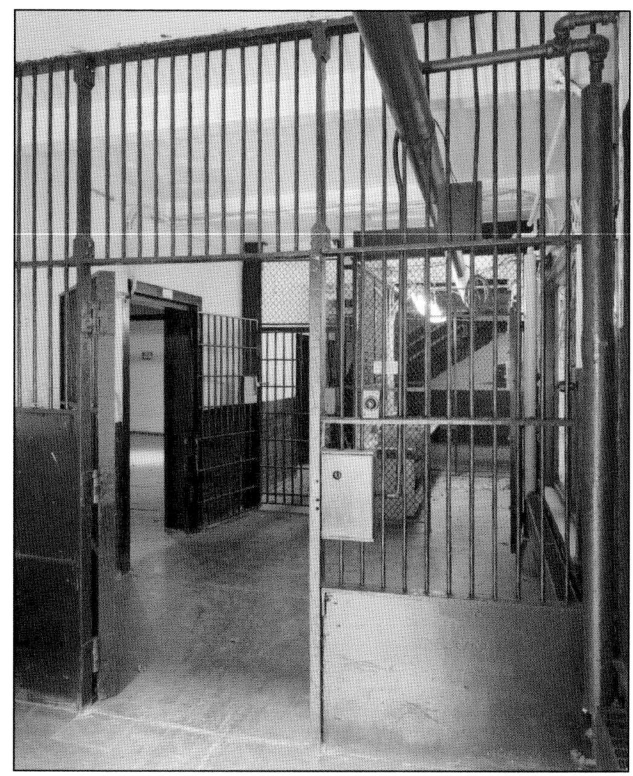

The maze of bars in this photograph was part of the jail's receiving area. (Courtesy of the Library of Congress.)

Court documents paint a bleak picture of the jail's cells: "The cells have four walls of stone; three of them are solid; the fourth wall, nearest the catwalk, has two openings, one a barred (and sometimes screened) window-like opening and the other a heavy, barred (and sometimes screened) door which swings on large hinges. The walls are cracked and flaked with repeated coats of paint; the floors are of composition tile; the walls and floor are damp and clammy. There are no heat outlets in the cells; heat is circulated by means of blowers at the end of the tiers; upper tier cells are extremely hot in the summertime and lower ones frigid in cold weather." Unused for years, the cells had deteriorated even further by the time these photographs were taken. (Courtesy of the Library of Congress.)

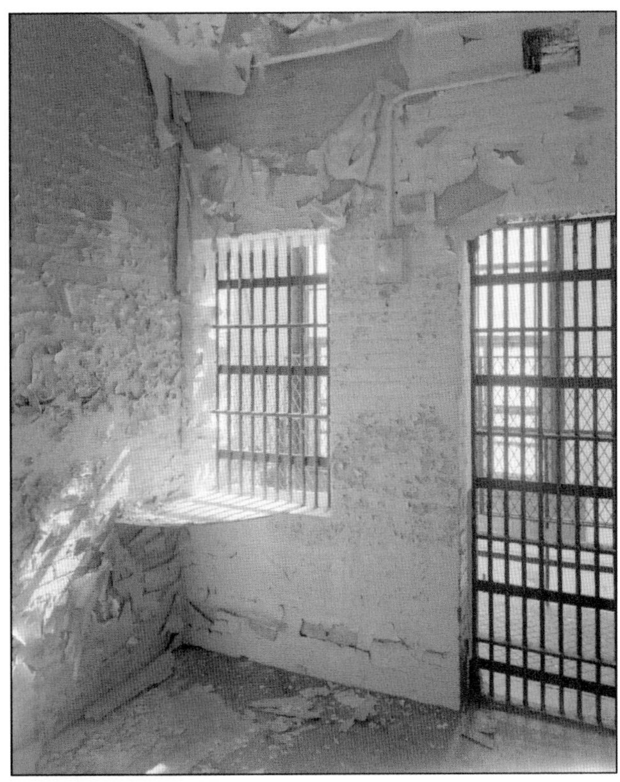

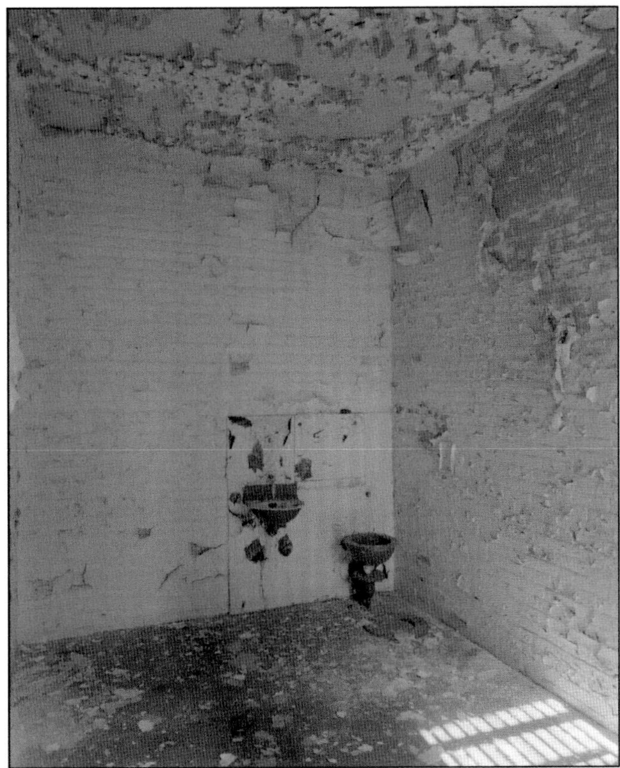

The Charles Street Jail suffered from overcrowding for years, with two prisoners often assigned to each cell. As Garrity's ruling notes, "Cell size is approximately 8' wide × 11' long × 10' high, and was designed and constructed for single occupancy. Nearly all of the usable floor space in cells is taken up by two iron-slatted cots which have no springs, are covered by old, worn and often soiled mattresses which have no protective covers and are in deplorable and unhealthy condition. The area between the cots is not sufficient to allow two men to pass each other." (Courtesy of the Library of Congress.)

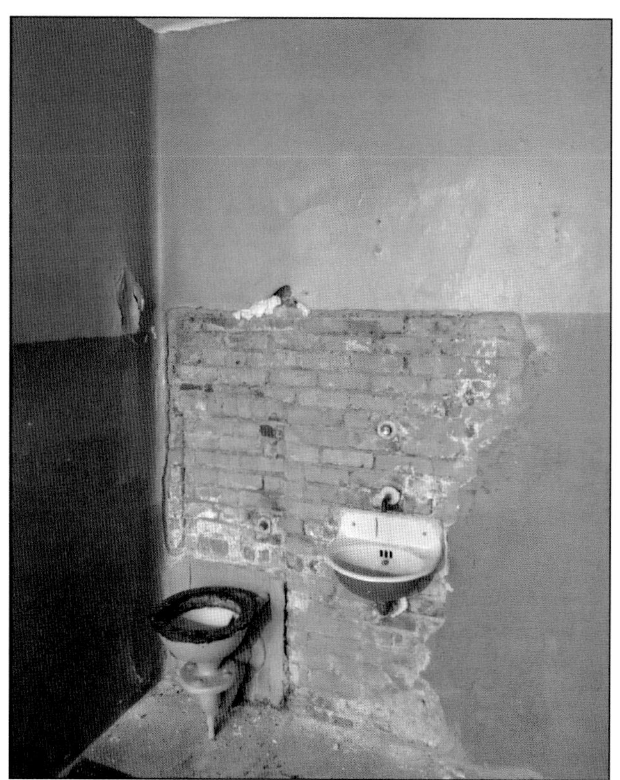

Condemning the jail's sanitary conditions, the verdict explains, "The plumbing system is antiquated, inadequate and impossible to repair economically . . . Toilets and sinks in the cells are corroded, filth-encrusted and often a serious health hazard. Toilet bowls are not covered and many have no seats . . . Flush valves in the toilet units are old and in need of repair or replacement, causing the toilets and sinks to get plugged up and to overflow frequently. Usually when this happens, the cells must be closed but some cells remain in use despite leaking toilets and sinks . . . There is no hot water in the cells." (Courtesy of the Library of Congress.)

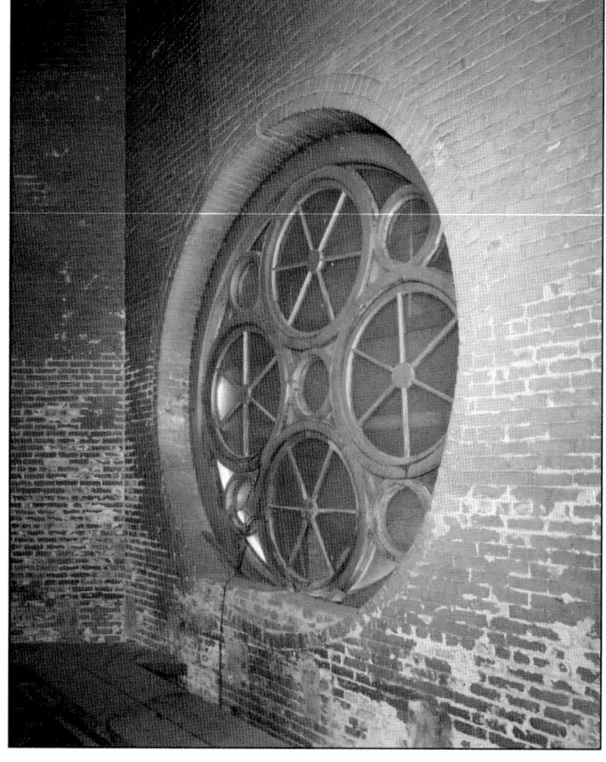

Despite the jail's dilapidated condition, vestiges of the original design remained intact. In this photograph, a sliver of light peeks around the edge of one of the boarded up ocular windows in the rotunda. (Courtesy of the Library of Congress.)

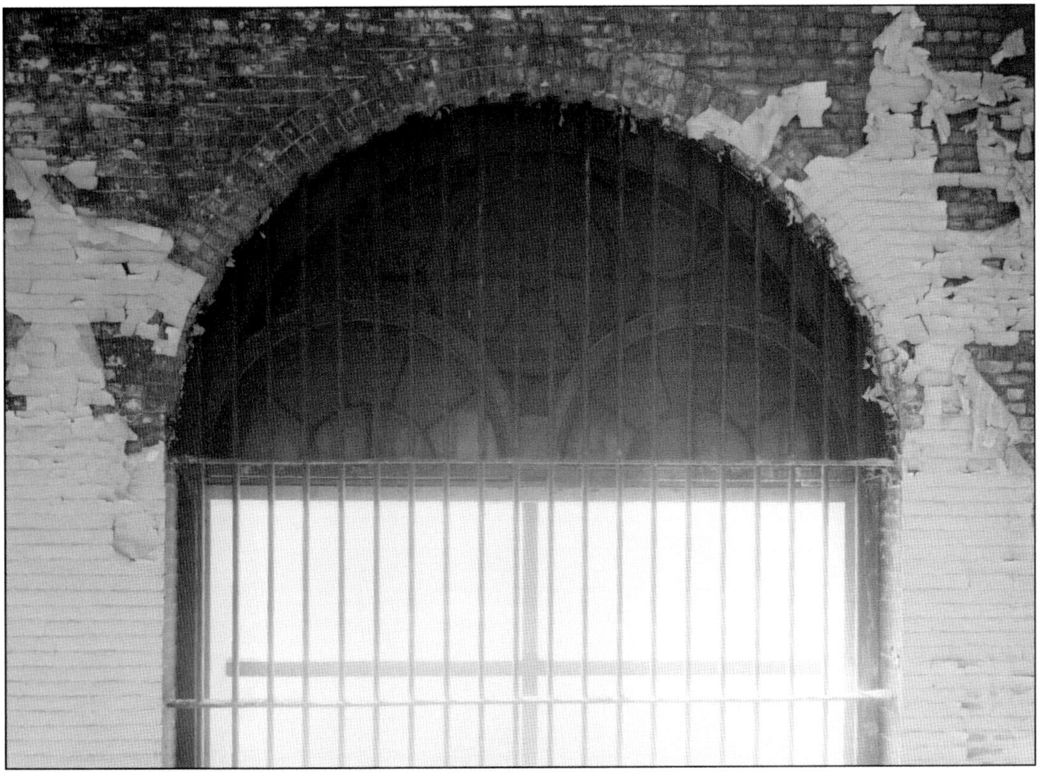

Throughout the jail, layers of lead-based paint were peeling from the walls and ceiling. (Courtesy of the Library of Congress.)

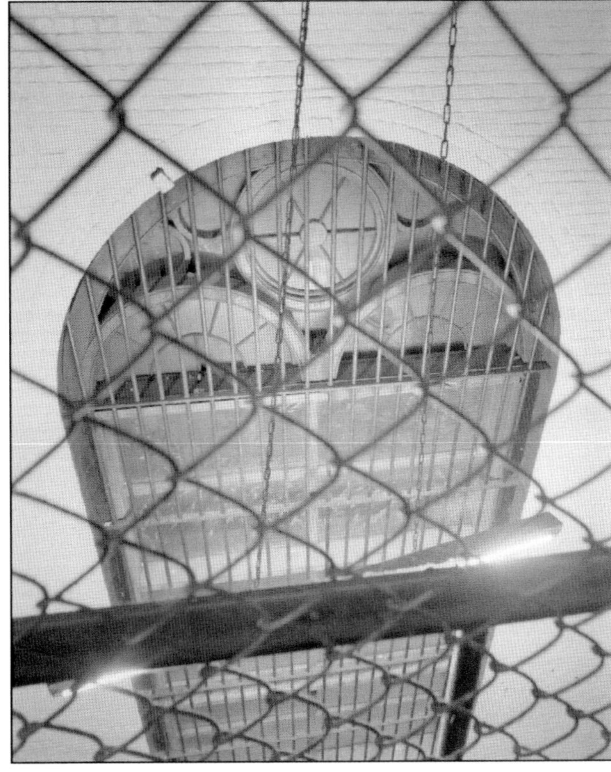

This image gives an idea of what an inmate would have seen while looking towards the outer walls of the jail from the catwalk. (Courtesy of the Library of Congress.)

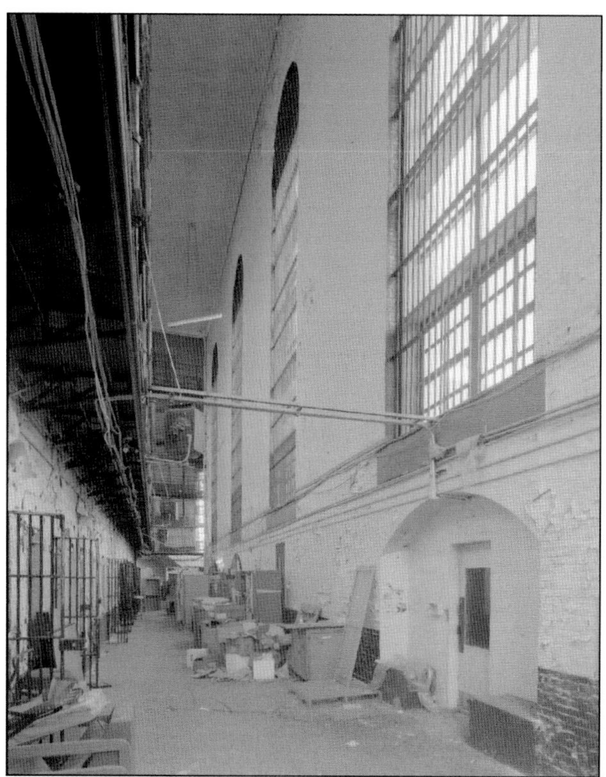

After all inmates were removed from the building, Massachusetts General Hospital used parts of the jail for storage of documents and equipment. (Courtesy of the Library of Congress.)

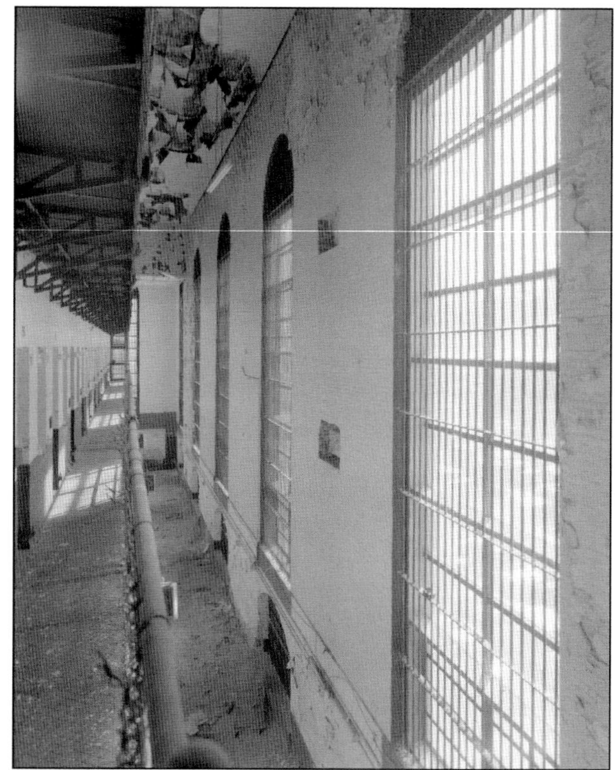

Almost as if it were serving a sentence of its own, the jail remained locked up and idle for about a decade before finally being given a second chance. (Courtesy of the Library of Congress.)

Eight

Transformation

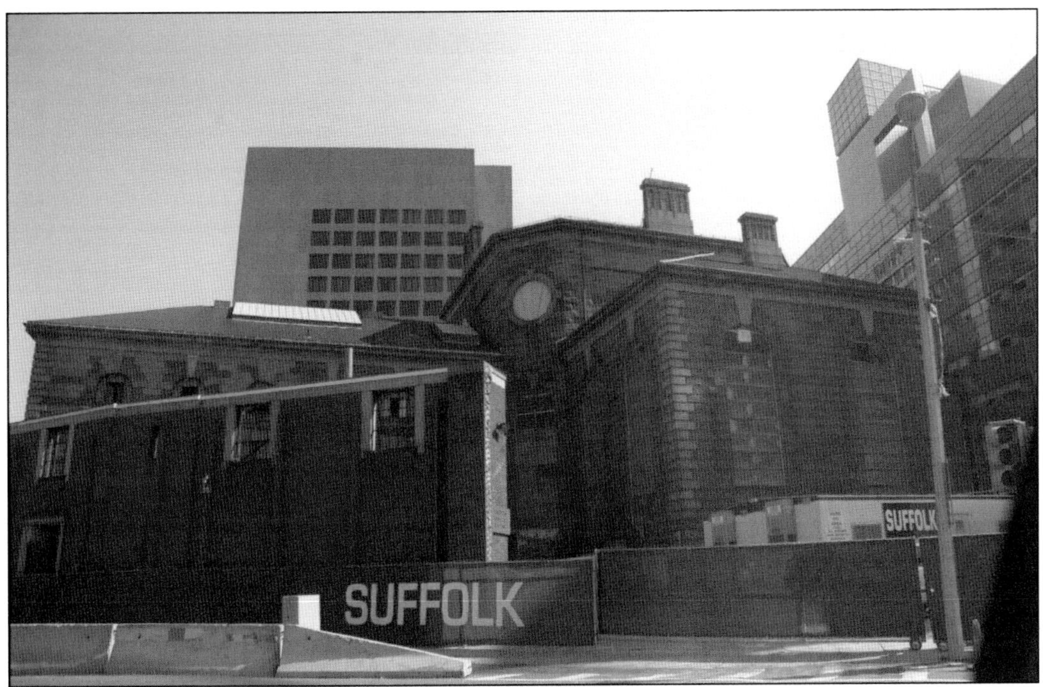

After taking possession of the Charles Street Jail in 1991, the Massachusetts General Hospital sought proposals for its reuse. In 2001, the development firm Carpenter & Company was selected to turn the former lockup into a luxury hotel. Cambridge Seven Associates, working with preservation architect Ana Beha Architects, led the architectural design for the adaptive reuse of the historic building. Suffolk Construction Company, along with many other firms, carried out the reconstruction and renovation. In this image, the building has been partially liberated from behind the high brick wall that hid it from public view for decades. (Courtesy of Suffolk Construction Company.)

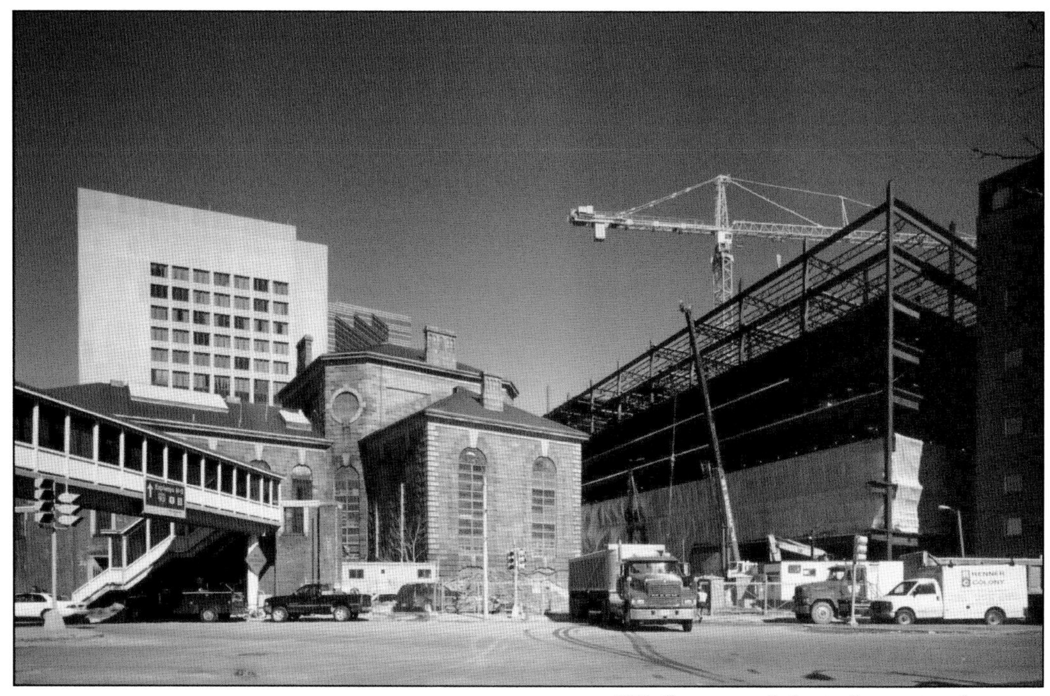

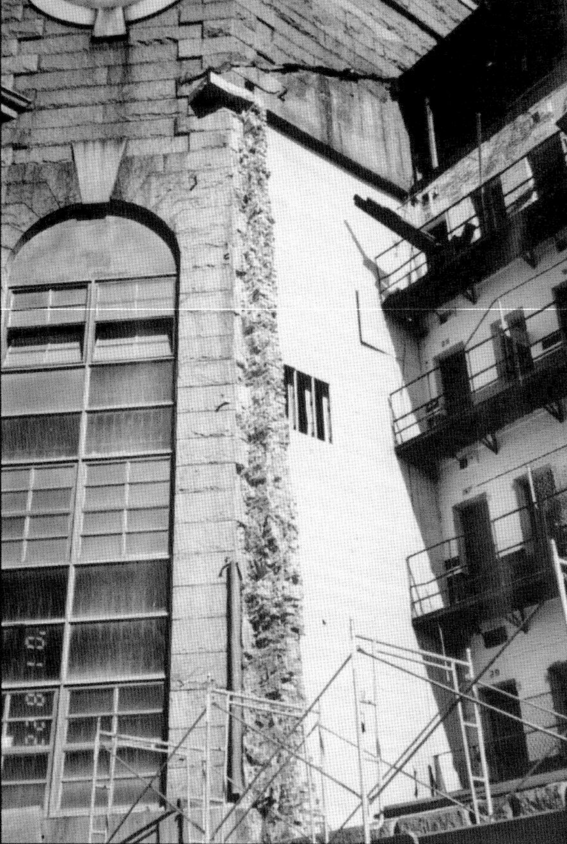

While most of the jail remained intact, the east wing was removed to make room for a new addition to the Massachusetts General Hospital, seen here under construction on the right. (Photograph by Kwesi Budu-Arthur, courtesy of Cambridge Seven Associates.)

With the outer wall of the east wing removed, the jail cells on the interior can be seen. In addition to holding prisoners, the cellblocks played a structural role in the building. The walls of the cells were load-bearing and helped support the roof. (Courtesy of the Library of Congress.)

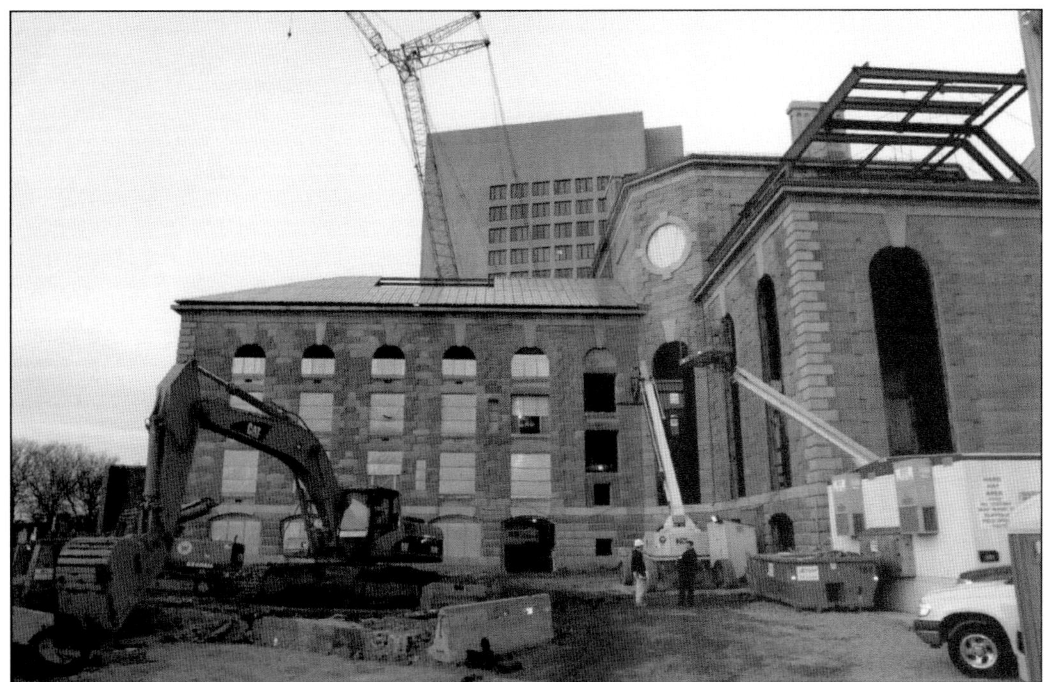

Converting the 150-year-old jail into a luxury hotel required completely gutting the interior. A temporary truss was built above the roof to hold it up while the load-bearing cellblocks were taken down and permanent roof supports were installed. (Courtesy of Suffolk Construction Company.)

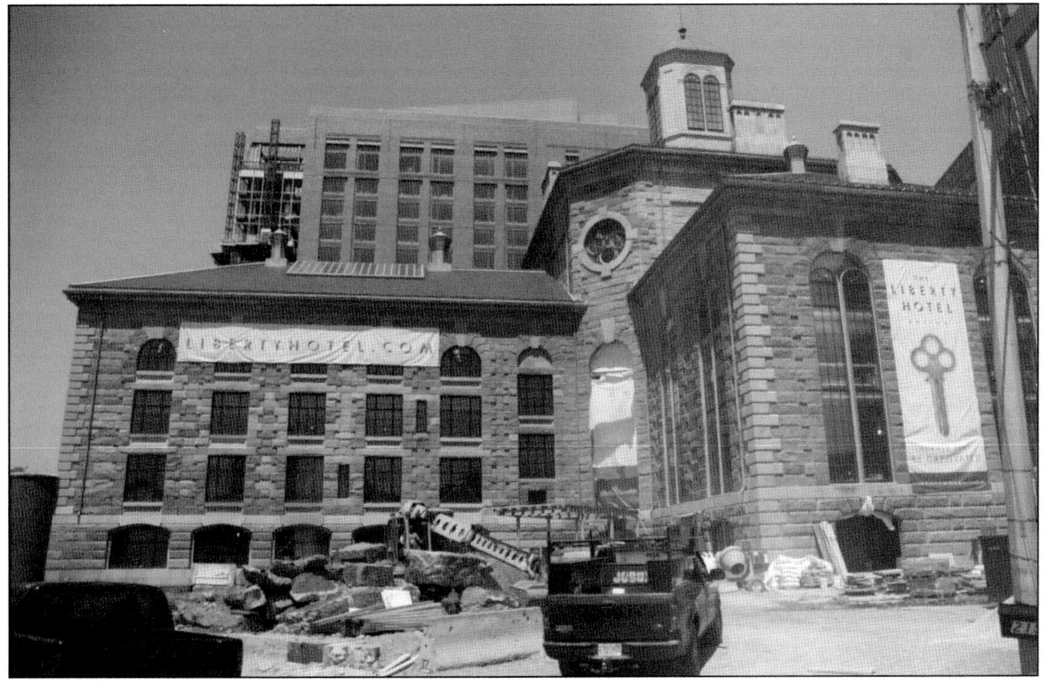

Windows were restored and replaced, and the granite exterior was scrubbed clean with soap, water, and plenty of elbow grease. To add 280 new guest rooms, Cambridge Seven Associates designed the adjoining hotel tower behind the former jail. (Courtesy of Suffolk Construction Company.)

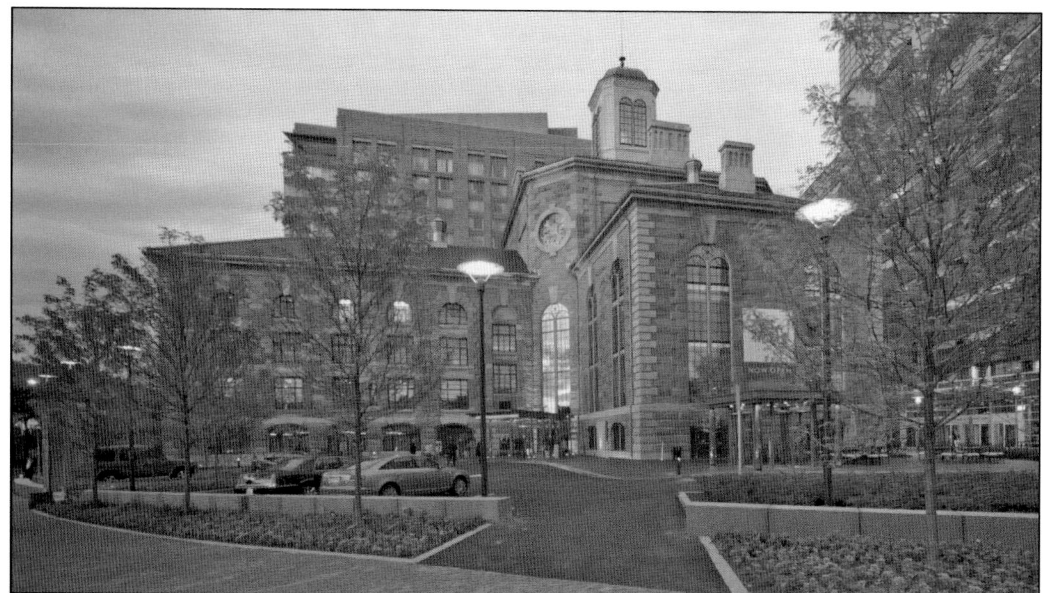

The painstaking restoration of the exterior was carried out in coordination with numerous historic and preservation agencies to ensure faithfulness to the original design. The striking transformation also included subtle memories of the building's former use. For example, the low garden walls in the foreground delineate where the high brick wall enclosing the jail yard once stood. (Photograph by Kwesi Budu-Arthur, courtesy of Cambridge Seven Associates.)

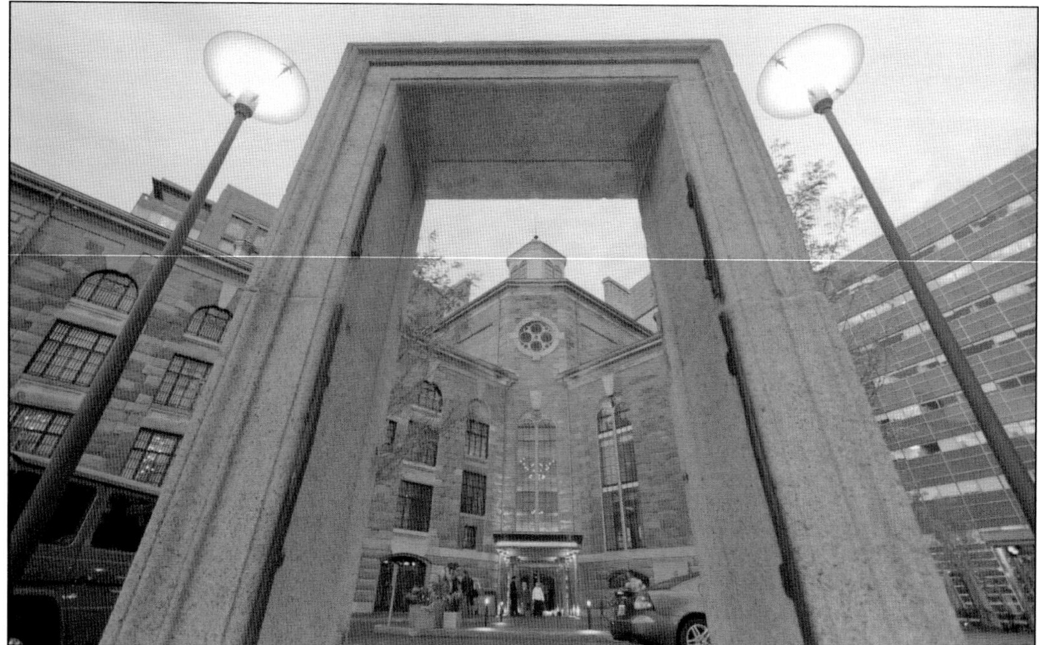

One of the challenges of the project, according to Carpenter & Company president Richard Friedman, was "how to preserve the 'jailness' of the building." Keeping elements such as the gateway from the wall that enclosed the jail yard was just one of many ways the renovation honored the building's previous life. (Photograph by Kwesi Budu-Arthur, courtesy of Cambridge Seven Associates.)

When it came to naming the hotel, Friedman says he "went through years of agony" as he considered jail-themed names such as Up the River and the Big House. Eventually, he came up with a name inspired by the opposite of incarceration—the Liberty Hotel. (Courtesy of the Liberty Hotel.)

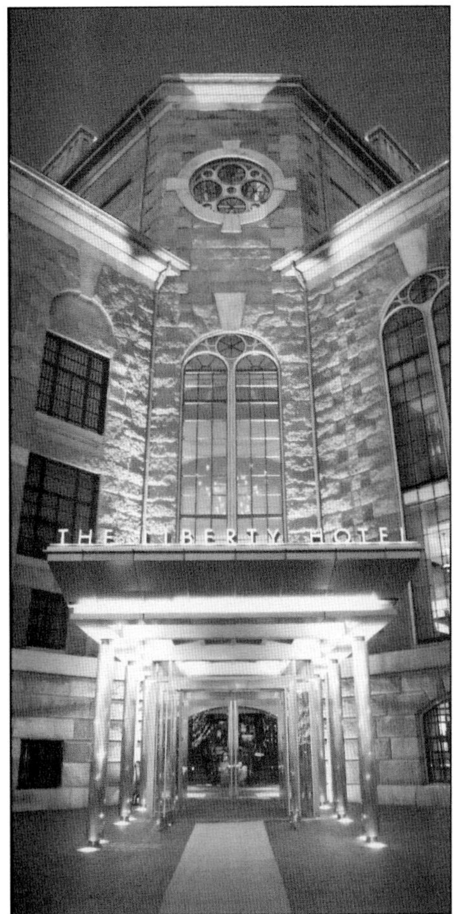

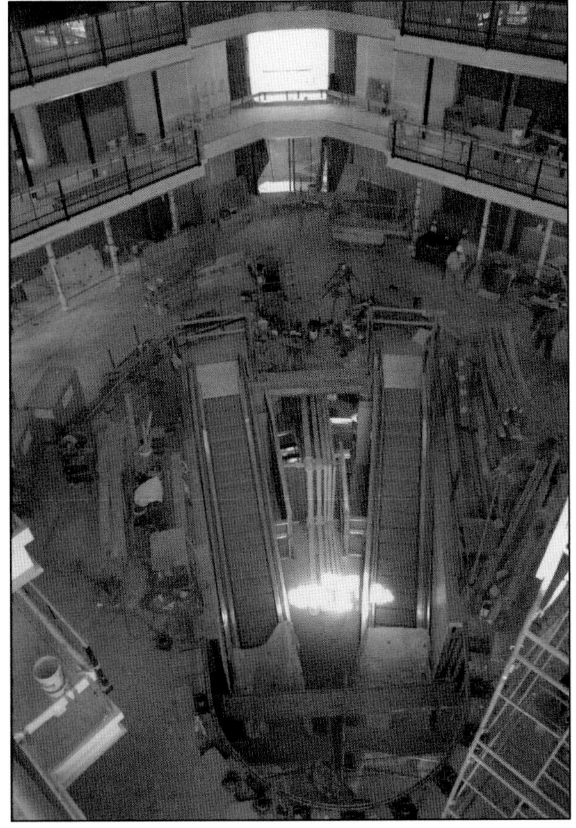

On the interior, the soaring, open rotunda where guards once watched over prisoners was turned into the hotel lobby. (Courtesy of Suffolk Construction Company.)

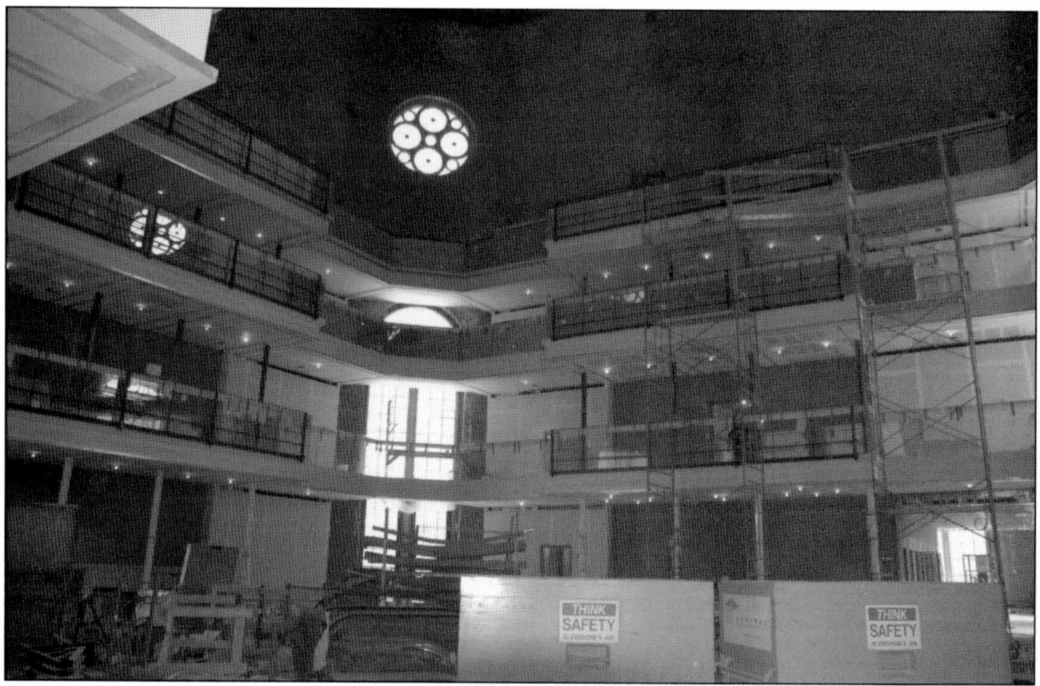

The narrow catwalks that encircled the rotunda were rebuilt into wider catwalks with spaces for visitors to gather or hold parties. (Courtesy of Suffolk Construction Company.)

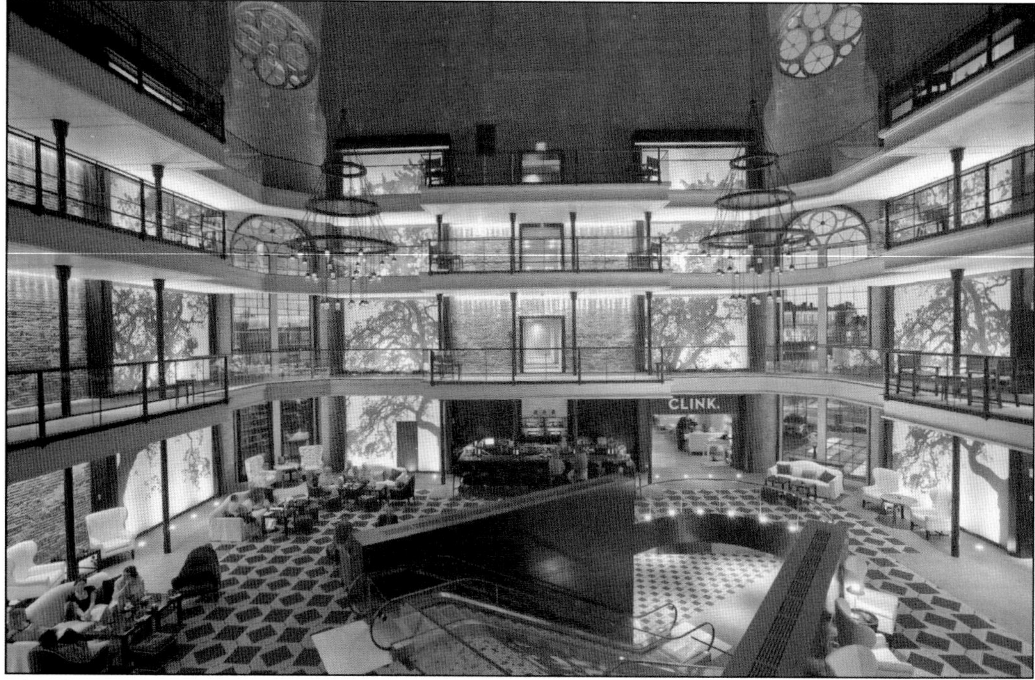

The formerly cold, stark rotunda is now an inviting space that includes many details from the old building. The balusters on the catwalk railings are original, while the columns are faithful replicas. The wood framing and glass in the ocular windows is also original. (Courtesy of the Liberty Hotel.)

A false ceiling that had been installed in the rotunda to conserve heat was removed, exposing the roof's wooden trusses. Steel supports were added for additional strength. (Photograph by Kwesi Budu-Arthur, courtesy of Cambridge Seven Associates.)

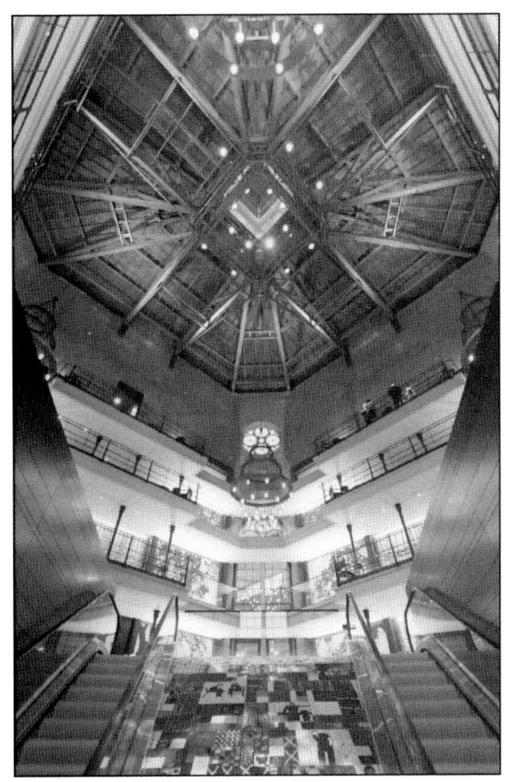

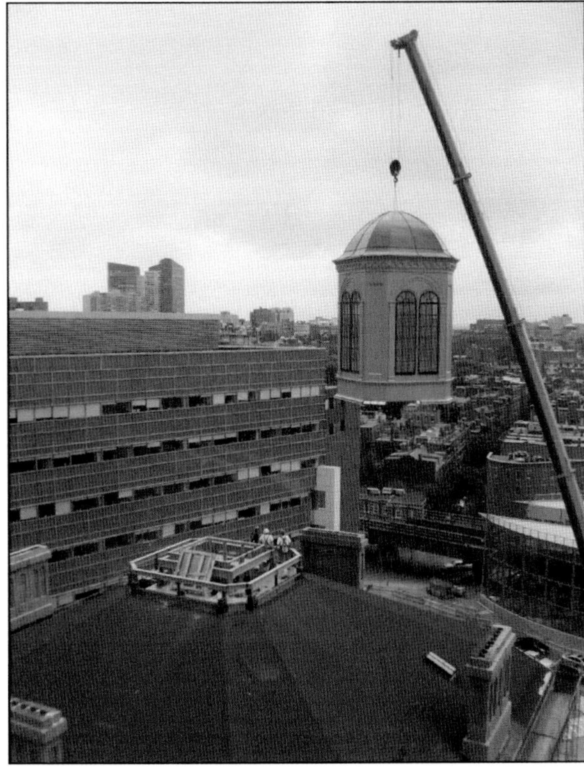

Gridley Bryant's original plans called for a large cupola atop the rotunda with windows that would admit light and air into the space below. To cut costs during construction, though, builders substituted a smaller clock tower. As part of the renovation, the team installed a cupola matching Bryant's original designs. (Photograph by David Wiborg, AIA, courtesy of Cambridge Seven Associates.)

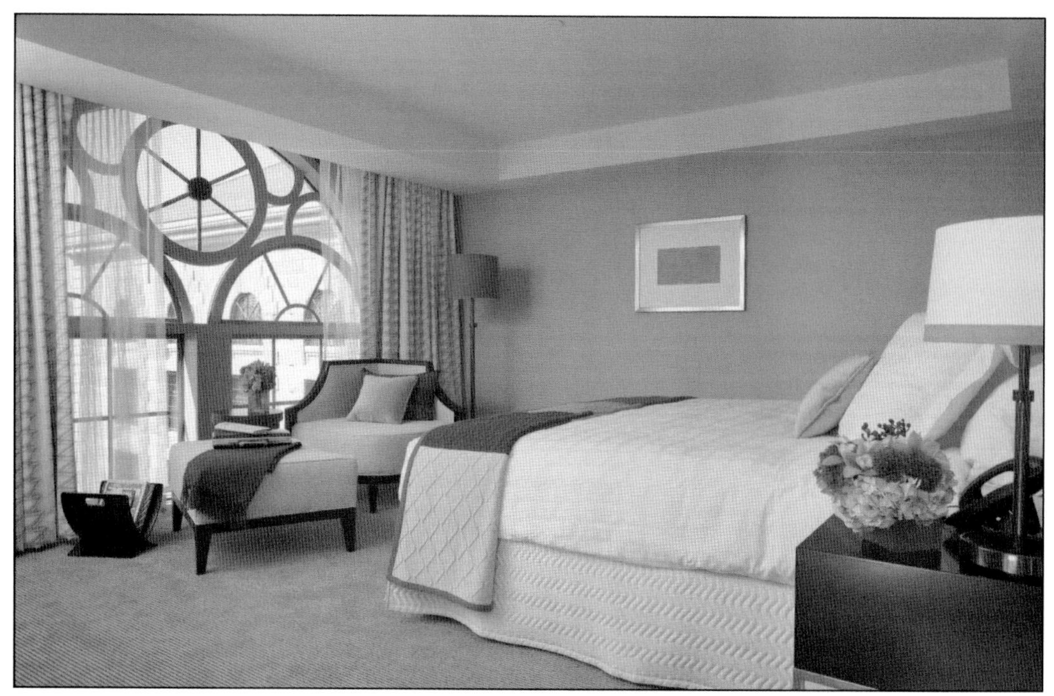

While most of the hotel's 298 guest rooms are located in the new tower connected to the former jail, 18 were created in the old building. Several feature Bryant's distinctive arched widows. (Courtesy of the Liberty Hotel.)

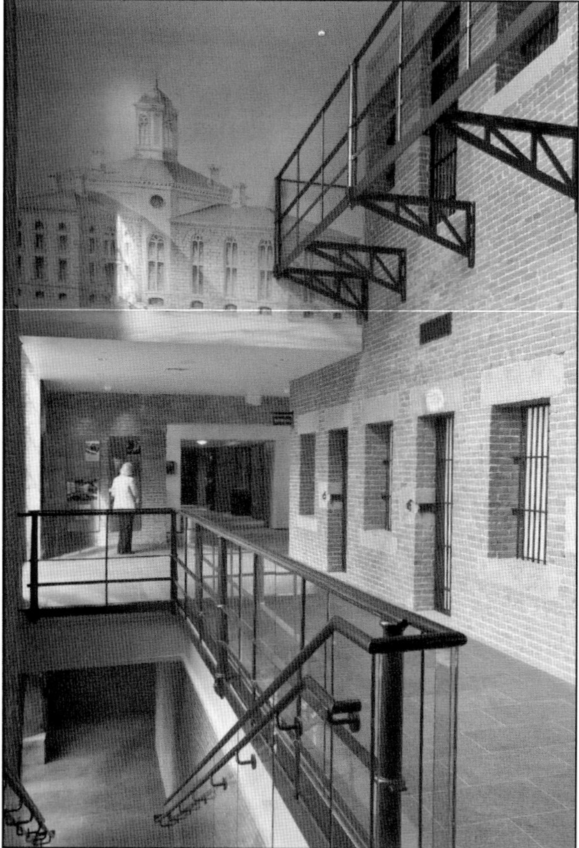

Part of the jail's north wing, which formerly housed women, now connects the old building to the new hotel tower. To preserve the character of the building, the developer and architects retained cells and a section of the original catwalk. (Photograph by Kwesi Budu-Arthur, courtesy of Cambridge Seven Associates.)

Jail cells in the south wing were gutted to create space for a restaurant. (Courtesy of Suffolk Construction Company.)

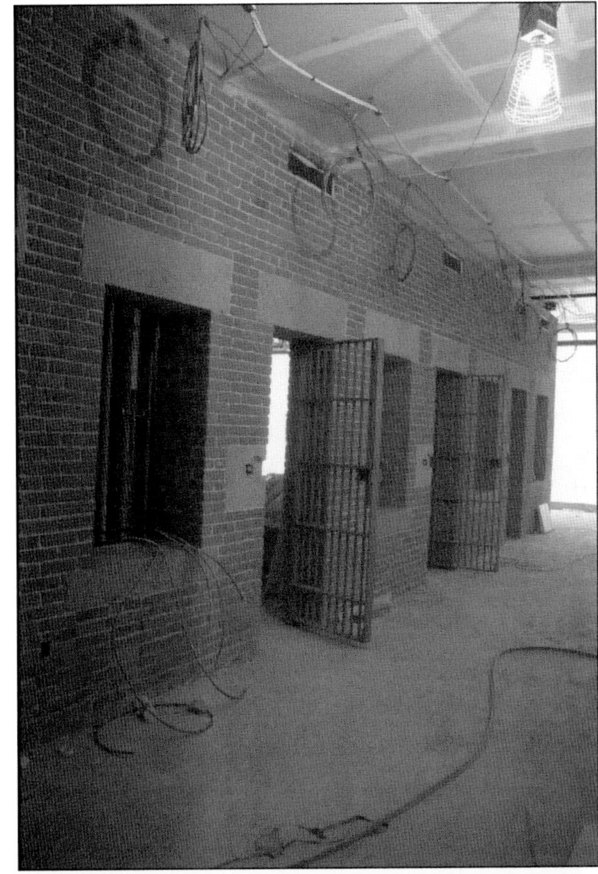

This image shows the same cellblock today. It is now part of a restaurant called Clink, where guests can order food unlike anything former inmates received. (Courtesy of the Liberty Hotel.)

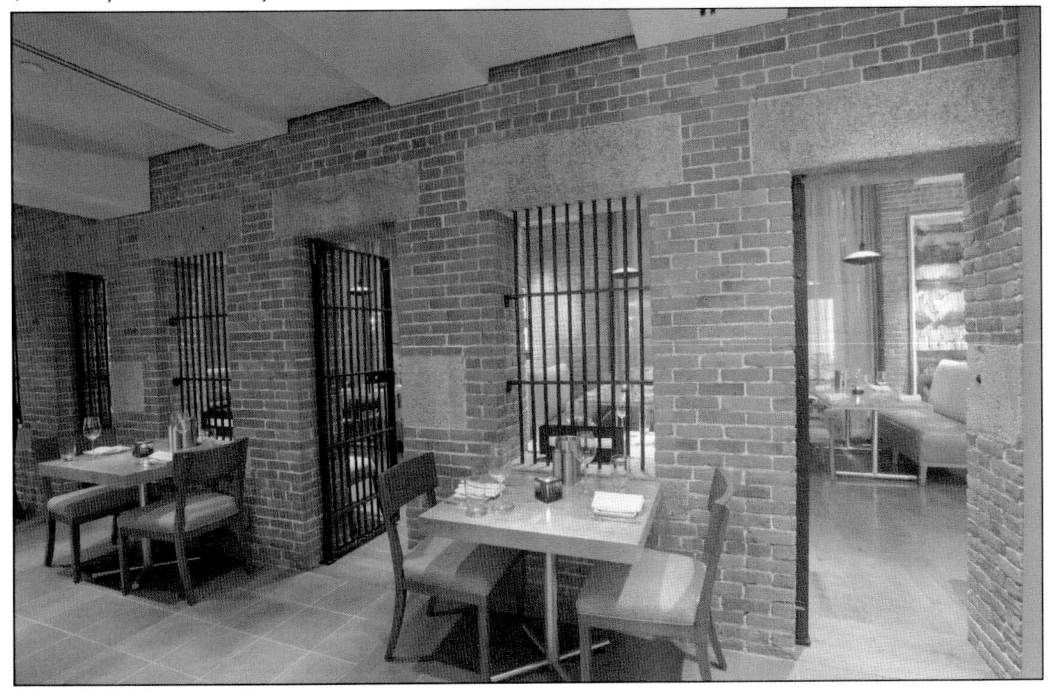

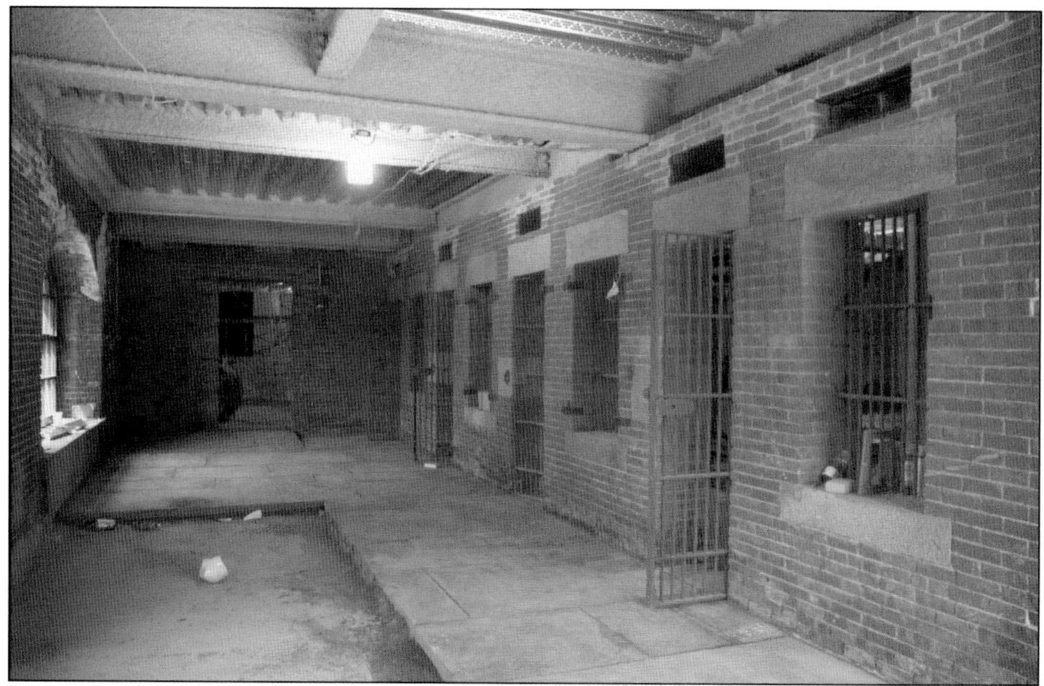

The cells on the ground floor beneath Clink were once part of the drunk tank, where people arrested for drunkenness were held. (Courtesy of Suffolk Construction Company.)

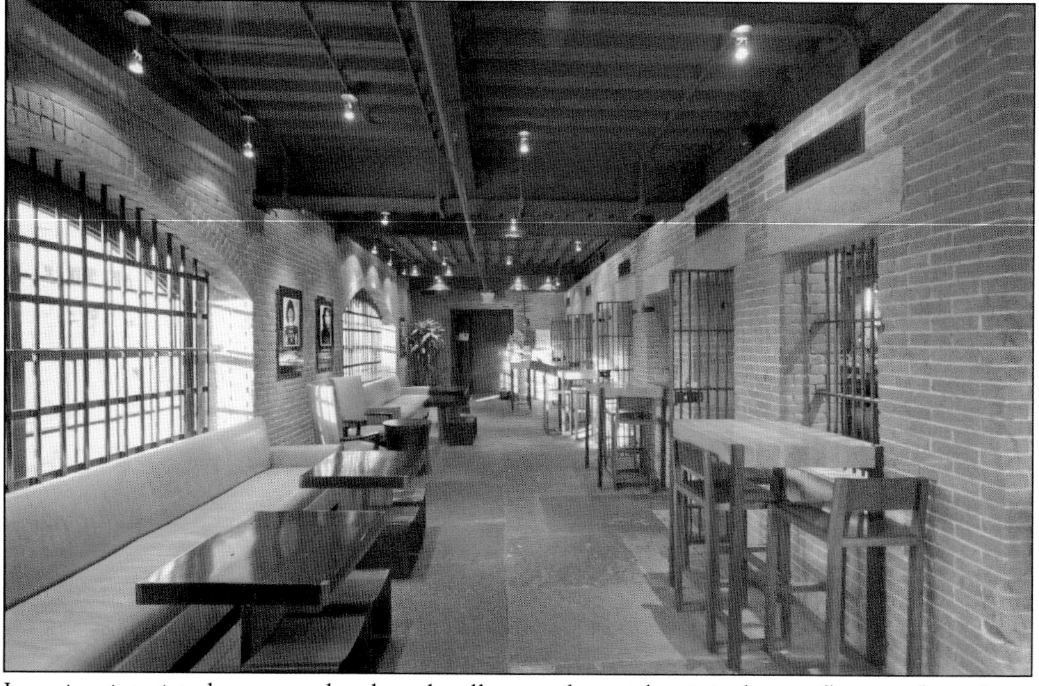

In an ironic twist, those same drunk tank cells, complete with original stone floors and iron bars, are now home to a watering hole called Alibi. (Photograph by Kwesi Budu-Arthur, courtesy of Cambridge Seven Associates.)

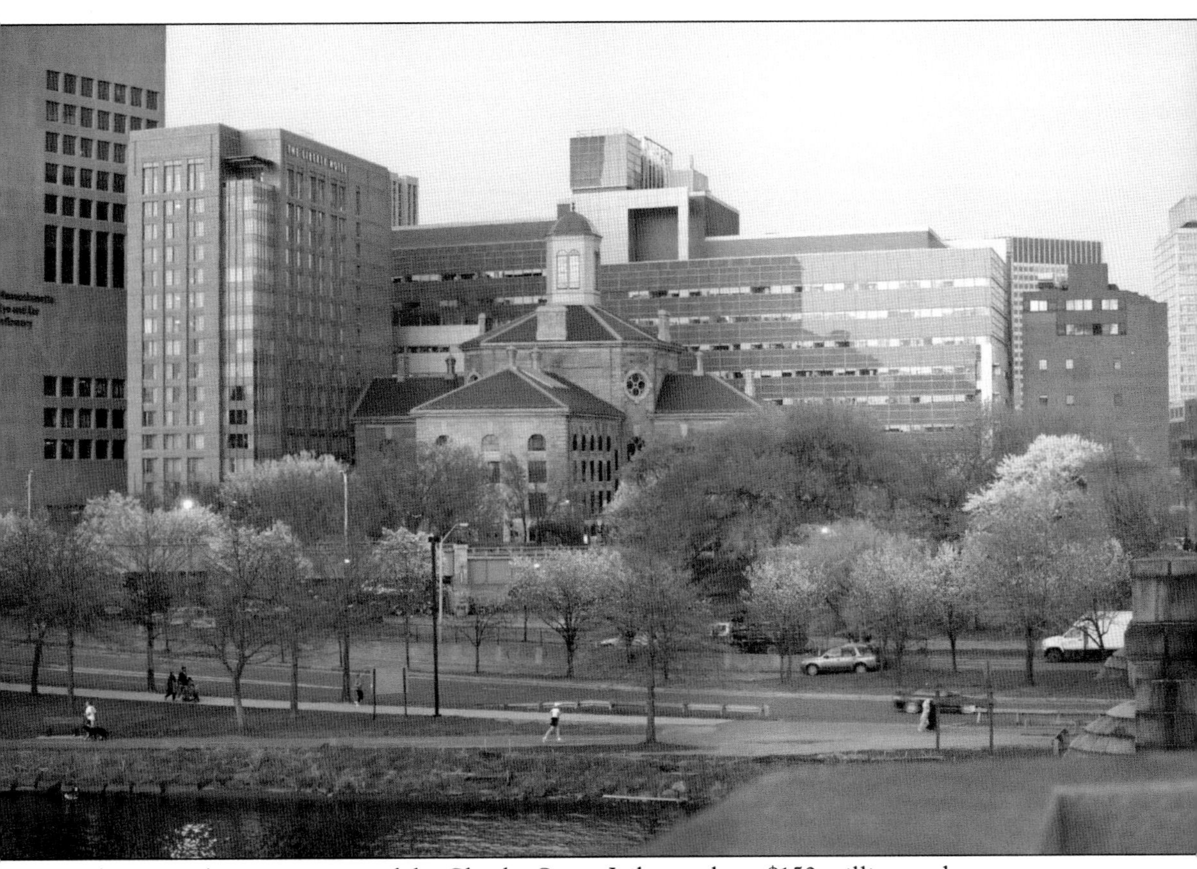

The meticulous renovation of the Charles Street Jail cost about $150 million and won numerous awards for design and preservation. While honoring the building's past, the renovation has also given the former jail a new life. "We took a place of sorrow and turned it into a place of joy," says principal architect Gary Johnson of Cambridge Seven Associates. (Photograph by Kwesi Budu-Arthur, courtesy of Cambridge Seven Associates.)

Consistent with our mission to preserve history on a local level, this book was printed in South Carolina on American-made paper and manufactured entirely in the United States. Products carrying the accredited Forest Stewardship Council (FSC) label are printed on 100 percent FSC-certified paper.

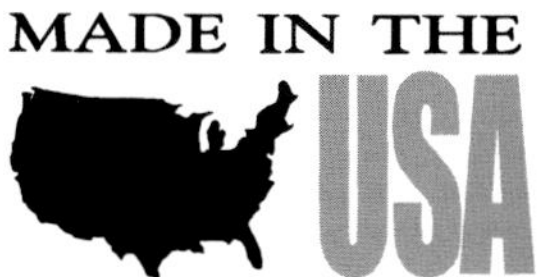